THE
DEMOGRAPHY
OF AFRICA

THE
DEMOGRAPHY
OF AFRICA

James D. Tarver

PRAEGER

Westport, Connecticut
London

Library of Congress Cataloging-in-Publication Data

Tarver, James D.
    The demography of Africa / James D. Tarver.
       p.   cm.
    Includes bibliographical references (p.   ) and index.
    ISBN 0–275–94885–4 (alk. paper)
      1. Africa—Population. 2. Demography—Africa.   I. Title.
    HB3661.A3T37   1996
    304.6′096—dc20   93–50729

British Library Cataloguing in Publication Data is available.

Library of Congress Catalog Card Number: 93–50729
ISBN: 0–275–94885–4

First published in 1996

Praeger Publishers, 88 Post Road West, Westport, CT 06881
An imprint of Greenwood Publishing Group, Inc.

Printed in the United States of America

The paper used in this book complies with the
Permanent Paper Standard issued by the National
Information Standards Organization (Z39.48–1984).

10 9 8 7 6 5 4 3 2 1

This book is dedicated to the millions of proud Africans, many of whom are illiterate and mired in poverty, who are striving for a more secure life. This book is also dedicated to the memory of my dear mother and father. I am especially grateful to my wife Olga Tarver and daughter Olga B. Bradley for their encouragement and inspiration. Lastly, I am indebted to scores of African demographers for their acute insights into demographic processes.

Contents

Tables

TABLES

Tables

Acknowledgements

I am indebted to the following for advice, comments, and suggestions:

Donald J. Adamchak, Kansas State University
Ghyasuddin Ahmed, University of Botswana
A. Bahri, United Nations Economic Commission for Africa
Gretchen Balanoff, Social Development Center
Delores Baldwin, Center for International Research, U.S. Bureau of the Census
Grace Barnas, Center for International Research, U.S. Bureau of the Census
Calvin L. Beale, U.S. Department of Agriculture
Donald J. Bogue, Social Development Center
Leon F. Bouvier, Tulane University
James W. Brackett, formerly Agency for International Development
Mattie Brandley, New York Public Library
Martin Brockerhoff, Westinghouse Social Sciences International
Debra C. Brown, Library of Congress
Kenneth R. Bryson, International Statistical Programs Center, U.S. Bureau of the Census
Alice Clague, United Nations
Anne R. Cross, Institute for Resource Development
Lincoln H. Day, Australian National University
Denise Dowell, formerly Population Reference Bureau
Richard A. Engels, U.S. Department of State, Muscat
Rita Gdula, Catholic University of America
Murray Gendell, Georgetown University
Jackie Gold, New York Public Library
K.T. de Graft-Johnson, United Nations Economic Commission for Africa

Gloria L. Hammond, Library of Congress
Larry Heligman, United Nations
Peter S. Heller, International Monetary Fund
Frank B. Hobbs, Center for International Research, U.S. Bureau of the Census
Dean Hoge, Catholic University of America
Peter D. Johnson, Center for International Research, U.S. Bureau of the Census
Debbie Jones, Catholic University of America
Paul R. Keith, Social Development Center
David Kelly, Library of Congress
Ung Soo Kim, Catholic University of America
Joanna Lawrence, Joanna's Graphics
Oey A. Meesook, The World Bank
Dominic Milazi, University of Bophuthatswana
H. Max Miller, University of Georgia
G. Nanjundappa, California State University
Richard Potts, National Museum of Natural History
Harry M. Rosenberg, National Center for Health Statistics
Patricia M. Rowe, Center for International Research, U.S. Bureau of the Census
William Seltzer, United Nations
Jacob S. Siegel, Georgetown University
Ram N. Singh, U.S. Department of Education
Gloria D. Steele, U.S. Department of Agriculture
C. Shannon Stokes, Pennsylvania State University
Felizardo Suzara, United Nations
Ralph Thomlinson, formerly California State University
Maria Turner, Catholic University of America

Many others, of course, assisted in various ways in completing this work.

1

Introduction to the
Study of African Demography

THE CONCEPT OF DEMOGRAPHY

Demography may be defined as the science of population. *Demos* is a Greek word meaning people and *graphy* refers to the writing, description, and representation in the field. The term *demography* was coined over a century ago (Guillard, 1855). The word *population* is much older and has a Latin derivative.

In the seventeenth and eighteenth centuries, during the days of Graunt, Petty, and Malthus, studies of births, deaths, and population growth were considered part of the discipline of political economy. Today, however, the study of human populations and their changing number and characteristics is considered to be a discipline in itself. Some scholars insist that demography is divided into two distinct branches: "formal" demography and "social" demography. In this context "formal" demography refers to mathematical analyses and model building.

Births, deaths, and migration, for example, are the three demographic variables that determine population growth. High fertility results in a young population and declining fertility increases the age of the population. Immigration and in-migration tend to lower the age of a population, while emigration and out-migration usually increase its age. Declining mortality usually results in a younger population. Thus, change in the age-sex composition of a population is a result of changes in fertility, the sex ratio at birth, mortality, and migration--variables that can be quantified and measured. The age-sex structure of a population may be considered as a demographic history of individuals living at any one time.

Some important measures of demographic change are the crude birth and death rates, which taken together indicate population increase. For example, the crude birth rate of Africa (number of births per 1,000 population) was 44.7 in the

1985-90 period. The African crude death rate for that period was 14.7, giving a natural increase rate of 30. Therefore, the annual rate of population increase in Africa was three percent, the highest of all major regions of the world.

Social demography, in contrast to the mathematical measurements of formal demography, encompasses all non-formal demographic analyses. Many of these population studies are strictly demographic in nature but others are interdisciplinary and relate demographic processes to social, economic, and other types of phenomena. This development in the field has led to the emergence of various interdisciplinary specializations such as economic demography and historical demography.

Economic demography includes many different economically related areas of study. Demographers in this specialty have investigated a number of interrelated subjects including population growth, population movements, and poverty. For example, some well-known studies have investigated population redistribution and economic growth (Kuznets, et al., 1964), immigration (Easterlin, 1982), and migration and urban development (Thomas, 1972).

Historical demography focuses on the study of periods predating modern censuses and registration systems (Ogden, 1987). It has reconstructed various characteristics of past populations and interpreted their underlying causes and consequences. Some of the prominent historical demography studies were of early Italian populations (Beloch, 1886), family reconstitution studies (Fleury and Henry, 1965), European marriage patterns (Hajnal, 1965), African slave trading (Lovejoy, 1983; Curtin, 1969), and fertility, mortality, and nuptiality trends in England for more than 300 years (Wrigley and Schofield, 1981).

John Graunt, who studied mortality in seventeenth century London, is generally considered the father of demography. His *Natural and Political Observations Made Upon the Bills of Mortality* (1662) was based upon the records of registers maintained by churches. He computed a crude life table and investigated the causes of death. The average length of life computed from Graunt's "Table of Survivors" was 18.2 years, but since Graunt's table was based upon imperfect data, it is impossible to determine the extent to which it reflected London's health conditions at that time. In addition to his contributions to the study of mortality, Graunt estimated London's population, its rate of growth, the sex ratio at birth, the number of women in the reproductive ages, and average family size (Graunt, 1939).

In the seventeenth century, "Political arithmetick" became the name of the new discipline population studies. This demographic term came from the title of a 1676 work by Sir William Petty, which was published posthumously (Petty, 1691). Petty computed the money value of man and the war losses of Ireland, as well as population estimates of London and rates of population growth. He also wrote extensively on the relation of demography to economic and political issues.

CONCERNS ABOUT POPULATION GROWTH, FAMINE, AND STARVATION

At the end of the eighteenth century, Thomas R. Malthus published his *Essay on the Principle of Population*, which contained two postulates: *first*, that food was necessary for the existence of man and *second*, that passion between the sexes was also necessary for the existence of man (Malthus, 1798). Malthus emphasized the increasing pressure of population on the means of subsistence. He was convinced that the population was increasing much more rapidly than the food supply, which would eventually result in massive destitution, and the wasting and exhaustion of certain natural resources.

According to this view, population was necessarily limited by the means of subsistence. Malthus stated that the population doubled every generation when its growth went unchecked; thus, the number of people would increase in each successive generation from one to two, to four, eight, 16, 32, 64, and on up to 128, then 256 by the eighth generation. However, the means of subsistence would increase only in an arithmetical ratio of one in each generation, such as one, two, three, and so on, reaching only nine by the eighth generation. Therefore, in two centuries the ratio of the population to subsistence would be 256 to nine and in three centuries 4,096 to 13. These statements were, of course, widely challenged and the *Essay* was so widely debated that it underwent six further editions, the last published in 1872.

Malthus presented two possible types of checks on population, positive checks and preventive checks. The only preventive check acceptable to him was moral restraint, which included the postponement of marriage as well as the avoidance of extramarital relations. In fact, Malthus considered moral restraint to be the only reasonable technique for reducing population growth. The positive checks he mentioned were cruel and devastating measures--war, famine, disease, epidemics, and misery.

Unfortunately, Malthus overlooked many crucial matters which affected his propositions, and he was subjected to many criticisms. For example, he did not anticipate the rapid technological advances that greatly increased agricultural production. The rapidly increasing and widespread destitution he feared never occurred. Since Malthus' day, populations have grown very rapidly. However, food production has generally kept pace except for brief periods in certain areas. Surpluses have usually occurred in many parts of the world with severe malnutrition being limited generally to drought-stricken areas.

Malthus also failed to foresee the great advances in standards of living that resulted from the ever-accelerating number of innovations and inventions. In addition, he did not anticipate the vast international migrations to the New World, which greatly alleviated population pressures in densely inhabited areas of Europe.

Malthusianism continues to be a concern, particularly in such African countries as Ethiopia and Sudan, as well as the rest of the Sahel region of north central Africa, where prolonged droughts and strife have resulted in famine, starvation, and mass population movements (Newman, 1975). Successive crop failures, epidemics, and other adversities also have severely reduced the population of Kenya and other countries at various times (Dawson, 1981; Helleiner, 1957). Millions of people in the world continue to suffer from hunger and malnutrition (Hendry, 1988). Whatever their exaggerations, Malthus' ideas still attract widespread attention today.

THE STUDY OF DEMOGRAPHY IN AFRICA

This book assesses and analyzes past, current, and probable future population trends and patterns in Africa, along with their underlying structures and implications: the full range of subjects essential to understanding the demography of Africa. This book was prepared specifically for scholars interested in studying Africa's rich, unique demographic history. Evidently modern man first appeared in Africa. Much later agriculture and the domestication of animals began, then African cities were first established around 3000 B.C.

During the long prehistoric and ancient periods Africa's population grew very slowly. From A.D. 14 to 1940, for example, the number of inhabitants increased from 23 million to 190 million. However, population growth greatly accelerated after World War II when biomedical and scientific agricultural discoveries were applied to combat disease and famine. Mortality rates declined while birth rates remained high, leading to a rapid annual population growth of three percent--the highest rate of all major regions in the world. When the African colonies got their independence millions moved into cities, resulting in Africa having the highest rates of urbanization in the world. The in-depth demographic characteristics and patterns which were a part of this long historic transformation are presented in this book.

Professional workers in central statistics offices, civil registration officers, ministry of health officials, and other African civil servants and population specialists should benefit from the demographic analyses and the presentations of pressing demographic problems, along with the proposed approaches being used to alleviate them.

DIVERSITY IN AFRICA

Unfortunately, many people remain unaware of the great diversity of Africa, believing it to have only a poor, rural, and homogeneous black population. Any such characterization is certainly a mistake because the continent is indeed one of many contrasts. Vast deserts, savannahs, and rain forests exist in Africa. Large, rapidly growing metropolises rise near villages and hamlets in which reside millions engaged in traditional, subsistence agriculture. At the same time, many others work in the mining of large mineral reserves. All these African people--whether urban or rural, industrial workers or white-collar workers--represent a wide variety of racial and ethnic groups.

United Nations Regions

The United Nations has classified the 56 African countries into five regions, based upon social and economic characteristics. The original classifications placed the entire continent into three regions (UN, 1949, 1958). Then, in 1963 the present five regional classifications were adopted (UN, 1966). The seven countries that border the Mediterranean Sea make up North Africa. The inhabitants of this region are predominantly of white racial stock, being descendants of people from southwestern Asia. Most are Muslims.

The Sahara Desert, the largest in the world, is the approximate boundary of North and South Africa. Approximately two million nomads of the Tuareg, Moor, Teda, and Fulani groups inhabit the Sahara Desert and the adjoining Sahel countries in upper sub-Saharan Africa (Norris, 1984). The 49 countries south of the Sahara are the home of most black Africans. In terms of the United Nations classification, four of the five regions (all except North Africa) are in sub-Saharan Africa. With the exception of a few million people of European and Asian descent in the Republic of South Africa and much smaller numbers elsewhere, black Africans inhabit this vast area of the continent, which includes both the mainland and a half dozen island countries.

Official Languages

There are more than a thousand ethnic groups in Africa speaking their own languages and dialects. Zaire, for example, has 700 languages and dialects, Nigeria 300, Chad 200, and Tanzania over 100 (Worldmark Encyclopedia, 1988). However, each country has designated one or more languages as its official language, and this great diversity creates language barriers. After independence most sub-Saharan countries adopted the language of the former European colonial power as the official language, while also retaining their own native language. The North African countries adopted Arabic as their official language. In addition to indicating the official language or languages of each African country, Appendix 1 also identifies the former colonial power and date of independence.

Seven different European countries, each with distinct languages, maintained African colonies well into the twentieth century. By 1914, for example, Ethiopia, which was ruled by its ancient monarchial system, and Liberia, a republic, were the only countries not under European domination. In 1847 Liberia became the first independent republic in Africa to receive slaves. From 1822 onwards it accepted slaves repatriated from America and uses English as the official language.

French and English are the most widely used official languages in Africa, followed by Arabic and Portuguese (Appendix 1). There are only about a half dozen countries with some other official language. Obviously, the multiplicity of official languages increases heterogeneity in Africa just as it does in Europe and Asia.

Independent Countries

For years the United Nations has recognized 55 separate countries in Africa. Eritrea, a former Italian colony in northern Ethiopia from 1890 to 1941, became an independent republic in 1993, making a total of 56 African countries. Of these, 53 are independent, and all are presently United Nations members. Some independent countries such as Lesotho, Morocco, and Swaziland are kingdoms, but most are republics. Of the three countries without independent status, Réunion has departmental status in the Republic of France, St. Helena is a dependent territory of Great Britain, and although Western Sahara (renamed Sahrawi) is a disputed territory, it is still recognized as Western Sahara by the United Nations.

Population Distribution

Geographically Africa is the largest major region in the world, with over 30 million square kilometers (more than eleven million square miles) of surface area. However, its countries vary greatly in size. For instance, a dozen of the largest countries are one million or more square kilometers in area. In contrast, a few small island countries are less than 1,000 square kilometers in area. In terms of variability in total population, St. Helena has about 7,000 inhabitants, whereas Nigeria has 109 million (UN, 1991, 1993).

Demographic Characteristics

There is also a great deal of variability in demographic characteristics both between and within countries. Crude birth and death rates are two of the most highly variable demographic characteristics. For instance, the crude birth rates of Malawi, Mali, and Uganda are over twice as high as those for Réunion and Mauritius. The variability of death rates among countries is even greater. For example, the crude death rates of Sierra Leone and Ethiopia are more than three times as high as in Tunisia and Kenya.

Great variability and diversity, of course, also exist in the demographic characteristics within countries. For instance, in South Africa the crude birth rate of blacks is more than twice that for whites, 40 compared with 16, respectively (the rate for South African Asians is 23). The difference in the crude death rates is somewhat less, 12 for blacks compared with 7.5 for whites.

Another example of the variability in the demographic characteristics within countries is in the economic activity rates of males and females among the approximately 20 Botswana census districts. The male economic activity rates range from 98 percent in Jwaneng to 60 percent in the North East census district. Females have slightly less variation, with a range of 29 percent of women economically active in the Ghanzi district to a high of 60 percent in the Orapa district.

Population Censuses

Population censuses were conducted in many African countries while they were still European colonies (Domschke and Goyer, 1986). The first population enumerations in Africa were administrative censuses begun in Réunion in 1690. Often these administrative censuses were simply head counts for military recruitment or taxes. The first complete African population census was taken on the island of Mauritius in 1735 under the administration of the French colonial governor (Lamy, 1977). The next country to conduct a population census was Seychelles in 1791, also under French colonial auspices (d'Espaignet, 1984). About ten other countries took their first census sometime before the twentieth century (Domschke and Goyer, 1986). Every population census taken in each African country between 1900 and 1970 is identified, by the year conducted, in Table 7 of the 1970 *Demographic Yearbook*, with the total enumerated population in each census also given (UN, 1971). It was only after independence that most African censuses included native Africans in their enumerations.

The early population censuses were neither as elaborate nor as accurate as recent censuses. Underenumeration occurred quite often, Africans were not even counted, and other deficiencies such as misstatements of age were common in many of them.

In censuses persons are classified on either a *de facto* or a *de jure* definition. *De facto* indicates where the person was the day the census was taken. *De jure* refers to the usual place of residence, regardless where the person was on the census day. At one time in some countries it was common to assign Africans to different residences based upon their ethnic allegiance. For example, the 1964 Botswana census was enumerated according to allegiance to central villages, not on a *de facto* basis. There has now been at least one population census taken in every African country with the first census conducted in Chad in 1993.

Data obtained from population censuses and surveys provide essential information for the study of the demographic structure and characteristics of the population, as well as their changing size and geographic distribution over time. Sample surveys may be taken much more inexpensively than censuses and have been extensively employed. For example, French government agencies took most of the early fertility surveys, beginning in the 1950s (Caldwell, 1974). In 1955-56 the United Nations and the government of Sudan jointly undertook its first sample survey in Africa as a pilot project to obtain demographic statistics (Johnson-Acsadi, 1987). Over the years there have been about 130 fertility surveys conducted in African countries, with the World Fertility Survey directing most since 1974 (London, et al., 1985). In addition, many other types of demographic surveys have been carried out.

In the past, practically every demographic survey was a retrospective study that asked such questions as the number of children ever born and the number of births and deaths occurring during specified periods. Such data often contained large errors (Blacker, 1974). As a result, multiround surveys were designed to overcome the serious shortcomings of single-round surveys (Van de Walle, 1974). These multiround surveys match individuals in successive rounds, usually taken every six months or every year, and account for population changes much more accurately than single-round retrospective surveys (Tarver, 1983).

Appendix 2 provides selected information about the most recently conducted population censuses in each African country. For information on earlier censuses, see Evalds (1985), Domschke and Goyer (1986), and Pinfold (1985).

Civil Registration Statistics

Population censuses and vital statistics provide essential information for demographic analysis. While modern African censuses generally tend to be relatively reliable, civil registrations (particularly births and deaths) are underreported in approximately 45 of the 56 countries. As a result, censuses in Africa usually ask questions about births and deaths occurring in the year preceding the census. In addition, most countries limit their marriage statistics exclusively to civil marriages. Since most Africans follow their traditional marriage customs and do not enter into civil marriages, their traditional marriages are excluded from the official civil registration statistics.

SUMMARY

This book is designed to provide a basic understanding of the major aspects of demography in Africa, its past, present, and future. It introduces the subject of population by presenting the demographic concepts, data, and techniques that measure various population phenomena. Mathematical equations have been used only for illustrative purposes in projecting populations. A mastery of these materials should provide sufficient background for further study of Africa's population. The references for each chapter serve as suggested readings that may be supplemented by many other relevant publications.

In this book the demographic characteristics of the 56 African nations are analyzed in a simple, straightforward manner. Since Eritrea was not an independent nation prior to 1990 the United Nations has not prepared separate population estimates for it. Therefore, it will be included with Ethiopia here.

For each characteristic, the countries were classified by their distinguishing features. Then, the patterns of the characteristics were described. Often individual countries were mentioned for specific reasons. In following this procedure, some countries may have been cited much more frequently than others because of their unique features but not because of any effort to emphasize specific countries at the expense of others.

REFERENCES

Beloch, Julius. 1886. *Die Bevölkerung der Griechisch-Römischen Welt*. Leipzig, Germany: Duncker and Humblot. (Reprinted, New York: Arno Press, 1979.)

Blacker, J.G.C. 1974. "The Estimation of Vital Rates from Census Data in Kenya and Uganda." In *Population in African Development*, edited by Pierre Cantrelle, vol. 1, 199-209. Liége, Belgium: Ordina Editions.

Caldwell, John C. 1974. *The Study of Fertility and Fertility Change in Tropical Africa*. Occasional Paper no. 7, Voorburg and London: International Statistical Institute and World Fertility Survey.

Curtin, Philip D. 1969. *The Atlantic Slave Trade: A Census*. Madison, WI: University of Wisconsin Press.

Dawson, Marc H. 1981. "Disease and Population Decline of the Kikuyu of Kenya, 1890-1925." In *African Historical Demography*, edited by Christopher Fyfe and David McMaster, vol. 2, 121-138. Edinburgh, Scotland: University of Edinburgh.

d'Espaignet, E.T. 1984. *The Population of Seychelles*. Victoria, Mahe: President's Office, Republic of Seychelles.

Domschke, Eliane and Doreen S. Goyer. 1986. *The Handbook of National Population Censuses, Africa and Asia*. Westport, CT: Greenwood Press.

Easterlin, Richard A. 1982. *Immigration*. Cambridge, MA: Harvard University Press.

Evalds, Victoria K. 1985. *Union List of African Censuses, Development Plans, and Statistical Abstracts*. New York: Hans Zell Publishers.

Fleury, Michel and Louis Henry. 1965. *Nouveau Manuel de dépouillement et d'exploitation de l'état Civil Ancien*. Paris: Institut National d'études Démographiques.

Graunt, John. 1939. *Natural and Political Observations Made Upon the Bills of Mortality*, edited by Walter F. Willcox. Baltimore, MD: Johns Hopkins Press. (Originally published in London, 1662.)

Guillard, Achille. 1855. *Eléments de statistique Humaine ou démographie Comparée*. Paris: Guillaumin.

Hajnal, John. 1965. "European Marriage Patterns in Perspective." In *Population in History*, edited by David V. Glass and D.E.C. Eversley, 101-143. London: Edward Arnold.

Helleiner, Karl F.   1957.   "The Vital Revolution Reconsidered."   *Canadian Journal of Economics and Political Science* 23: 1-9.

Hendry, Peter. 1988. *Food and Population: Beyond Five Billion.* Population Bulletin, vol. 43. Washington, DC: Population Reference Bureau, Inc.

Johnson-Acsadi, Gwendolyn. 1987. "Fertility and Family Planning." *Population Bulletin of The United Nations*, Nos. 19/20, 44-62.

Kuznets, Simon S. et al. 1957-64. *Population Redistribution and Economic Growth: United States, 1870-1950.* 3 vols. Philadelphia, PA: American Philosophical Society.

Lamy, G. 1977. "The Demographic Situation in Mauritius." Seminar Paper on Population Growth and Development Planning, ECA/UNFPA. Rose Hill, Mauritius.

London, Kathy A. et al. 1985. "Fertility and Family Planning Surveys: An Update. "*Population Reports*, Series M, number 8. Baltimore, MD: Johns Hopkins University.

Lovejoy, Paul E. 1983. *Transformations in Slavery.* Cambridge: Cambridge University Press.

Malthus, Thomas R. 1798. *An Essay on the Principle of Population as It Affects the Future Improvement of Society, with Remarks on the Speculations of Mr. Godwin, M. Condorcet, and other writers.* London: Johnson.

Newman, James L. 1975. *Drought, Famine, and Population Movements.* Syracuse, NY: Syracuse University.

Norris, H.T. 1984. "Indigenous Peoples of the Sahara." In *Key Environments-Sahara Desert*, edited by J.L. Cloudsley-Thompson, 311-324. Oxford, England: Pergamon Press.

Ogden, P.E. 1987. "Historical Demography." In *Historical Geography: Progress and Prospect*, edited by Michael Pacione, 217-249. London: Croom Helm.

Petty, William. 1691. *Political arithmetick: or a discourse concerning the value of lands, people, buildings....As the same relates to every country in general, but more particularly to the territories of His Majesty of Great Britain and his neighbours of Holland and Zealand and France.* London: R. Clavel.

Pinfold, John R. 1985. *African Population Census Reports.* Oxford, England: Hans Zell Publishers.

Tarver, James D. 1983. *Multi-Round Demographic Survey, 1980/1981: Migration in Cyprus.* Nicosia, Cyprus: Ministry of Finance.

Thomas, Brinley. 1972. *Migration and Urban Development.* London: Methuen.

United Nations. 1949. *World Population Trends, 1920-1947.* New York.

_____. 1958. *The Future Growth of World Population.* New York.

_____. 1966. *World Population Prospects as Assessed in 1963.* New York.

_____. 1971. *1970 Demographic Yearbook.* New York.

_____. 1991. *World Population Prospects 1990*. New York.

_____. 1993. *World Population Prospects, 1992 Revision*. New York.

Van de Walle, Etienne. 1974. "The Role of Multi-Round Surveys in the Strategy of Demographic Research." In *Population in African Development*, edited by Pierre Cantrelle, vol. 1, 301-308. Liége, Belgium: Ordina Editions.

Worldmark Encyclopedia of the Nations. 1988. *Africa*, vol. 2. New York: Worldmark Press.

Wrigley, E.A. and R.S. Schofield. 1981. *The Population History of England: 1541-1871*. Cambridge, MA: Harvard University Press.

2

World Population Growth

Throughout history the population growth of different areas has been quite varied: rapid in certain periods, practically stationary in others, and at other times actually declining. These changes have been closely linked with political and social stability and unrest, as well as the availability of resources. Obviously, there were widely fluctuating populations usually characterized by high fertility and mortality and erratic shifts in migration. Epidemics, plagues, famines, and natural disasters took large tolls of human lives at different times, and patterns of population change varied greatly among different areas. Recently other factors, such as industrialization, urbanization, public health advances, and biomedical discoveries, have profoundly affected population change and distribution.

PREHISTORIC AND ANCIENT POPULATIONS

Paleontologists believe that human beings developed first in Africa. For example, during the approximate five billion years of the earth's history, traces of the human species existed in Africa throughout the great Pleistocene geological period (Butzer, 1971). Fossilized remains of a bipedal primate (*Australopithecus afarensis*), an ancestor of modern man, have been found in a geological stratum formed nearly four million years ago in Ethiopia and Tanzania (Johanson and Eddy, 1982). The earliest evidence of more modern human beings, the skeletal remains of *Homo erectus* and his stone tools, which are approximately one to two million years old, were found in Olduvai Gorge in Tanzania (Leakey, 1961).

In preparing prehistoric population estimates, Beloch and others chose the date of Augustus Caesar's death, A.D. 14, as a benchmark for estimating the population near the beginning of the Christian era. The reason for choosing this reference date was that A.D. 14 represented an important turning point in the population settlement and distribution of the Western world (Beloch, 1886). By A.D. 14 the coastal areas of the central and eastern Mediterranean had been fully settled, and the population density of the Levant region of Syria, Lebanon, and Palestine had nearly reached its maximum level. The attractive frontiers for future migration and settlement lay in Gaul, in northwestern Europe, where Julius Caesar had made earlier explorations. For this reason, population estimates for A.D. 14 reflect the distribution at one of the most important periods in the ancient history of the Western world (Usher, 1956).

The long period of population history from the beginning of human existence until the death of Augustus in A.D. 14 is the time about which we know the least concerning changing numbers, composition, and distribution of the world's people (Beloch, 1886). Demographic data for the first hundreds of thousands of years of human existence are but sketchy estimates. However, the precision of such estimates tends to improve gradually with the passage of time, even though most estimates remained deficient as to accuracy and detail until modern times.

Population estimates for various dates during prehistoric times indicate that the rate of growth probably speeded up as the period ended. Early groups of nomadic hunters and gatherers were small in size and particularly subject to the hazards of severe climatic changes. Archaeologists believe that hunters-gatherers kept their numbers well below the food-carrying capacities of the areas they occupied (Shaw, 1981). Thus, they may have had a slightly higher standard of living and fewer communicable diseases than some early agriculturalists.

In the prehistoric period mortality was usually quite high, and there is evidence that men outlived women. Certainly, lives were very short, and fossil remains suggest that many lives ended in violence. Under these extreme, primitive conditions, population growth was very slow and frequently erratic (UN, 1973).

Angel (1947) estimated the longevity of prehistoric people in Greece to be only 18 years. A later estimate for the Roman period at the beginning of the Christian era was a life expectancy at birth of 22 years (Pearson 1901-02). The average length of life almost doubled from prehistoric days to the Middle Ages. For example, Halley's life table for Breslau (now Wroclaw), Poland, gave a life expectancy at birth of 33.5 years for the 1687-91 period. Then, the life expectancy at birth remained practically stationary for another 200 years. Within the last 150 years longevity has almost doubled, with Japan now having an average life expectancy at birth of 79 years (UN, 1991). In fact, more than 60 countries and territories have life expectancies at birth of 70 years or more.

Improved living conditions and technological improvements in agriculture, medicine, and public health have been important factors in increasing longevity. However, it does not appear that the increase in longevity has been due to any inherited trait or characteristic.

Death rates have declined since prehistoric days as average life expectancy increased. The declining mortality levels may be approximated from life expectancies. For example, early man's life expectancy of 18 years implies a crude death rate of 56 per 1,000 population. When life expectancy increased to 22 years, the crude death rate fell to 45. For a life expectancy of 33.5 years, the implied crude death rate was 30. Finally, as in the case of Japan, a life expectancy of 79 years implies a crude death rate of 13 per 1,000 population.

Fertility levels had to be very high for replacement of the population in the prehistoric era, with estimated crude birth rates of 50-60 per 1,000 population, with females rearing at least three daughters on the average. Obviously birth rates fluctuated from time to time in different areas.

There were somewhere between five and 10 million people on earth when agriculture and the domestication of animals began about 10 thousand years ago in the Tigris and Euphrates Valleys of Mesopotamia following the final retreat of the glaciers (Deevey, 1960). The agricultural revolution developed in Egypt's Lower Nile Valley soon after. These developments made it possible to support denser populations than in the hunting and gathering societies that preceded them. The sedentary way of life greatly expanded food supplies, and advances in agriculture eventually produced surpluses.

The rate of population growth accelerated somewhat after the adoption of agriculture and the domestication of animals, as these advances resulted in much greater, more dependable food supplies in the new agricultural settlements. Tool making, metallurgy, and other technological developments enabled people to live in increasingly larger settlements, which resulted in some division of labor and improvements in standards of living. In some instances the sedentary life increased birth rates, and higher population densities of agriculturalists raised death rates by causing sanitation problems and increasing exposure to communicable diseases (Lee, 1972). The latter part of the prehistoric period was marked by slow, widely fluctuating population gains from area to area, somewhat greater than those prior to the beginning of agriculture.

Cities first appeared around 3500 to 3300 B.C. near the Nile and the Tigris and Euphrates Rivers, marking the beginning of urbanization in the world. Around 1650 B.C., Avaris, Egypt, was the first city to reach 100,000 inhabitants (Chandler, 1987). Not long afterward, the Mesopotamian cities of Babylon and Nineveh for a time surpassed the size of all other cities of the world. Significantly, these gains in cities reflect the general population growth occurring throughout the two earliest areas of agricultural production and urbanization. Notwithstanding the early and impressive demographic, social, and economic developments in the Nile Valley, Egypt was destined to be exploited by a succession of foreign invaders beginning with the Hyksos rulers from Asia around 1650 B.C. They were followed, in succession, by Persians, Greeks, Romans, Arabs, and Turks, invaders who occupied this country for more than 2,000 years. During this time its population declined nearly 75 percent as a result of exploitation, disruption of the economy, and social disintegration.

The two most populous countries in Asia were experiencing divergent population trends during this period. For example, the population of China in A.D. 2 was estimated to be 71 million (Durand, 1960). For the next 1700 to 1800 years, it experienced marked fluctuations due to dynastic growth and decay. In 300 B.C. India was thought to have had between 100 and 140 million inhabitants (Nath, 1929). A series of calamities resulted in heavy population losses and the population remained relatively stable for almost 2,000 years.

POPULATION BEFORE 1650

It took all of human history before the death of Augustus in A.D. 14 for the world population to reach an estimated quarter of a billion. Then, during the next 16-17 centuries it nearly doubled, going from about 260 million in A.D. 14 to 516 million in 1650 (table 2.1). However, practically all of this growth occurred after the year 1000.

Much of this period prior to A.D. 1000, the Dark Ages, was characterized by general stagnation. There were great fluctuations and dislocations of the population in some regions. Armed invasions occurred in the western Roman Empire, central and western Europe, and parts of Asia and Africa, along with dynastic successions in China. Famines and pestilence led to political and economic crises in those areas. Eastern, northern, and western Africa experienced instability during this time. Barbaric invasions exercised restraining influences on fertility in some areas of the world, and epidemics were factors in increasing mortality. For example, the Justinian plague, lasting from A.D. 542 to 600, may have taken as many as 100 million lives throughout the world (UN, 1973). As a result, the world population during this thousand-year period was relatively constant. Actual population losses in Europe and Asia occurred during the Dark Ages (table 2.1). On the other hand, Latin America, the former Soviet republics, and Africa (but only the areas south of the Sahara) experienced population gains, being the regions of the world least affected by the prevailing turmoil characteristic of that period.

The economic recovery and expansion that began in the eleventh century was accompanied by population growth in most areas of the world. From 1000 to 1650 the devastating effects of various wars, famines, and plagues (such as the Black Death which struck Europe and North Africa around 1350) certainly had restraining effects upon population growth. Even so, the world's population increased 85 percent, or by nearly a quarter of a billion persons, between 1000 and 1650.

POPULATION FROM 1650 TO 1950

Population growth accelerated during this period at an ever increasing rate (Durand, 1967). For example, the rate of growth of the world's population rose from an estimated average annual rate of 0.3 percent in the years 1650-1750 to 0.8 percent from 1900 to 1950, and the 1950 population was nearly five times that of 1650. All major regions except Africa and Oceania had steadily increasing numbers of inhabitants throughout this period. From 1650 to 1800 the number of inhabitants was fairly stable with a slight dip in 1750 (table 2.2).

The industrialized European countries had a lower rate of population growth from 1900 to 1950 than in the years 1850-1900. On the other hand, Africa, Asia, and Latin America, the three developing regions, had comparatively larger population gains in 1900-50 than in 1850-1900 due to relatively high birth rates and small to moderate declines in mortality. Biomedical and scientific agricultural discoveries in the industrialized nations were applied to combat disease and famine in the developing nations after World War II. Medical discoveries were employed worldwide to conquer such fatal communicable diseases as yellow fever, smallpox, whooping cough, tetanus, tuberculosis, and diphtheria. Swamps infested with mosquitoes were sprayed with the insecticide DDT to control malaria and yellow fever. With birth rates increasing in Africa, the resulting decline in mortality led to rapid population growth.

Many important social and economic events occurred in this 300-year period that had profound impacts upon the world's population. Divergent patterns and trends in birth and death rates led to contrasting population growth patterns in the rapidly industrialized developed countries and in the poor developing countries. The Industrial Revolution, which began in England in the eighteenth century, provided thousands of new employment opportunities at increased real wages. Marriage rates rose and birth rates increased until they reached their peak in the early 1800s. Very large population gains occurred in England and in most western European countries until around 1890 to 1920, when birth rates dropped. In Ireland, Romania, and Albania, fertility declined after 1920. The rapid population growth in Europe was over, but it was yet to begin in the developing countries.

This generalized pattern of population change in the developed countries is known as the demographic transition (Thompson, 1929; Notestein, 1945). However, it is still questionable whether the demographic transition is applicable to Africa (Henin, 1971).

Africa had low rates of population growth between 1750 and 1900, during which time the developed countries were industrializing and registering record population gains (table 2.2). Population growth accelerated in Africa in 1900-50, but it was not until after 1970 that record rates of population increase occurred as a result of rising birth rates and declining death rates. Although Africa's birth and death rates probably increased for awhile after colonization, mortality rates did not decline appreciably until after World War II.

POPULATION GROWTH BETWEEN 1950 AND 1990

The rate of growth of the world's population continued to increase slightly through 1965-70, when it leveled off and began to drop gradually (table 2.3). Overall, nearly 2.8 billion people were added to the world's population between 1950 and 1990, with 87 percent of the growth occurring in the developing countries. Moreover, the number of inhabitants in the developing countries more than doubled, while the number in developed countries grew by 45 percent. By 1990, over three-quarters of the world's population were living in the developing countries (UN, 1991, 1993).

Latin America was the most rapidly growing of all major regions in the 1950-70 period. Africa was second, while Europe was the slowest growing. Between 1970 and 1990 Africa had the highest rate of population growth and Latin America dropped to second. Changes in the levels of birth and death rates in Africa and Latin America accounted for shifts in growth patterns. For example, Africa had around 45 births and 15 deaths per 1,000 population in 1985-90, giving it a natural increase of 30 per 1,000 population, the highest of all major regions. High birth rates, falling death rates, and increased life expectancy resulted in large population gains and a three percent annual growth rate.

Asia, with nearly 60 percent of the world's inhabitants, had a population increase of over 1.7 billion, or over 125 percent, between 1950 and 1990. Western Asia was the most rapidly growing region, with a gain of over 200 percent. China, the most populous country in the world, had a population growth of 105 percent. India, the second most populous country, grew by nearly 140 percent, whereas Japan had only a 48 percent gain.

Currently, the population of East, Middle, and West Africa is increasing at an annual rate of 3.0 to 3.2 percent, while North and South Africa's annual growth rate is 2.4 to 2.6 percent. From 1950 to 1990 North Africa's population increased by nearly 90 million, which was more than 170 percent, while sub-Saharan Africa's population grew 331 million, or 195 percent. The changing patterns of birth and death rates account for the comparatively higher population gains in sub-Saharan Africa. For instance, the sub-Saharan crude birth rate remained constant between 46 and 48, but the North African crude birth rate declined about 20 percent to under 40. Moreover, the crude death rates of all five regions in Africa fell 40 to 50 percent between 1950 and 1990.

FUTURE POPULATION

According to UN population projections, Africa is expected to have nearly 1.6 billion inhabitants in 2025, a gain of 955 million or 150 percent since 1990, and it will continue to be the most rapidly growing region of the world (table 2.3). In contrast, Europe is projected to have the smallest relative increase with three percent.

Table 2.1
World Population Estimates, by Major Region, A.D. 14-1650 (in millions)

Region	Population by Year									
	A.D. 14	350	600	800	1000	1200	1340	1500	1600	1650
WORLD TOTAL	256	254	237	261	280	384	378	427	498	516
Africa	23	30	37	43	50	61	70	85	95	100
Asia	184	185	168	173	172	242	186	225	297	305
North America								1	1	1
Latin America	3	5	7	10	13	23	29	40	14	12
Europe	40	28	19	29	31	45	77	62	72	75
Oceania	1	1	1	1	1	1	2	2	2	2
Former Soviet Republics	5	5	5	5	13	12	14	12	17	21

Source: Compiled from various series of A.D. 14-1650 population estimates.

Table 2.2
World Population Estimates, by Major Region, 1650-1950 (in millions)

Region	Population by Year							
	1650	1700	1750	1800	1850	1900	1940	1950
WORLD TOTAL	516	641	728	906	1171	1608	2295	2516
Africa	100	100	95	90	95	120	191	222
Asia	305	414	475	597	741	915	1244	1377
North America	1	1	1	6	26	81	144	166
Latin America	12	12	11	19	33	63	130	166
Europe	75	86	113	146	208	296	380	393
Oceania	2	2	2	2	2	6	11	13
Former Soviet Republics	21	26	31	46	66	127	195	180

Source: Compiled from various series of 1650-1950 population estimates.

Table 2.3
World Population, by Major Region, 1950-2025 (in millions)

Region	Population by Year					
	1950	1970	1990	2000	2025
WORLD TOTAL	2516	3698	5292	6261	8504
Developed Regions	832	1049	1206	1264	1354
Developing Regions	1684	2649	4086	4997	7150
Africa	222	362	642	867	1597
Asia	1377	2102	3113	3713	4912
North America	166	226	276	295	332
Latin America	166	286	448	538	757
Europe	393	460	498	510	515
Oceania	13	19	26	30	38
Former Soviet Republics	180	243	289	308	352

Source: Compiled from United Nations, *World Population Prospects 1990*
(Sales No. E.91.XIII.4).

21

Population growth in Asia, the most populous region of the world, is likely to be very high during the period from 1990 to 2025. For example, the projected gain is 1.8 billion people, bringing the total Asian population to 4.9 billion in 2025. China is projected to have 1.5 billion people in 2025, and India is likely to have 1.4 billion. In comparison, Africa, while projected to be the most rapidly growing major region in the world, will be the second most populous region in 2025 with only a third as many people as Asia.

Recent long-range projections indicate that Africa's population may exceed three billion by the year 2125 (UN, 1992). This medium fertility assumption shows that Africa will be the most populous major region of the world at that time. India is projected to have 1.9 billion inhabitants and China will be third largest, with less than 1.4 billion, both considerably less than projected for Africa.

SUMMARY AND IMPLICATIONS

The demographic transition that occurred in developed countries at different times under differing circumstances resulted in low birth and death rates as well as low rates of population growth. In Africa death rates have declined but birth rates have been increasing in some countries. The stage of the demographic transition which Africa is currently in is the transitional growth phase with comparatively high rates of population growth of three percent annually.

An important and relevant question, of course, is whether Africa will ever complete the demographic transition it has begun. Obviously, there are several uncertainties. First, the birth rates of the developed countries were never as high as those in Africa. Thus, the African fertility levels must fall absolutely and comparatively much more to reach low levels. Second, except in South Africa, the region is not entering a definite Industrial Revolution, which would greatly alter the underlying customs and social and economic conditions of families.

Apparently, the nature of the future demographic transition in Africa will differ in some respects from the experiences of the developed countries. For example, the decline in the birth rates of developed countries came from family limitation practices that were primarily due to individual choices made in response to social and economic realities of the era. In Africa, however, family planning programs and national population policies are attempting to stem the unprecedented population growth. In both instances there have been increases in fertility during the early stages of modernization. It may require many generations to complete the demographic transition in Africa by achieving low birth rates and low rates of population growth. Nevertheless, fertility declines in Kenya, Zimbabwe, Botswana, Sudan, and Senegal have been noted in recent contraceptive surveys which seem to indicate that general declines in birth rates are likely to occur.

REFERENCES

Angel, J. Lawrence. 1947. "The Length of Life in Ancient Greece." *Journal of Gerontology* 2: 18-24.

Beloch, Julius. 1886. *Die Bevölkerung der Griechisch-Römischen Welt*. Leipzig, Germany: Duncker and Humblot. (Reprinted, New York: Arno Press, 1979.)

Butzer, Karl W. 1971. *Environment and Archeology: An Ecological Approach to Prehistory*. Chicago: Aldine-Atherton.

Chandler, Tertius. 1987. *Four Thousand Years of Urban Growth*. Lewiston, New York: St. David's University Press.

Deevey, Edward S. Jr. 1960. "The human population." *Scientific American* 203: 195-204.

Durand, John D. 1960. "The population statistics of China, A.D. 2-1953." *Population Studies* 13: 209-256.

Durand, John D. 1967. "The Modern Expansion of World Population." *Proceedings of the American Philosophical Society* 111: 136-159.

Henin, Roushdi A. 1971. "On the Applicability of the Theory of Demographic Transition to African Countries." In *The Demographic Transition in Tropical Africa*, 15-26. Paris: Development Centre of the Organization for Economic Co-operation and Development.

Johanson, Donald C. and Maitland A. Eddy. 1982. *Lucy: The Beginnings of Humankind*. New York: Warner Books.

Leakey, Louis B. 1961. *The Progress and Evolution of Man in Africa*. London: Oxford University Press.

Lee, Richard B. 1972. "Population Growth and the Beginnings of Sedentary Life Among the !Kung Bushmen." In *Population Growth: Anthropological Implications*, edited by Brian Spooner, 330-342. Cambridge, MA: M.I.T. Press.

Nath, Pran. 1929. *A Study in the Economic Condition of Ancient India*. London: Royal Asiatic Society.

Notestein, Frank W. 1945. "Population: The Long View." In *Food For the World*, edited by Theodore W. Schultz, 36-57. Chicago: University of Chicago Press.

Pearson, Karl. 1901-02. "On the Change in Expectation of Life in Man During a Period Circa 2000 Years." *Biometrika* 1:261-264.

Shaw, Thurston. 1981. "Towards a Prehistoric Demography of Africa." In *African Historical Demography*, edited by Christopher Fyfe and David McMaster, vol. 2, 581-606. Edinburgh, Scotland: University of Edinburgh.

Thompson, Warren S. 1929. "Population." *American Journal of Sociology* 34: 959-975.

Usher, Abbott Payson. 1956. "The History of Population and Settlement in
  Eurasia." In *Demographic Analysis*, edited by Joseph J. Spengler and Otis
  Dudley Duncan, 3-25. Glencoe, Il: Free Press.
United Nations. 1973. *The Determinants and Consequences of Population
  Trends*, vol. 1. New York.
_____. 1991. *World Population Prospects 1990.* New York.
_____. 1992. *Long-Range World Population Projections: Two Centuries
  of Population Growth, 1950-2150.* New York.
_____.   1993. *World Population Prospects, The 1992 Revision.* New
  York.

3

Population Growth in Africa

Africa has undoubtedly experienced the longest period of external domination and subjugation of any major region in the world. Many of these outside influences greatly restrained population growth and depleted the number of its inhabitants. However, other external influences, especially in this century, have greatly increased Africa's population.

PREHISTORIC POPULATIONS

The prehistoric population estimates for Africa are mainly for Egypt. When Alexander the Great conquered Egypt in 332 B.C., the total population was estimated to have been seven million. In the second century B.C. the Romans destroyed Carthage, which was the largest African city on the western Mediterranean and had approximately 200,000 inhabitants. By the first century B.C. the Romans had completely occupied North Africa, controlling Egypt on the east as well as the 4,000 miles of territory west to the Atlantic Ocean and north of the Sahara. During their occupation, the Romans imported large quantities of farm products from North Africa.

Some prehistoric population estimates of Africa have been made from 3000 B.C. going back as far as two million years (Shaw, 1981). According to Shaw, Africa's total population was about five million in 3000 B.C. when nonagricultural towns and cities were first appearing, and there were about two million people around 10,000 B.C. when permanent agriculture began. The population estimate for 500,000 years ago was less than half a million. Two million years ago, when most of the earth's inhabitants presumably lived in Africa, the total population was around a quarter of a million (Shaw, 1981).

POPULATION TO 1650

Africa's population was estimated to have been 23 million at the death of Augustus in A.D. 14 (table 2.1). By 1650 Africa's population had increased to 100 million, a fivefold gain since A.D. 14. Practically all of this growth occurred in the large area south of the Sahara, and about half of the growth took place after the year 1000. Of course, the different population figures are strictly estimates, but most appear reasonable and consistent with changes over time.

North Africa

Egypt and the Maghreb area of northwestern Africa were the two sites of the earliest urban population centers in North Africa, although urbanization was much earlier in Egypt. By the fourth century B.C. a flourishing civilization was emerging in the Nile Delta. Around 3500 B.C. the Kingdom of Pharaohs was formed, which persisted for about 3,000 years. The Cush culture in Sudan, which began about 1700 B.C., evolved from Egypt.

Permanent agriculture and the domestication of animals eventually created surpluses of food in the Nile region. Towns and cities grew in size as population increased. Egypt soon became the most urbanized country in the ancient world. For example, Memphis was the world's largest city around 3000 B.C. Later, Avaris, Thebes, and Alexandria were the largest cities in the world at various times before the Christian era. Egypt is the only African country for which separate population estimates have been made for various estimate dates between A.D. 14 and 1650. In A.D. 14 it had an estimated seven million inhabitants, the same as at the time of Alexander the Great's invasion in 332 B.C. Then the population dropped to a low of two million in 1200 and remained at three million from 1500 to 1650. During these long years of foreign invasions and misrule, Egypt's population first drastically declined then remained almost stationary.

The Berbers were the earliest settlers in the western Mediterranean region of Africa, arriving there before 2000 B.C. Northwestern Africa became a rich agricultural area, producing large quantities of olives and wheat, and the Berbers were very active in the trans-Saharan trade in the West African countries. In 814 B.C. the Phoenicians founded the city-state of Carthage on the bay of Tunisia, which developed a thriving trade and was considered to be the richest city in the world. By 146 B.C. mercantile and territorial competition with the Romans resulted in war and destruction of Carthage, which had reached a population of about 200,000 (Charles-Picard, 1961). By A.D. 1000 central and western North Africa had around one million inhabitants, which increased to about four million by 1500.

Sub-Saharan Africa

Thousands of years ago, members of the Bantu language group, which originated in the Congo River basin, began their long complex migrations throughout most of the middle, eastern, and southern regions of sub-Saharan black Africa. The farthest point of their movement was reached in South Africa shortly after the death of Augustus Caesar in A.D. 14. As the Bantus moved, their culture was adopted by the indigenous inhabitants along the way. These Bantu migrants were largely responsible for populating the area south of the Sahara, and they also changed the hunting and gathering cultures they found to cultivation and pastoral economies, as well as disseminating their knowledge of iron-working.

Although reliable population estimates are lacking for the regions and countries south of the Sahara during the period following the Bantu migration, it is known that the area as a whole experienced gradual gains from 12 million in A.D. 14 to 79 million in 1500. East Africa sustained increases from the middle of the thirteenth century to the end of the fifteenth century. Sizeable migrations into eastern and southern Africa contributed to population growth in these two regions. However, West Africa is believed to have suffered population losses because of unsettled conditions resulting from unrest and warfare.

Although slave trading was to have a significant effect upon the population of Africa before it ended, its impact before 1600 is believed to have been rather small. It is estimated, for example, that trans-Atlantic slave trading reduced the African population by no more than 400,000 prior to 1600, with the majority of the people sold into slavery coming from West Africa and Angola (Lovejoy, 1982, 1983).

POPULATION FROM 1650 TO 1950

Africa was characterized by high birth rates throughout this period--and by high death rates during most of it--resulting in a relatively constant population until 1850. There was some growth after 1850, but it was not until 1900-50 that Africa's population growth began to accelerate. From 1900 to 1950, for example, the annual rate of growth was approximately 1.7 percent, which was about the same rate of increase as that in the United States until the onset of the worldwide economic depression in the 1930s. Numerous epidemics and plagues in Africa during the 1900-30 period kept the number of inhabitants relatively stable.

A thorough study of the British colonial population in this period shows that the number of inhabitants in British West Africa remained nearly constant during the first quarter of this century, then increased thereafter (Kuczynski, 1948). On the other hand, the population of British East Africa was thought to have declined in the first quarter of this century, then increased afterwards (Kuczynski, 1949;

Martin 1953, 1961).

During the latter part of this period both North and sub-Saharan Africa had moderately high rates of population growth. The first Egyptian census showed 6.7 million inhabitants in 1882, an increase of approximately four million since 1650. With high birth rates and declining death rates, population increases continued, with the 1947 Egyptian census enumerating 19 million. Algeria, Morocco, and Tunisia also experienced substantial gains. For instance, the number of inhabitants in Algeria rose from 2.0 million in 1845 to 7.5 million in 1948, and the population of Tunisia grew from 2.0 million in 1921 to 3.2 million in 1946. Annual growth rates in the Republic of South Africa were around two percent between 1911 and 1950.

Nonetheless, several major factors tended to reduce Africa's population growth from 1650 to 1950: slave trading, European colonization that introduced contagious fatal diseases, and general unrest accompanying colonialism.

Slave Trading

African slaves were cheap and plentiful, and nearly 20 million were sold in trade across the Atlantic Ocean, the Sahara Desert, the Red Sea, and the Indian Ocean. For example, Lovejoy (1983) estimated that 11.7 million slaves were imported to the Americas between 1450 and 1900--6.1 million from 1701 to 1800, the peak period. Moreover, Austen (1979) estimated that the total slave trade by Arabs came to million, with the largest number being sold from 900 to 1400. Of this total, 4.8 million were sold as part of the trans-Saharan trade, 1.6 million were forcibly deported from Red Sea ports, and 0.8 million went to the East African coast. This provides an overall estimate of approximately 19 million African slaves traded. Almost 60 percent of those sent to the Americas came from West Africa and most of the rest from middle and southeastern Africa.

The impact of the slave trade upon African societies has been a subject of lively debate among scholars. One point of view is that the relatively small numbers exported exerted a comparatively minor influence upon the total population and the economies (Ogden, 1987). A contrasting view is that serious adverse demographic and economic consequences resulted. According to one scholar, slave trading reduced the actual 1880 sub-Saharan population by about half, or more than 100 million persons (Inikori, 1982). Similarly, it has been claimed that the two million slaves taken by the Portuguese from Angola left the country helpless and in shambles, that Portuguese criminals were hired to divide the natives into warring factions, and that conditions in Mozambique were just as vicious (Oliver and Fage, 1972).

Obviously, slave trading altered the age-sex structure of village populations in Africa. First, slaves were young, with few being over 30 years of age. Second, the majority were males, particularly those in the trans-Atlantic trade. However, in the slave trade by Arabs there was a definite preference for women and children. Often women were priced twice as high as men. Of course, the demographic effects of slave exportation varied with the number, age, and sex of those captured. Many villages disappeared after the raids, with all survivors scattering. In any event, slave trading left large proportions of very young and old people in many depopulated villages, with relatively few in the most productive young adult ages. Both Manning (1981, 1982) and Thornton (1980) have shown that the demographic effects of the trading of slaves were significant. Thornton, for example, found that the sex imbalances in Angolan villages conformed closely to the sex ratios of the slaves sold in the trans-Atlantic trade.

Effects of Diseases

Infectious diseases transmitted by Europeans proved fatal to thousands of Africans in the same way as they did to certain populations in the Americas who were reduced by diseases of European origin (Willcox, 1940). Europeans introduced such crops as maize, cassava, sweet potatoes, tobacco, and pineapple from the Americas, but they also introduced influenza, measles, and some strains of smallpox and other communicable diseases. For example, the influenza pandemic that reached the continent of Africa initially through Freetown, Sierra Leone, in August, 1918 cost the lives of about 1.35 million Africans in less than a year (Patterson, 1981). This outbreak proved to be the most deadly catastrophe that ever occurred in Africa in such a brief period of time and took about 30 million lives worldwide.

Apparently, the population of Kenya declined from 1890 to 1925 due to the ravages of epidemics introduced by Europeans, famines, and plagues (Dawson, 1981). Smallpox epidemics that followed the 1892 and 1898-1900 famines wiped out the entire populations of many Kikuyu and Masai villages, taking the lives of at least ten percent of all the country's inhabitants. After these disasters a devastating cerebrospinal meningitis epidemic swept through the Kikuyu territory in 1913. Then, after World War I, many military servicemen returned with malaria, dysentery, and other diseases. In Kenya a famine followed the continent-wide influenza pandemic of 1918-19, which was followed in 1919-20 by a plague. Rinderpest outbreaks and locust swarms occurred several times, resulting in the worst famine experienced in years. From a tenth to one-half of the weakened inhabitants of many villages died either from starvation, dysentery, smallpox, influenza, meningitis, malaria, or some other affliction related to the famine. Uganda and Tanzania were depopulated in the same way (Clark, 1977).

At the Cape of Good Hope in South Africa the deadly smallpox epidemics came much earlier than in eastern Africa. In fact, three major smallpox epidemics occurred in the eighteenth century: one in 1713, another in 1755, and a third in 1767 (Ross, 1977). The epidemics of 1713 and 1755 ravaged the entire Cape and practically wiped out the Khoi Culture.

Political Strife and Unrest

The nineteenth century, especially, was one of maneuvering and quarreling among European nations for trading rights, and political and strategic control, over various African territories. Forced labor and taxes, such as the hut tax levied by the British in 1898 in Sierra Leone, created unrest. Forced labor was required of Burkina Faso natives in the Côte d'Ivoire. Often a territory occupied by one European country was made up of warring factions. This was a continuous source of strife. For example, in South Africa the Boer War and Zulu raids uprooted literally thousands from their homes. These struggles, not only with Europeans but among Africans themselves, served throughout colonial rule as checks on population growth in many areas, even though declining death rates led to population growth in the latter part of the 1650 to 1950 period.

POPULATION GROWTH BETWEEN 1950 AND 1990

The high birth rates between 1950 and 1990, coupled with declining death rates, resulted in Africa's population more than doubling, going from 222 million in 1950 to 642 million in 1990. Between 1970 and 1980, for the first time in history, Africa had the highest rate of population growth of all major regions in the world (Tarver and Miller, 1986). From 1985 to 1990 Africa had the highest birth rate of all major regions of the world, a crude rate of 45 per 1,000 population. Its crude death rate was still the highest, but it had dropped to 15, yielding a rate of population increase of three percent per year, which indicates a doubling in the size of the population in 23 years.

From 1950 to 1990 West and East Africa, already the two most populous regions, had the highest proportionate population gains. North and Middle Africa had the next highest, and South Africa had the lowest relative gains. Generally, population increases in the 55 individual African countries were exceedingly high during this period. For instance, the number of inhabitants tripled in a few countries and, in about half of the countries, the population doubled. Throughout the period, however, birth rates were declining slightly. The unprecedented growth was due, in part, to medical and hygiene breakthroughs reducing mortality, particularly infant mortality, and extending life expectancy. Rates of population growth rose in this short period from 2.2 percent in 1950-55 to 3.0 percent in 1985-90 as death rates declined and birth rates in sub-Saharan Africa remained somewhat constant.

The population of Africa more than doubled between 1950 and 1990 despite the unfavorable and unstable political, social, and economic climate that prevailed. First, it was during this period that all African nations, except South Africa and Egypt, obtained their independence from the European colonial powers. Libya, which had been under an Anglo-French military government since the defeat of Italy in 1943, was the third colony to obtain its independence in 1951. While South Africa became independent in 1910 and Egypt in 1922, Morocco and Tunisia followed with their independence from France in 1956. Sudan also obtained its independence from Great Britain in 1956. Most remaining French colonies achieved their independence in the 1960s. Finally, Zimbabwe obtained its independence in 1980, over 500 years after the Portuguese settled the Cape Verde Islands in 1462 and more than 300 years after the Dutch settled the Cape of Good Hope in 1652.

African countries have experimented with a wide variety of political systems and institutions since their recent independence. There have been one-party political systems, multiparty political systems, socialist and Marxist governments, and civilian and military rule, along with many sudden and violent changes in government (McGowan and Johnson, 1984). Although political instability was not conducive to population and economic growth, large population increases occurred nevertheless.

Over the years guerrilla warfare, ethnic conflicts, and political oppression, as well as other forms of strife, have forced millions of Africans to seek asylum in other African countries. Part of this involuntary immigration is only temporary, as some refugees eventually return home. The rest of the forced immigration becomes permanent for refugees who settled in the country of their asylum. In 1975, an estimated 1.2 million African refugees were outside their home country, with 460,000 Angolans in Zaire (UNHCR, 1989, 1990). By 1980, Africa had more refugees than any other major region of the world, over three million, with more than a million Ethiopian refugees in Somalia and half a million in Sudan. In addition, prolonged domestic strife in many countries has been exacerbated by drought and famine to swell the numbers of refugees. At the end of 1987 half of Africa's 3.6 million refugees had sought asylum in either Somalia, Sudan, or Ethiopia. By 1989 there were nearly 4.6 million political and economic refugees in Africa, the largest number of all major regions in the world. Guerrilla activity and unrest in Mozambique led to over one million fleeing to Malawi, Zimbabwe, and Zambia. The Tutsi people's policy of genocide toward the Hutu people has created long-standing tensions in Burundi and Rwanda, and has driven as many as 100,000 Hutus to squalid refugee camps.

FUTURE POPULATION

Projections of the world population indicate that Africa will be the most rapidly growing region at least until 2025. While the total world population is expected to increase by 60 percent, the number in Africa is expected to more than double, going from 642 million in 1990 to nearly 1.6 billion in 2025. The young age structure of the African population will insure large increases until 2025 and beyond.

In practically every African country, projected population increases to 2025 are very large. For example, UN projections indicate that, by 2025, five of the 20 most populous countries in the world will be in Africa. Nigeria, which is projected to have 280 million residents, will be the sixth most populous country in the world. Ethiopia is likely to have over 127 million, Egypt and Zaire about 90-100 million each, and Tanzania and Kenya between 80 and 85 million each.

Altogether, half a dozen African countries are projected to have at least a fourfold increase in the number of their inhabitants by 2025. Nearly 30 countries are expected to triple their population and about 15 to double. East, Middle, and West Africa are projected to have the highest population increases of all regions, and North and South Africa will have the lowest.

Should Africa be fortunate and escape a really devastating AIDS epidemic, its population may very well reach three billion by 2125 (UN, 1992). So, in less than 150 years, the number of inhabitants may be approximately five times its present number and Africa would become the most populous major region in the world. These possibilities, of course, raise many perplexing questions.

SUMMARY AND IMPLICATIONS

The implications of the very rapid projected population growth in Africa are far-reaching. Future standards of living and per capita income depend upon both future population growth and future economic growth. There is always a possibility that future rates of population increase will exceed rates of economic growth, resulting in declining per capita incomes and standards of living (World Bank, 1985, 1986). Family planning programs and national governmental policies are now being employed to limit population growth.

As a consequence of increasing rates of population growth and mounting population pressures, more and more African countries want to lower their fertility rates. The World Fertility and Contraceptive Prevalence Surveys show that 20 percent of all North African couples and only 10 percent of sub-Saharan couples use contraceptive techniques.

About three-fourths of the African countries are presently participating in various family planning programs. Most governments encourage private planned parenthood associations to carry out various phases of the programs. In some countries as many as eight or 10 agencies and organizations may coordinate in this effort. Governments often integrate family planning in their maternal and child health services by emphasizing birth spacing for health reasons.

In addition to active family planning programs, many African governments have taken legal measures to reduce fertility. For example, some countries have raised the legal age for marriage. Others have outlawed polygamy. Some countries also now limit child allowances for government officials to no more than three or four children and some limit the number of maternity leaves.

The emphasis upon family limitation has achieved some success in Mauritius,

Tunisia, and a few other countries in recent years. Development efforts that integrate the improvement of the status of women with family planning programs offer many possibilities.

REFERENCES

Austen, Ralph A. 1979. "The Trans-Saharan Slave Trade: A Tentative Census." In *The Uncommon Market: Essays in the Economic History of the Atlantic Slave Trade*, edited by H.A. Gemery and J.S. Hogendorn, 23-76. New York: Academic Press.

Charles-Picard, Gilbert and Colette Charles-Picard. 1961. *Daily Life in Carthage at the Time of Hannibal*. New York: Macmillan.

Clark, Colin. 1977. *Population Growth and Land Use*. London: The Macmillan Press.

Dawson, Marc H. 1981. "Disease and Population Decline of the Kikuyu of Kenya, 1890-1925." In *African Historical Demography*, edited by Christopher Fyfe and David McMaster, vol. 2, 121-138. Edinburgh, Scotland: University of Edinburgh.

Inikori, J.E. 1982. *Forced Migration*. New York: Africana Publishing Company.

Kuczynski, Robert R. 1948. *Demographic Survey of the British Colonial Empire: West Africa*, vol. 1. London: Oxford University Press.

_____. 1949. *Demographic Survey of the British Colonial Empire: East Africa*, vol. 2. London: Oxford University Press.

Lovejoy, Paul E. 1982. "The Volume of the Atlantic Slave Trade: A Synthesis." *Journal of African History* 23: 473-501.

_____. 1983. *Transformations in Slavery*. Cambridge: Cambridge University Press.

Manning, Patrick. 1981. "The Enslavement of Africans: A Demographic Model." *Canadian Journal of African Studies* 15: 499-526.

_____. 1982. *Slavery, Colonialism and Economic Growth in Dahomey, 1640-1960*. Cambridge: Cambridge University Press.

Martin, C.J. 1953. "Natural Increase of the African Population of British East Africa." *Population Studies* 7: 181-199.

_____. 1961. "Population Census Estimates and Methods in British East Africa" and "Estimates of Population Growth in East Africa, with Special Reference to Tanganyika and Zanzibar." In *Essays on African Population*, edited by K.M. Barbour and R.M. Prothero, 17-30 and 49-62. London: Routledge & Kegan Paul.

McGowan, Pat and Thomas H. Johnson. 1984. "African Military Coups d'Etat and Underdevelopment: A Quantitative Historical Analysis." *The Journal of Modern African Studies* 22: 633-666.

Ogden, P.E. 1987. "Historical Demography." In *Historical Geography: Progress and Prospect*, edited by Michael Pacione, 217-249. London: Croom Helm.

Oliver, Roland and John D. Fage. 1972. *A Short History of Africa*. Middlesex, England: Penguin Books.

Patterson, K. David. 1981. "The Demographic Impact of the 1918-19 Influenza Pandemic in Sub-Saharan Africa: A Preliminary Assessment." In *African Historical Demography*, edited by Christopher Fyfe and David McMaster, vol. 2, 403-431. Edinburgh, Scotland: University of Edinburgh.

Ross, Robert. 1977. "Smallpox at the Cape of Good Hope in the Eighteenth Century." In *African Historical Demography*, edited by Christopher Fyfe and David McMaster, Vol. 1, 416-428. Edinburgh, Scotland: University of Edinburgh.

Shaw, Thurston. 1981. "Towards a Prehistoric Demography of Africa." In *African Historical Demography*, edited by Christopher Fyfe and David McMaster, vol. 2, 581-606. Edinburgh, Scotland: University of Edinburgh.

Tarver, James D. and H. Max Miller. 1986. "Patterns of Population Growth in Africa." *African Studies* 45: 43-60.

Thornton, John. 1980. "The Slave Trade in Eighteenth Century Angola: Effects on Demographic Structures." *Canadian Journal of African Studies* 14: 417-27.

United Nations. 1992. *Long-range World Population Projections: Two Centuries of Population Growth 1950-2150*. New York.

United Nations High Commissioner for Refugees. 1989, 1990. *Fact Sheets*, vol. 3, no. 2 and vol. 4. no. 1. Geneva.

Willcox, Walter F. 1940. *Studies in American Demography*. Ithaca, NY: Cornell University Press.

The World Bank. 1985. *World Development Report 1984*. New York: Oxford University Press.

_____. 1986. *Population Growth and Policies in Sub-Saharan Africa*. Washington, DC: World Bank.

4

Fertility of the African Population

More than 143 million children were born throughout the world in 1991. When this figure is converted to an overall birth rate, it is equivalent to 27 children for each 1,000 people that year (table 4.1). This measure is the crude birth rate--the number of live births in a given year per 1,000 total population. It is very useful because it expresses the frequency of live births of an entire population as a single number and several different areas can be compared simultaneously.

In 1991 nearly 30 million children were born in Africa. Even though the African children born in 1991 comprised only 20 percent of the total, this continent nevertheless had a crude birth rate of 44, the highest in the world (table 4.1). In some African countries, such as Malawi and Rwanda, birth rates were still increasing as late as 1980, whereas in most areas of the world the rates were falling (Henin, et al., 1982).

Birth rates were generally high in prehistoric days although they fluctuated from time to time. While the rates have tended to decline over the years, there have been many instances where they actually increased in the early phases of modernization. Fertility rates rose during the early stages of industrialization in many western European countries (Wrigley and Schofield, 1981; Petersen, 1960). In the Kalahari desert of Southern Africa, both fertility and mortality levels among the Dobe !Kung rose when they began living sedentary lives and engaging in permanent agriculture (Howell, 1979; Lee, 1972). Similar increases are thought to have occurred in colonial Africa. Fertility, for example, increased in Zaire in the early stages of modernization beginning in World War II (Romaniuk, 1980) and at the beginning of the century in Sudan (O'Brien, 1987). Other examples occurred in Kenya (Henin, et al., 1982; Dawson, 1987), in Ghana (Kpedekpo, 1971), and in Tanzania (Turshen, 1987; Koponen, 1986).

FERTILITY CONCEPTS AND MEASUREMENT

Lorimer (1954) studied the fertility levels of populations not using birth control and found them with somewhat lower than expected rates. Later, Henry (1961) used the term *natural* to describe reproductive behavior unaffected by deliberate family limitation practices, a policy which some religious bodies strongly advocate. However, in the measurement of fertility by any rate, all live births are counted regardless of whether family limitation practices were present or not.

Since fertility usually plays the most dominant role in population change, much effort has been devoted to refining methods to measure it precisely. Several different rates have been developed, including various crude, corrected, specific, and standardized rates. The basic data for these fertility measures are population censuses, surveys, and vital statistics registrations.

There are two types of fertility measures. *Period* fertility rates refer to short periods of time, usually one year. The measurement of fertility by the various period rates will be discussed first. *Cohort* fertility rates measure the reproductive performance of women as they pass through their childbearing years until they complete their families. Thus, cohort fertility is based upon reproductive histories and reflects the size of completed families.

PERIOD FERTILITY RATES

Crude Birth Rate

Of all the different fertility rates this is the simplest and most frequently used measure. It is defined as the annual number of live births per 1,000 population. The total midyear population is used as the denominator whenever possible. In countries with less than 90 percent of their births registered, the number of births should be corrected if possible for incompleteness of registration before calculating crude rates.

Crude birth rates in Africa, as in the world as a whole, have generally followed a steadily declining trend since 1950. On the other hand, in eastern, middle, and western Africa birth rates have remained at the very high levels of 46 to 49 (tables 4.1 and 4.2). The high rates for countries like Burundi and Niger have remained about constant, while the rates for Benin, Rwanda, and Malawi have actually risen. In contrast, Morocco, Egypt, and South Africa have experienced small declines. Despite the overall high fertility in Africa several countries in Middle Africa had comparatively low fertility levels due to venereal disease (Bongaarts, et al., 1984). For example, ten countries had relatively high infertility, with the percentage of childless women at the end of their childbearing years ranging from 11 in Chad to 32 in Gabon (Frank, 1983).

The crude birth rate is certainly a simple, concise measure. However, it has its shortcomings. For example, the denominator used in computing the rate may include relatively large numbers of children and adults not in the childbearing ages.

General Fertility Rate

The general fertility rate is a more precise measure than is the crude birth rate because the denominator is limited to women in the childbearing ages. This measure is defined as the annual number of live births per 1,000 women in the reproductive ages. In the computation of the general fertility rates in table 4.3 the ages of 15 to 49 were used.

Africa's general fertility rates have remained approximately constant since 1950. Whereas the general fertility rate of the world as a whole dropped from 153 in 1950-55 to 112 in 1985-90, Africa's rate declined from 207 to 200, practically no change (table 4.3). Kenya, the country with the highest recognized overall fertility in 1980-85, also had the highest 1985-90 general fertility rate with 264. There were at least 230 children per 1,000 women in the childbearing ages of 15 to 49 in Malawi, Uganda, Tanzania, Nigeria, Niger, and Rwanda--high fertility rates by any standard.

Child-Woman Ratios

This fertility measure is usually calculated when reliable birth data are unavailable. It reflects the relative number of children under five years of age per 1,000 women of childbearing ages, usually 15-49 years of age. Both the numerator and denominator for this measure come from the same population census.

This index serves as an indirect measure of fertility and ordinarily is used only when birth statistics are lacking. The ratio is based upon the survivors of births during the five years preceding the census and includes the effects of infant and childhood mortality. Children 0-4 years of age are usually underenumerated in population censuses, which also affects the reliability of the ratios. Therefore, child-woman ratios must be interpreted with caution for they are affected by factors other than fertility.

Kenya's child-woman ratio of 1,004 in 1985 stands out very prominently, as it is exceptionally high (table 4.3). Moreover, its child-woman ratios steadily increased from about 800 in 1950. The ratios for Rwanda, Nigeria, Uganda, and Libya were more than 900 in 1985. Most other countries had child-woman ratios of 700 or more, with only a handful of countries experiencing declining ratios since 1950.

Total Fertility Rates

The total fertility rate estimates the number of children a group of women will bear during their lifetimes, assuming that the age-specific birth rates at a particular time remain constant. Also, it assumes that all women will survive throughout their childbearing years. Therefore, mortality has no effect upon these rates. The total fertility rate is generally considered to be the most sensitive and best single cross-sectional fertility measure. However, when age-specific birth rates change markedly over time the total fertility rate may provide poor estimates of family size.

In computing total fertility rates live births are classified by age of mother, usually into about seven five-year groups beginning with 15-19 years and ending with 45-49 years of age and over. Then, age-specific birth rates are calculated by taking the number of live births occurring annually to mothers of each five-year age group, dividing by the total number of women in each respective age group, then multiplying by 1,000. Next, the age-specific birth rates are summed and multiplied by five to obtain total fertility rates.

Africa's high total fertility rates have been relatively constant since 1950. The rate dropped only from 6.7 in 1950-55 to 6.2 by 1985-90 (table 4.4). In contrast, the total fertility rate of the world declined nearly 30 percent, from 5.0 to 3.5, in the same period (table 4.4).

Assuming a continuation of the age-specific birth rates during 1985-90, the average number of children that African women will have is 6.2 in their lifetimes. The comparable figure for European women is 1.7 and that for North American women, 1.8, about a third as many.

Women in Rwanda can expect more than eight children during their lives, the highest of all African countries and throughout the world (Yemen is second highest with 8.0) (table 4.4). In Malawi and the Côte d'Ivoire women are likely to have an average of 7.5 children.

Gross Reproduction Rate

The gross reproduction rate is derived from the total fertility rate and is used to estimate the number of girls women will bear during their childbearing years should they give birth to daughters at the age-sex specific rate of a designated base year. Like the total fertility rate, the gross reproduction rate assumes that females will live throughout their childbearing years. This rate may be obtained by multiplying the percentage of all female births by the total fertility rate.

The gross reproduction rates for 1985-90 show that each African woman had, on the average, 3.07 daughters (table 4.3). It is obvious that the present generation of females is bearing more than enough daughters to replace themselves even though mortality is excluded from the computational technique. These relatively large numbers of newborn girls will, of course, accelerate population growth.

Table 4.1
Crude Birth Rates in the Major Regions of the World, 1991
(number of live births per 1,000 total population)

Major Region	Crude Birth Rate
WORLD TOTAL	27
Developed Regions	14
Developing Regions	30
Africa	44
Northern Africa	37
Western Africa	46
Eastern Africa	48
Middle Africa	45
Southern Africa	35
Asia	27
Western Asia	36
Southern Asia	33
Southeast Asia	28
East Asia	20
North America	16
Canada	15
United States	17
Latin America	28
Central America	31
Caribbean	26
South America	27
Europe	13
Northern Europe	14
Western Europe	12
Eastern Europe	14
Southern Europe	11
Oceania	19
Former Soviet Republics	18

Source: Compiled from Population Reference Bureau, *1991 World Population Data Sheet*.

Table 4.2
Crude Birth Rates of African Countries, 1950-90

Country	Rates, By 5-Year Periods					
	1950-55	1960-65	1970-75	1975-80	1980-85	1985-90
AFRICA	49	49	47	46	45	45
Algeria	51	50	48	45	41	36
Angola	50	49	48	48	47	47
Benin	43	48	49	49	49	49
Botswana	49	53	52	53	49	49
Burkina Faso	51	51	50	47	47	47
Burundi	49	45	44	45	47	48
Cape Verde	51	49	39	35	39	40
Cameroon	44	45	46	46	47	48
Central African Republic	44	43	43	45	46	46
Chad	45	46	45	44	44	44
Comoros	47	52	49	48	48	48
Congo	44	45	46	46	46	46
Côte d'Ivoire	53	53	51	51	50	50
Djibouti	50	50	50	49	48	47
Egypt	49	45	38	39	39	35
Equatorial Guinea	42	41	42	43	43	44
Ethiopia	52	50	48	48	45	49

Table 4.2 (Continued)

Country	Rates, By 5-Year Periods					
	1950-55	1960-65	1970-75	1975-80	1980-85	1985-90
Gabon	30	31	31	31	34	39
Gambia	47	51	49	49	48	47
Ghana	48	48	46	45	45	44
Guinea	55	52	52	52	51	51
Guinea Bissau	41	40	41	42	43	43
Kenya	53	53	53	54	51	47
Lesotho	42	43	42	42	42	41
Liberia	48	50	48	47	47	47
Libya	48	49	49	47	46	44
Madagascar	48	48	46	46	46	46
Malawi	52	55	57	57	57	56
Mali	53	52	51	51	51	51
Mauritania	48	48	47	47	47	46
Mauritius	47	43	26	27	22	19
Morocco	50	50	46	39	37	36
Mozambique	46	47	46	45	46	45
Namibia	45	46	45	45	44	44
Niger	54	53	52	52	52	52

41

Table 4.2 (Continued)

Country	Rates, By 5-Year Periods					
	1950-55	1960-65	1970-75	1975-80	1980-85	1985-90
Nigeria	51	52	49	49	49	49
Réunion	39	40	31	26	24	24
Rwanda	47	51	53	53	52	51
St. Helena			Not Available			
São Tomé & Príncipe			Not Available			
Senegal	49	50	49	49	47	46
Seychelles			Not Available			
Sierra Leone	48	48	49	49	48	48
Somalia	49	48	48	52	53	50
South Africa	43	42	36	34	33	32
Sudan	47	47	47	47	46	45
Swaziland	50	49	48	47	47	47
Togo	47	48	46	45	45	45
Tunisia	46	47	37	36	34	31
Uganda	51	49	50	50	53	52
Tanzania	49	52	51	51	51	51
Western Sahara			Not Available			
Zaire	47	47	47	46	45	46

Table 4.2 (Continued)

	Rates, By 5-Year Periods					
Country	1950-55	1960-65	1970-75	1975-80	1980-85	1985-90
Zambia	50	49	49	52	51	51
Zimbabwe	52	52	49	44	43	42

Source: Compiled from United Nations, *World Population Prospects 1990*

(Sales No. E.91.XIII.4).

In 1985-90 females in Rwanda were likely to have four daughters each, the largest number of infant daughters per woman of all African countries (table 4.3). The estimated number of girls per woman was 3.6 to 3.7 in Malawi and Uganda. In every country except Mauritius, the 1980-85 gross reproduction rates were one or more.

Net Reproduction Rate

Net reproduction rates are also derived from total fertility rates. This fertility measure gives the number of daughters a cohort of newborn girls will bear throughout their lifetimes, assuming fixed age-specific birth and death rates. In one perspective, the net reproduction rate is a measure of the extent that a cohort of newly born girls will replace themselves, assuming an indefinite continuation of a set of age-specific birth and mortality rates. For instance, a net reproduction rate of 1.0 indicates the precise replacement of the population, a rate above 1.0 indicates a growing population, and a rate of less than 1.0 indicates a declining population.

Worldwide, the net reproduction rate declined from 1.65 in 1950-55 to 1.43 in 1985-90 even though the population continued to grow. Africa, on the other hand, experienced an increase, with its net reproduction rate rising from 1.91 in 1950-55 to 2.30 in 1985-90. Each newly born African girl is expected to bear 2.30 infant girls at a time when 1.0 indicates an exact replacement of the population.

Thus, for Africa the net reproduction rates are over twice that required for replacement (table 4.3). In Rwanda the net reproduction was 2.89. Libya, Kenya, and Côte d'Ivoire all have net reproduction rates of 2.8. The fertility rates presented above are all considered to be period measures. For most purposes the total fertility rate is thought to be the most sensitive and useful period measure.

COHORT RATES OF FERTILITY

Cohort fertility is based upon the reproductive history of women expressed in completed family size. The cohort fertility measures resemble total fertility rates. However, they reflect childbearing over a period of many years, whereas the total fertility rate is based upon performance during one year. Reproductive histories of women may be constructed from various records. Usually, however, these histories are based upon information reported by individuals in population censuses and surveys. The United Nations, for example, recommends that questions on both the number of children born alive and the number of children living be included in population censuses.

In both population censuses and surveys retrospective questions are asked about the number of children ever born to each woman. The histories are, therefore, complete only for women 50 years of age and over. Understatements, particularly of deceased children, are frequently made due to faulty recall. Too, children who have left the parental home are often forgotten. Older women with large families are most likely to underreport. According to one prominent demographer, the accuracy of reporting the number of children ever born in the African countries tends to vary inversely with the age of the mother (Brass, et al., 1968).

The errors inherent in single-round, retrospective fertility surveys have been described by several demographers (Blacker, 1974). Since the number of children ever born are underreported, the resulting reproductive histories generally have limited usefulness. For example, in censuses taken between 1950 and 1977, 28 African countries reported the number of children born alive and the number of females 45 years of age and over. The average size of completed families ranged from 2.5 in Zambia to 7.0 in Malawi. Obviously, completed family size was understated by at least four children in some of the 28 countries.

THE INFLUENCE OF KINSHIP, ETHNICITY, AND FAMILY PATTERNS ON FERTILITY

African villages were traditionally characterized by strong extended family and kinship ties under a social organization which encouraged high fertility. Africans acquire prestige by having large numbers of children. The desire for large numbers of children transcends their economic value in agricultural activities. It has a lot to do with life-force and the deep belief that children are the guarantors of immortality (Tempels, 1969).

Kinship and ethnic groups have different attitudes about family planning practices. In the past the Hutus and Tutsis of Rwanda, for example, have relied upon traditional breast-feeding patterns to maintain a stable population, as less than five percent of the women of reproductive ages used modern contraceptive methods. However, the recent rapid disappearance of traditional breast-feeding practices in Rwanda, which became too old fashioned there, resulted in it having the highest fertility levels of all African countries. In contrast fertility has declined in some African countries due, in part, to marital disruption resulting from long separations of wives from their migrant laborer husbands. This employment system has created a new role for wives, that of household heads operating farms with their children.

Polygyny is still common in some parts of western and west-central Africa, where probably 25 to 50 percent of the married men have more than one wife. Polygynous marriages enable chiefs and wealthy men to accumulate many wives and offspring, thereby enlarging the size of the kinship group over which they have influence. Usually the kinship structure of these polygynous societies results in marriages between relatives, usually cousins. Men marry much younger women and they usually rear many children who are half-brothers and sisters.

Table 4.3
General, Gross, and Net Reproduction Rates of African Countries and Child-Woman Ratios

Country	General Fertility Rates 1985-90	Child-Woman Ratios 1985	Gross Reproduction Rates 1985-90	Net Reproduction Rates 1985-90
AFRICA	200		3.07	2.30
Algeria	183	791	2.65	2.32
Angola	207	791	3.15	2.12
Benin	228	875	3.50	2.39
Botswana	214	879	3.50	2.92
Burkina Faso	209	775	3.20	2.22
Burundi	204	777	3.35	2.31
Cameroon	189	773	3.40	2.59
Cape Verde	130	712	2.75	2.49
Central African Republic	190	750	3.05	2.23
Chad	191	738	2.90	1.98
Comoros	201	833	3.43	2.66
Congo	194	733	3.10	2.42
Côte d'Ivoire	213	878	3.65	2.80
Djibouti			3.25	2.28
Egypt	139	643	2.21	1.80
Equatorial Guinea	183	717	2.90	2.00
Ethiopia	217	816	3.34	2.22
Gabon	158	578	2.46	1.86
Gambia	206	742	3.20	2.09
Ghana	212	858	3.15	2.44
Guinea	200	754	3.45	2.19

Table 4.3 (Continued)

Country	General Fertility Rates 1985-90	Child-Woman Ratios 1985	Gross Reproduction Rates 1985-90	Net Reproduction Rates 1985-90
Guinea Bissau	173	673	2.85	1.81
Kenya	264	1004	3.45	2.80
Lesotho	173	704	2.85	2.36
Liberia	222	891	3.35	2.47
Libya	211	902	3.35	2.83
Madagascar	196	793	3.25	2.52
Malawi	230	826	3.74	2.47
Mali	218	761	3.50	2.31
Mauritania	226	869	3.20	2.19
Mauritius	82	412	.98	.93
Morocco	132	627	2.35	1.98
Mozambique	197	747	3.15	2.16
Namibia	199	793	3.00	2.41
Niger	232	886	3.50	2.35
Nigeria	232	913	3.40	2.51
Réunion	71	331	1.20	1.17
Rwanda	233	926	4.10	2.89
Senegal	203	782	3.20	2.21
Sierra Leone	196	706	3.20	2.02
Somalia	213	815	3.25	2.20
South Africa	161	686	2.20	1.88
Sudan	197	811	3.15	2.28
Swaziland	212	843	3.20	2.56
Tanzania	232	898	3.50	2.70
Togo	199	804	3.24	2.48
Tunisia	124	574	2.00	1.79
Uganda	230	912	3.60	2.70

Table 4.3 (Continued)

Country	General Fertility Rates 1985-90	Child-Woman Ratios 1985	Gross Reproduction Rates 1985-90	Net Reproduction Rates 1985-90
Zaire	198	802	3.00	2.29
Zambia	220	888	3.55	2.72
Zimbabwe	216	781	2.87	2.37

Source: Compiled from United Nations, *World Population Prospects 1990*
(Sales No.E.91.X111.4) and *Demographic Yearbook 1986*
(Sales No. E.87.XIII.7).

While the overall size of some polygynous families often is quite large, the fertility of women in these marriages is lower on the average than of women in monogamous unions (Pebley and Mbugua, 1989).

FERTILITY AND SOCIOECONOMIC STATUS

Education, occupation, and income are the three basic indicators of socioeconomic status most often used in the study of fertility and family size. Family size has been found to vary consistently with each of these three variables (Weller and Bouvier, 1981).

Education

Studies uniformly show an inverse relationship between fertility and education. The World Fertility Survey, for instance, found that the average number of children per woman declined as her education increased (World Fertility Survey, 1984). In Ghana, for example, the number of children ever born was inversely related to the education of the mother (Ghana Fertility Survey 1979-1980, 1983b).

In Botswana women with completed families now have about five children, compared to seven in 1981 (Tarver and Miller, 1986). Family size dropped to 4.6 children for women who had completed primary school and to slightly over three for those with secondary or university study (Botswana Survey, 1985, 1989).

Many female students postpone marriage and childbearing. When they do so, the size of families declines as education and age at marriage increases, for age at marriage is inversely related to size of family (Cleland and Hobcraft, 1985). Beyond age 20 each extra year of marriage delay is usually associated with an overall fertility reduction. Furthermore, highly educated females are the most likely to practice family limitation.

Occupation

The most prestigious workers (those in the white-collar and professional occupations) have the lowest fertility, and unskilled workers and agricultural laborers have the highest fertility (Ghana Fertility Survey 1979-1980, 1983b). Professional workers not only have the highest educational attainment of all occupational groups but also the highest average incomes. Their fertility is also low because they not only marry at older ages but they are likely to use effective family limitation practices. For example, the evidence indicates that women who worked in the modern urban market economy, those in high status occupations, and those away from home or for non-family employers have comparatively low fertility (World Fertility Survey, 1984).

Income

Families with high incomes tend to have the smallest number of children (Egyptian Fertility Survey, 1983a). Individuals with high incomes also tend to have high levels of educational attainment as well as knowledge of contraception. Generally, high-income families are concentrated in urban areas of Africa and have smaller family orientations than poor rural families who are more concerned with abundant child labor and old-age security.

Income and wealth in its various forms are negatively associated with fertility. Increasing income generally stimulates higher educational aspirations, which delays marriage and results in a diminishing need for child labor. According to one economist, the short-run effect of an increase in income is to raise fertility, especially in very low income groups (Simon, 1977). However, the long-term effect of increases in income, economic development, and modernization is to reduce fertility (Simon, 1974).

RECENT FERTILITY TRENDS

Both the crude birth rates (table 4.2) and the total fertility rates (table 4.4) indicate that Africa's overall fertility levels changed very little during the past 40 years. Although declines occurred in northern and southern Africa they were largely offset by increases in eastern, middle, and western Africa.

Recently some rather significant declines occurred in a few of the African countries with historically high fertility. Perhaps the most noteworthy decline was in Kenya, which was once thought to have the highest birth rate in the world. Other African countries have also experienced major fertility and infant mortality declines in recent years.

In Kenya the total fertility rate declined from 8.1 children per woman in 1974-77 to 7.7 in 1983 to 6.7 during 1984-89 (*Kenya Survey*, 1980, 1984, 1989). For Zimbabwe the total fertility rate fell from 6.5 in 1983 to 5.5 in 1985-88 (*Zimbabwe Survey*, 1985, 1989). Also, Botswana's total fertility rate declined from 7.1 in 1981 to 6.5 in 1984 then to 5.0 during 1983-88 (*Botswana Family Health Survey*, 1989). The fertility declines in Kenya, Zimbabwe, and Botswana are attributable mainly to increased contraceptive use and child spacing.

In Senegal the total fertility rate dropped from 7.1 in 1978 (Senegal Survey, 1981) to 6.6 in 1986 (Senegal Survey, 1988). Sudan had a total fertility rate of 6.0 in 1978-79 (*Sudan Survey*, 1982), which fell to 5.0 during 1984-89 (*Sudan Survey*, 1990). The fertility decline for Sudan is closely associated with increases in the age at first marriage.

Increases in contraceptive uses and later marriages, however, have not been the only important factors in reducing fertility in these countries. The extension of comprehensive health care systems, which facilitated population control programs, has also been an important factor. When child survival increases couples can have only the number of children they actually desire. During the past decade declines in infant mortality accompanied fertility declines in Kenya. Probably the most important factor responsible for recent fertility declines was increased education, especially among women. Age at marriage increases with education, delaying childbearing and thereby reducing the size of the family. Increased employment opportunities for women, particularly in urban areas, is also associated with declines in fertility.

Obviously, birth rates haven't fallen throughout Africa, for about a dozen countries still have total fertility rates of 7.0 or more. In these countries fertility has either increased or remained approximately constant since 1950. At present Rwanda, rather than Kenya, has the highest fertility in Africa followed by Malawi, Côte d'Ivoire, and Uganda. Ethiopia's fertility rose in the early 1980s, especially in the rural areas. These increases were attributed to various improvements in health which occurred in the early stages of modernization.

Major declines in fertility have occurred in other African countries. For example, total fertility rates in the North African countries of Algeria, Egypt, Morocco, and Tunisia have fallen 25 to 30 percent since 1950. Fertility has also fallen about the same in South Africa but only about 15 percent in Cape Verde. However, the greatest declines of all were in Mauritius and Réunion, where total fertility rates dropped to about 2.0.

Further fertility declines will, of course, occur in the future, for more than half of all governments desire to lower their birth rates and some have established target figures for contraceptive use and total fertility rates in future years. Obviously, the population policies of some countries will prove much more effective than in others (Sadik, 1991).

FERTILITY AND FAMILY PLANNING SURVEYS

Years ago African governments became increasingly concerned about the high rates of population growth and the accompanying social and economic problems. As a result, a large number of fertility surveys were carried out, the first ones being in the mid-1950s. The majority of the early African fertility surveys were in francophone countries by or with the cooperation of the French National Institute of Statistics and Economic Studies, beginning with the Guinea Survey of 1954-55 (Caldwell, 1974). Between 1960 and 1973, 85 fertility surveys were carried out in 34 different African countries which were designed to determine the underlying nature of fertility and provide information useful in developing population policies (Duncan, 1973). After 1974 the fertility and family planning surveys were conducted by the World Fertility Survey and the Contraceptive Prevalence Surveys (London, et al., 1985). Beginning in 1984 the Demographic and Health Surveys assumed responsibility for these studies (Fisher and Way, 1988). In all, there have been 140 fertility surveys undertaken in about 40 of

Table 4.4
Total Fertility Rates of the World and the African Countries, By Five-Year
Periods, 1950-90

Regions and Countries	5-Year Periods					
	1950-55	1960-65	1970-75	1975-80	1980-85	1985-90
WORLD TOTAL	5.0	5.0	4.5	3.8	3.6	3.5
Developed Regions	2.8	2.7	2.2	2.0	1.9	1.9
Developing Regions	6.2	6.1	5.4	4.5	4.2	3.9
Africa	6.7	6.8	6.6	6.5	6.4	6.2
Eastern Africa	6.8	6.9	7.0	7.1	6.9	6.9
Burundi	6.8	6.8	6.8	6.8	6.8	6.8
Comoros	6.3	6.9	7.0	7.0	7.0	7.0
Djibouti	6.6	6.6	6.6	6.6	6.6	6.6
Ethiopia	6.7	6.7	6.8	7.0	6.5	6.8
Kenya	7.5	8.1	8.1	8.1	7.9	7.0
Madagascar	6.6	6.6	6.6	6.6	6.6	6.6
Malawi	6.8	7.0	7.4	7.6	7.6	7.6
Mauritius	6.3	5.7	3.3	3.1	2.5	2.0
Mozambique	6.2	6.4	6.5	6.5	6.5	6.4
Réunion	5.7	5.7	3.9	3.4	2.8	2.4
Rwanda	7.1	7.7	8.3	8.5	8.5	8.3
Somalia	6.6	6.6	6.6	6.6	6.6	6.6
Uganda	6.9	6.9	7.0	7.2	7.3	7.3
Tanzania	6.7	6.9	7.0	7.1	7.1	7.1
Zambia	6.6	6.6	6.9	7.2	7.2	7.2
Zimbabwe	7.2	7.5	7.2	6.6	6.2	5.8
Middle Africa	5.9	6.0	6.1	6.2	6.2	6.2
Angola	6.4	6.4	6.4	6.4	6.4	6.4
Cameroon	5.7	5.9	6.4	6.6	6.7	6.9
Central African Republic	5.5	5.7	5.7	5.9	6.1	6.2
Chad	5.8	6.0	6.0	5.9	5.9	5.9
Congo	5.7	6.0	6.3	6.3	6.3	6.3
Equatorial Guinea	5.5	5.5	5.7	5.7	5.8	5.9
Gabon	4.1	4.1	4.3	4.4	4.5	5.0
Zaire	6.0	5.9	6.1	6.1	6.1	6.1

52

Table 4.4 (Continued)

Regions and Countries	5-Year Periods					
	1950-55	1960-65	1970-75	1975-80	1980-85	1985-90
Northern Africa	6.8	7.1	6.4	6.0	5.7	5.1
Algeria	7.3	7.4	7.4	7.2	6.4	5.4
Egypt	6.6	7.1	5.5	5.3	5.1	4.5
Libya	6.9	7.2	7.6	7.4	7.2	6.9
Morocco	7.2	7.2	6.9	5.9	5.4	4.8
Sudan	6.7	6.7	6.7	6.7	6.6	6.4
Tunisia	6.9	7.2	6.2	5.7	4.9	4.1
Southern Africa	6.5	6.5	5.6	5.2	5.0	4.7
Botswana	6.5	6.9	6.9	7.0	7.1	7.1
Lesotho	5.8	5.8	5.7	5.7	5.8	5.8
Namibia	5.9	6.0	6.1	6.1	6.1	6.1
South Africa	6.5	6.5	5.5	5.1	4.8	4.5
Swaziland	6.5	6.5	6.5	6.5	6.5	6.5
Western Africa	6.8	6.9	6.9	6.9	6.9	6.9
Benin	6.8	7.0	7.1	7.1	7.1	7.1
Burkina Faso	6.9	6.7	6.7	6.5	6.5	6.5
Cape Verde	6.6	7.0	7.0	6.7	6.3	5.6
Côte d'Ivoire	6.9	7.3	7.4	7.4	7.4	7.4
Gambia	6.1	6.5	6.5	6.5	6.5	6.5
Ghana	6.9	6.9	6.6	6.5	6.5	6.4
Guinea	7.0	7.0	7.0	7.0	7.0	7.0
Guinea Bissau	5.1	5.1	5.4	5.6	5.8	5.8
Liberia	6.3	6.7	6.8	6.8	6.8	6.8
Mali	7.1	7.1	7.1	7.1	7.1	7.1
Mauritania	6.5	6.5	6.5	6.5	6.5	6.5

Table 4.4 (Continued)

Regions and Countries	5-Year Periods					
	1950-55	1960-65	1970-75	1975-80	1980-85	1985-90
Niger	7.1	7.1	7.1	7.1	7.1	7.1
Nigeria	6.8	6.9	6.9	6.9	6.9	6.9
Senegal	6.7	7.0	7.0	7.0	6.7	6.5
Sierra Leone	6.1	6.3	6.5	6.5	6.5	6.5
Togo	6.6	6.6	6.6	6.6	6.6	6.6

Source: Compiled from United Nations, *World Population Prospects 1990* (Sales No. E.91.XIII.4).

Africa's 55 countries. The information collected provides the largest body of knowledge about Africa's fertility and family planning ever accumulated. Contraceptive use was found to be definitely associated with fertility declines in developing countries.

SUMMARY AND IMPLICATIONS

Over the years two different types of policies have evolved to reduce population growth in the developing countries of Africa (Van de Walle, et al., 1988). On the one hand, family planning programs have proven effective in slowing population growth. On the other hand, various economic development programs have been helpful in reducing the birth rates of developing countries. Experience has shown that both types of policies are compatible and effective. Each policy complements the other although at times one has been advocated at the exclusion of the other.

The prospects for any sudden decline in population growth in Africa do not appear promising. However, the prospects for a gradual decline in the future do seem promising based upon recent fertility declines in a few countries. One reason for this optimistic view is that three-fourths of the African governments are supporting family planning programs and related comprehensive health programs. As the educational attainment and employment of women increase fertility will decline and declines in infant mortality will tend to reduce high fertility.

REFERENCES

Blacker, J.G.C. 1974. "The Estimation of Vital Rates From Census Data in Kenya and Uganda." In *Population in African Development*, edited by Pierre Cantrelle, vol. 1, 199-209. Liége, Belgium: Ordina Editions.

Bongaarts, John, Odile Frank, and Ron J. Lesthaeghe. 1984. "The Proximate Determinants of Fertility in sub-Saharan Africa." *Population and Development Review* 10: 511-537.

Botswana Family Health Survey II 1988. 1989. Columbia, MD: Central Statistics Office and Institute for Resource Development/Macro Systems, Inc.

Botswana Family Health Survey 1984. 1985. Columbia, MD: Family Health Division, Ministry of Health and Westinghouse Public Applied Systems.

Brass, William et al. 1968. *The Demography of Tropical Africa.* Princeton, NJ: Princeton University Press.

Caldwell, John C. 1974. *The Study of Fertility and Fertility Change in Tropical Africa* Occasional Paper no. 7. Voorburg and London: International Statistical Institute and World Fertility Survey.

Cleland, John G. and John Hobcraft. 1985. *Reproductive Change in Developing Countries.* London: Oxford University Press.

Dawson, Marc H. 1987. "Health, Nutrition, and Population in Central Kenya, 1890-1945." In *African Population and Capitalism: Historical Perspectives*, edited by Dennis D. Cordell and Joel W. Gregory, 201-217. Boulder, CO: Westview Press.

Duncan, William G. 1973. *The Nature and Content of Fertility Surveys Conducted Throughout the World Since 1960* Occasional Paper no. 1. Voorburg and London: International Statistical Institute and World Fertility Survey.

Enguête Démographique et de Santé Sénégal 1986. 1988. Columbia, MD: Direction de la Statistique and Institute for Research Development/Westinghouse.

Enquête Sénégalese Sur la Fécondité, 1978. 1981. Dakar, Senegal: Rapport National d'Analyse, vol. 1 and 2, Direction de la Statistique.

Frank, Odile. 1983. "Infertility in Sub-Saharan Africa: Estimates and implications." *Population and Development Review* 9: 137-144.

Fisher, Andrew A. and Ann A. Way. 1988. "The Demographic and Health Surveys Program: An Overview." *International Family Planning Perspectives* 14: 15-19.

Henin, Roushdi A., Ailsa Korten, and Linda H. Werner. 1982. *Evaluation of Birth Histories: A Case Study of Kenya* Scientific Report number 36. Voorburg and London: International Statistical Institute and World Fertility Survey.

Henry, Louis. 1961. "Some Data on Natural Fertility." *Eugenics Quarterly* 8: 81-91.

Howell, Nancy. 1979. *The Demography of the Dobe !Kung.* New York: Academic Press.

Kenya Contraceptive Prevalence Survey 1984. 1984. Nairobi, Kenya: Central Bureau of Statistics, Ministry of Finance and Planning.

Kenya Demographic and Health Survey 1989. 1989. Columbia, MD: National Council for Population and Development and the Institute for Resource Development/Macro Systems, Inc.

Kenya Fertility Survey 1977-78, first report. 1980. 2 vols., Nairobi, Kenya: Ministry of Economic Planning and Development, Central Bureau of Statistics.

Koponen, Juhani. 1986. "Population growth in historical perspective--the key to changing fertility." In *Tanzania: Crisis and Struggle for Survival*, edited by Jannik Boesen et al., 31-57. Uppsala, Sweden: Scandinavian Institute of African Studies.

Kpedekpo, G.M.K. 1971. "The Extent and Nature of Existing Statistical Data for the Measurement of Demographic Transition in Tropical Africa." In *The Demographic Transition in Tropical Africa*, 43-49. Paris: Development Centre of the Organization for Economic Co-operation and Development.

Lee, Richard B. 1972. "Population Growth and the Beginnings of Sedentary Life among the !Kung Bushmen." In *Population Growth: Anthropological Implications*, edited by Brian Spooner, 330-342. Cambridge, MA: M.I.T. Press.

London, Kathy A. et al. 1985. "Fertility and Family Planning Surveys: An Update." *Population Reports*, Series M, number 8. Baltimore, MD: Johns Hopkins University.

Lorimer, Frank. 1954. *Culture and Human Fertility*. Zurich, Switzerland: UNESCO.

O'Brien, Jay. 1987. "Differential High Fertility and Demographic Transition: Peripheral Capitalism in Sudan." In *African Population and Capitalism: Historical Perspectives*, edited by Dennis D. Cordell and Joel W. Gregory, 173-186. Boulder, CO: Westview Press.

Pebley, Anne and Wariara Mbugua. 1989. "Polygyny and Fertility in Sub-Saharan Africa." In *Reproduction and Social Organization in Sub-Saharan Africa*, edited by Ron J. Lesthaeghe, 338-364. Berkeley, CA: University of California Press.

Petersen, William. 1960. "The Demographic Transition in the Netherlands." *American Sociological Review* 25: 334-47.

Romaniuk, Anatole. 1980. "Increase in Natural Fertility During the Early Stages of Modernization: Evidence from an African Case Study, Zaire." *Population Studies* 34: 293-310.

Sadik, Nafis, ed. 1991. *Population Policies and Programmes: Lessons Learned from Two Decades of Experience*. New York: United Nations Population Fund.

Simon, Julian L. 1974. *The Effects of Income on Fertility*. Chapel Hill, NC: Carolina Population Center.

_____. 1977. *The Economics of Population Growth*. Princeton: Princeton University Press.

Sudan Demographic and Health Survey 1989-1990. 1990. Khartoum, Sudan: Department of Statistics and Demographic Health Surveys,Institute for Resource Development/Macro Systems, Inc.

Sudan Fertility Survey 1978-79. 1982. Khartoum, Sudan: Ministry of National Planning.

Tarver, James D. and H. Max Miller. 1986. "Women Head Botswana's Households." *Population Today* 14: 4-9.

Tempels, Placide. 1969. *Bantu Philosophy*. Paris: Presence Africaine.

Turshen, Meredith. 1987. "Population Growth and the Deterioration of Health: Mainland Tanzania, 1920-1960." In *African Population and Capitalism: Historical Perspectives*, edited by Dennis D. Cordell and Joel W. Gregory, 187-200. Boulder, CO: Westview Press.

Van de Walle, Etienne, Patrick O. Ohadike, and Mpembele D. Sala-Diakanda. 1988. *The State of African Demography*. Liége, Belgium: International Union for the Scientific Study of Population.

Weller, Robert H. and Leon F. Bouvier. 1981. *Population, Demography, and Policy*. New York: St. Martin's Press.

World Fertility Survey. 1983a. *The Egyptian Fertility Survey, 1980* Socio-Economic Differentials and Comparative Data from Husbands and Wives, vol. 3. Voorburg and London: International Statistical Institute.

_____. 1983b. *The Ghana Fertility Survey, 1979-1980: A Summary of Findings*. Voorburg and London: International Statistical Institute.

_____. 1984. *Major Findings and Implications*. Voorburg and London: International Statistical Institute.

Wrigley, E.A. and R.S. Schofield. 1981. *The Population History of England: 1541-1871*. Cambridge, MA: Harvard University Press.

Zimbabwe Demographic and Health Survey 1988. 1989. Harare, Zimbabwe and Columbia, MD: Zimbabwe Central Statistical Office and the Institute for Resource Development/Macro Systems, Inc.

Zimbabwe Reproductive Health Survey 1984. 1985. Harare, Zimbabwe and Columbia, MD: Zimbabwe National Family Planning Council and Westinghouse Public Applied Systems.

5

Mortality in Africa

Even though Africa's death rates have fallen more rapidly than the death rates in other regions, this continent still has the highest mortality of all major regions in the world, with a life expectancy of only 52 years in 1985-90. Evidence indicates that Africa's average life expectancy at birth may be increasing about half a year per calendar year (UN, 1982a). Impoverishment and other constraints have made rapid mortality declines impossible.

CAUSES OF DEATH

The major causes of death are closely related to a country's stage of development and industrialization. The first diseases that people in developing countries are able to conquer are the infectious and parasitic diseases. As their standard of living rises and new medical techniques are adopted, deaths due to respiratory diseases are brought under control. As the result of the saving of lives primarily at the younger ages, the population eventually grows older and deaths due to degenerative diseases progressively increase. Then, circulatory ailments (vascular and heart disease) and cancer become the principal causes of death.

In Africa infectious and parasitic diseases and respiratory ailments are still major causes of death among children. The progressive increase in mortality control at the youngest ages has the same effect as increasing the birth rate and continues to enlarge the proportional size of the youthful population.

Each year the UN *Demographic Yearbook* publishes the number of deaths of a few selected African countries classified by cause of death as identified in the Eighth Revision of the International Classification of Diseases (ICD). The 50 separate causes of death were combined into the following 14 major groups as shown in Table 5.1 (WHO, 1967).

The percentage of deaths classified as due to "symptoms, senility, and ill-defined conditions" may be used as a measure of the quality of the reporting of cause of death. Cause-of-death certification has been very successful in some developed countries, where no more than one percent of all deaths are classified as symptoms, senility, and ill-defined conditions. This term is used for those deaths where the cause has not been diagnosed. However, in many African countries, where the cause of one-half or more of the total deaths are not diagnosed, the tabulations have limited value. For example, in Egypt in 1979, 62 percent of all deaths were not diagnosed by cause (table 5.2).

The World Health Organization recommends a standard method of medical diagnosis and coding procedures used in processing death certificates. The certifying medical attendant is instructed to determine the sequence of morbid events leading to death, then establish the underlying cause. When there is more than one cause the medical examiner is to specify the primary one. The comparability of the tabulations of deaths by cause from country to country depends not only upon the skills of certifying medical attendants in correctly diagnosing the cause of death but also upon the accuracy of the coder in classifying the proper cause of death on the certificate. Studies indicate a great deal of variability in specifying accurate medical certification as well as in coding. Even though the cause is very difficult to determine in some cases, the World Health Organization urges extreme care in the certification of cause to reduce the number of deaths classified as due to "ill-defined conditions" to an absolute minimum.

To illustrate recent trends, the patterns of four major causes of death identified in the Eighth Revision of the ICD will be examined for five African countries--Angola, Cape Verde, Egypt, Kenya, and the Republic of South Africa. Two causes of death (infectious and parasitic diseases and diseases of the respiratory system) are highly characteristic of the less advanced developing countries with young populations. The other two causes (neoplasms or cancer and diseases of the circulatory system) are degenerative diseases characteristic of advanced developing and developed countries with older populations.

These examples are highly selective but they do show definite changes in causes of death that are underway in African countries. Except for Egypt, the cause of death tabulations are fairly reliable, even though a third of the deaths in Cape Verde and a quarter of those in Angola were not diagnosed by cause (table 5.2).

The Republic of South Africa was chosen, not because its mortality patterns are representative of Africa, but because its white, coloured, and Asian populations have somewhat higher standards of living than Africans in Angola, Cape Verde, Kenya, and Egypt. These higher standards of living should, therefore, be reflected in certain mortality structures (table 5.2).

In 1970 Kenya was probably typical or perhaps slightly more advanced than most African countries in terms of health conditions. Over 40 percent of all deaths in that country were due to infective and parasitic diseases. It also had a comparatively high proportion who died from respiratory diseases. In contrast, only two percent of the white South Africans died from parasitic diseases. Obviously, they also had much higher levels of living than the poor Africans in Kenya. Moreover, relatively fewer white South Africans died of respiratory diseases than Africans in Kenya, and coloureds and Asians in South Africa.

The higher standard of living among whites in South Africa is, however, directly associated with relatively high rates of heart disease and cancer. For example, they had the highest percentage of deaths due to diseases of the circulatory system and to neoplasms of all population groups in the five countries. In contrast, Angola and Kenya had the lowest percentages of deaths caused by neoplasms and circulatory diseases. These contrasting cause-of-death patterns may be attributed largely to different styles of living and varying stages of development.

Generally, the patterns of changes in the major causes of death in the African countries are consistent with the trends observed elsewhere. Mortality from infectious and parasitic diseases, and respiratory diseases, declined with development as mortality from degenerative diseases increased. Nevertheless, Africa still faces many serious diseases and health problems such as nutritional deficiencies, malaria, river blindness, filariasis, and bilharziasis (UN, 1982a).

On the basis of the death structure of high mortality populations, Lopez and Hull (1983) predicted cause-specific death rates from overall crude death rates. Their regression technique provides a procedure for estimating the cause of death structure from crude death rates in the African countries. This technique is also useful for the study of causes of death in countries in different stages of development, and particularly in developing countries in the early stages of epidemiological transition. Also, the mortality structure is quite different for the older populations of more developed countries than for developing countries with large youthful populations (Preston, 1976).

ACQUIRED IMMUNE DEFICIENCY SYNDROME

Recent advances in health care in many parts of Africa have been overshadowed by the appearance of AIDS, which was first diagnosed there in the late 1970s (WHO, 1990a,b). Promiscuity is the main cause of the spread of the HIV virus over a large area of Africa (Simonsen, et al., 1988; Ahmed, 1988). Blood transfusions and the use of unsterilized needles probably played a less important role in the transmission of the disease.

Even though the estimates of the number of HIV infections and AIDS cases in Africa differ somewhat it is thought that there are approximately five million HIV infections in sub-Saharan Africa and a half million infants have been born infected with HIV (WHO, 1990a,b). About a third of the 15 to 49 year olds in the large urban agglomerations of eastern and middle Africa are infected with HIV, with Uganda having an estimated 750,000 inhabitants with HIV infections (WHO, 1990a,b).

Probably half a million AIDS cases have occurred in Africa, which is more than half of all cases worldwide. This disease is mainly concentrated in middle and eastern Africa, but increasing numbers of AIDS cases are being reported from West Africa, particularly Côte d'Ivoire (Clavel, et al., 1987). Quite likely more than 50,000 have already died of AIDS. Future AIDS deaths are expected to increase the number of infant, childhood, and adult mortalities, thereby reducing the rate of population growth accordingly.

Most Africans with AIDS are heterosexual, as the disease affects approximately equal numbers of men and women. Moreover, most are in the mature economically productive ages of 20 to 40. In some areas AIDS is popularly known as the "slim disease" because those who contract it suffer painful wasting away of body tissues by uncontrolled weight loss. In addition, AIDS is accompanied by chronic diarrhea and prolonged fever. There is definitely a serious AIDS threat in Africa and governments have been urged to adopt comprehensive health policies to cope with the rapidly accelerating HIV virus, which may even result in severe population losses.

LIFE TABLES

The life table is a rigorously constructed statistical instrument designed for measuring the mortality of a population. John Graunt is credited with developing the first life table in the seventeenth century, based upon mortality data obtained from parish records in London. His crude table showed a life expectancy at birth of 18.2 years (Graunt, 1939). Edmond Halley's life table for the city of Breslau, Germany, which covered the years 1687-91, is considered the earliest authentic table (Halley, 1693).

A life table shows the probability of surviving from any given age to any subsequent age. It may be complete, abridged, current, or a generation life table.

Abridged Life Tables

A set of abridged life tables were constructed for the Island of Mauritius during 1982-84 by five-year age groups (Kumari, Undated). This life table is quite reliable, for death registrations and census enumerations are relatively accurate in Mauritius. Life tables were computed separately for males and females and mortality rates were used to derive the other life table functions. The average remaining lifetime of each person who survives to the beginning of each age interval is known as life expectancy.

Table 5.1
Causes of Death Classified According to the Eighth Revision of the
International Classification of Diseases (1965)

I. Infective and parasitic diseases

II. Neoplasms

III. Endocrine, nutritional, and metabolic Diseases

IV. Diseases of the blood and blood-forming organs

V. Diseases of the nervous system and sense organs

VI. Diseases of the circulatory system

VII. Diseases of the respiratory system

VIII. Diseases of the digestive system

IX. Diseases of the genitourinary system

X. Complications of pregnancy, childbirth, and the puerperium

XI. Congenital anomalies

XII. Certain causes of mortality in early infancy

XIII. Symptoms, Senility, and ill-defined conditions

XIV. Accidents, poisonings, and violence (external cause)

Source: World Health Organization, *Manual of the International Statistical Classification of Diseases, Injuries, and Causes of Deaths*, Vol. 1, 1967.

Table 5.2

Percent of All Deaths Due to Major Causes for Selected Countries and Years

	Country					
Cause of Death	Kenya	South Africa Coloured and Asiatic	White	Angola	Egypt	Cape Verde
	1970	1971	1971	1973	1979	1980
I	43	25	2	27	3	20
II	2	7	16	2	2	6
III	2	2	1	2	1	3
IV	1	--	--	3	--	1
V	2	1	--	1	--	1
VI	6	20	42	7	13	16
VII	13	14	9	9	9	8
VIII	2	1	3	3	1	1
IX	--	1	1	1	--	--
X	1	--	--	1	--	--
XI	1	1	1	3	1	2
XII	3	7	3	4	4	4
XIII	19	11	12	26	62	34
XIV	5	10	10	11	4	4
TOTAL	100	100	100	100	100	100

Source: Compiled from United Nations, *Demographic Yearbook 1979*
(Sales No. E/F.80.XIII.1), *Demographic Yearbook 1983*
(Sales No. E/F.84.XIII.1), and *Demographic Yearbook 1984*
(Sales No. E/F.85.XIII.1).

Life tables are essential for many different types of demographic analyses in Africa. They are needed to derive survival rates, project mortality, and study the changing life expectation.

In countries with defective and incomplete data other methods of constructing abridged life tables have generally been used. One widely used method for the African countries has been the Brass logit or standard life tables (Brass, et al., 1968, 1975). Carrier and Hobcraft (1971) and Sullivan (1972) have made methodological contributions to these techniques.

Complete Life Tables

Complete life tables calculate all functions for each single year of age, not by five- or ten-year age groups. There are two sets of complete life tables which are quite significant for the study of mortality in Africa. First, interpolated complete life values were calculated from abridged UN model life tables (Heligman and Pollard, 1980; UN, 1982b). In the other case, abridged life tables were first computed for the Island of Mauritius, then single-year-of-age values were calculated, using Beer's coefficients (Kumari, 1974).

The construction of complete life tables is much more complicated than for abridged life tables because functions must be calculated for each single year of age. Basic death, population, and birth data must be adjusted for inconsistencies, biases, and errors, which usually disappear in five-year age groups. These computations may prove to be quite laborious. Defective data make it impossible to construct complete life tables for many African countries by conventional methods. Although abridged life tables are not as precise as complete life tables, they provide sufficiently accurate figures for most demographic purposes in African countries.

CHANGES IN LENGTH OF LIFE SINCE ANCIENT TIMES

Estimates of the life expectancy of prehistoric and ancient man in Africa were made from human fossils found in caves in the Maghreb region of northwestern Africa and later from Egyptian mummies. Estimates of longevity were made at different cave sites in Algeria and Morocco, which yielded an overall average of 21.1 years for the early Maghreb population in the middle Paleolithic period. One of the most prominent sites was the Taforalt cave in Morocco, which was inhabited for more than 1,500 years (Ferembach, 1962). The average expectation of life of the individuals in the Taforalt cave was 21.4 years.

The Egyptians had an estimated life expectancy at birth of 28.7 years during the period that they were under Roman rule about 2,000 years ago (Russell, 1958). Longevity in Rome at that time was 22 years, which was lower than in Egypt (Pearson, 1901-02). Scholars believe that Rome was a very unhealthy place to live at that time. Increases in longevity in Italy were comparatively slow. In fact, Italian life expectancy did not reach 35 years until 1870 (Cipolla, 1965).

By 1930 most of the devastating epidemics and plaques in Africa had subsided (Dawson, 1981; Patterson, 1981; Ross, 1977). Life expectancy at birth for Egyptians in the 1927-37 intercensal period was estimated to be just about 30 years (Kiser, 1944). Over the 2,000-year period since Roman occupation Egypt had suffered greatly from the domination by various foreign rulers, and health and living conditions had deteriorated. However, by 1950-55 Egypt and the Maghreb countries had life expectancies at birth of 42 to 45 years, increases that resulted mainly from the application of modern health and medical care after World War II.

With few exceptions mortality rates steadily declined in Africa since the 1940s. Now every country in North Africa except Sudan has a life expectancy of 60 years or more. Historically, West Africa had the highest mortality and life expectancy continues to be comparatively low in that area. Sierra Leone, for example, has an average life expectancy at birth of only 41 years and a crude death rate of 23 in 1985-90. However, the greatest relative declines in mortality occurred in Réunion and Mauritius, which have the highest expectation of life at birth--approximately 70 years, compared to 52 years for Africa as a whole during 1985-90 (table 5.3).

MAJOR TRENDS IN SELECTED DEATH RATES

Patterns of change in infant and early childhood mortality rates, crude death rates, and maternal death rates in Africa are important indicators of mortality. Definite declines occurred in each of these three measures of mortality.

Infant and Early Childhood Mortality Rates

The age patterns of child mortality vary substantially in the developed and developing countries of the world. In the developed countries 85 percent of all deaths among children under five years occur to infants under one year of age. However, in developing countries infant mortality accounts for about two-thirds of all deaths to children under five years of age.

In Africa the deaths of children under five years of age account for nearly half of all deaths (UN, ECA, 1985). There are three different age groups under five years to consider in early childhood mortality. The first group reflects neonatal deaths to children under one month of age, when they face the highest risk of dying in their very first hours and days of their lives. Most neonatal deaths are due to congenital abnormalities and injuries occurring during parturition. Neonatal deaths account for about 30 percent of all early childhood mortality (Lopez and Hull, 1983).

In the post-neonatal period of one to 11 months malnutrition, respiratory, and diarrheal diseases claim about 30 to 40 percent of the infant lives. After age one infectious and parasitic diseases, such as measles and diphtheria, account for about 25 percent of all early childhood deaths.

Infant and early childhood mortality are major preoccupations of Africans, as this continent has the highest mortality probabilities at these ages of all major regions of the world (table 5.4). There have, however, been some major improvements in the survival of African children during the past 15 years (UN, 1988). For example, the infant mortality rate declined from 137 in 1970-75 to 103 in 1985-90. Also, the probability of an African child dying before age five dropped from 233 in 1970-75 to 167 in 1985-90. Nevertheless, these major declines in Africa are overshadowed by the low mortality levels of the developed regions of the world. In the developed countries the probability of dying in infancy is about 15 out of every 1,000 children. The comparable figure for Africa is 103, about seven times as high. In the developed countries of the world fewer than 20 out of every thousand children die before reaching age five. In Africa the probability of dying before their fifth birthday, is 167 which is over eight times as high as in the industrialized countries.

Child mortality probabilities are available only for selected African countries over a 20-year span, which provide some approximate comparisons (table 5.5). For example, Sierra Leone in West Africa has the highest mortality levels in the world, with infant mortality probabilities of 206 per thousand births and 364 per thousand children under five years of age (table 5.5). Gambia, Malawi, and Mali have infant mortality probabilities of 180 and over, and child mortality probabilities of at least 300 (table 5.5). In contrast, Mauritius and Réunion have the lowest infant and childhood mortality in Africa, with 30 or fewer deaths per 1,000 children. Between these extremes are Algeria, Botswana, Cape Verde, South Africa, and Tunisia, with infant mortality probabilities under 80 per thousand live births.

Most African nations have made great commitments to health programs designed to reduce infant and child mortality by using immunization and rehydration techniques (UNICEF, 1988). The year 1986, for example, was declared the African Year of Immunization with the objective of immunizing children against the six major childhood diseases: diphtheria, tetanus, tuberculosis, whooping cough, measles, and poliomyelitis. A number of African countries have established immunization goals for their children.

Thousands of African children have been victims of diarrhea-induced dehydration. Many governments such as Egypt initiated programs to popularize the use of oral rehydration salts.

Several studies have been made of the socioeconomic aspects of infant mortality in Africa (Rutstein, 1983, 1984). Caldwell (1979) found that the mother's education was consistently the most important variable in accounting for infant mortality differentials. He showed that the probability of the survival of a child was directly related to his mother's formal education. Also, income has been found to be inversely related to child mortality in Kenya (Anker and Knowles

1980) and child mortality was found to be lower in urban than in rural areas (Farah and Preston, 1982).

Crude Death Rates

The average annual number of deaths per 1,000 population in Africa dropped from 27 during 1950-55 to 15 in 1985-90 (table 5.3). The death rates in North Africa declined 50 percent during this 30-year period, from 25 to 11. In sub-Saharan Africa the southern region had the lowest crude death rate in 1985-90, with 10 per 1,000 population. The other three regions had death rates of 16-17 per one thousand population.

Generally, medical and public health care programs have been successfully applied in Africa in the prevention and control of infectious diseases. In many instances international agencies have been instrumental in introducing programs for the control of disease and improved sanitation. For example, the introduction of antibiotics resulted in mortality declines from typhoid fever, pneumonia, and intestinal diseases.

Maternal Mortality Rates

Maternal mortality rates reflect the risk of dying from complications of pregnancy, childbirth, and the puerperium. Usually, the maternal mortality rate is defined as the number of deaths from puerperal causes per 100,000 live births. The risk of maternal mortality rises as the number of children a mother has borne increases. Also, mothers with short spacing between births have higher risks, and women who experienced malnutrition in childhood or adolescence often have difficulties in childbirth. Apparently, many of the maternal deaths in Africa are due to complications resulting from improperly performed abortions (Kwast, et al., 1986). In Addis Ababa abortion was the most frequent cause of death of women.

Only about half a dozen African countries reported any figures on maternal deaths during the last decade and those for Egypt are considered to be the only reliable ones (UN, 1990). There, the maternal mortality rate declined from 823 in 1978 to 785 in 1982. However, the age-sex specific mortality rates of many African countries have shown that the death rates of women in some of the reproductive ages were higher than for men (UN, 1982a).

Complications of childbirth are among the leading causes of death of women of childbearing ages in all developing countries. Africa has the highest maternal mortality rate of all major regions of the world, with 640 deaths per 100,000 live births (table 5.6). The rates for Asia and Latin America are 420 and 270, respectively. West Africa not only has the highest maternal mortality rate in Africa but in the entire world as well (WHO, 1986).

Table 5.3
Changes in Crude Death Rates[1] and Life Expectancy at Birth, 1950-90

Regions and Countries	Crude Death Rates			Life Expectancy		
	1950-55	1970-75	1985-90	1950-55	1970-75	1985-90
WORLD TOTAL	20	12	10	48	59	64
Developed Regions	10	9	10	66	71	74
Developing Regions	24	13	10	42	55	61
Africa	27	19	15	38	46	52
Eastern Africa	28	20	16	37	45	51
Burundi	25	21	18	39	43	48
Comoros	24	18	13	40	48	54
Djibouti	31	23	18	33	41	47
Ethiopia	32	23	21	33	41	44
Kenya	25	17	11	41	51	58
Madagascar	27	19	14	38	47	54
Malawi	31	24	21	36	41	47
Mauritius	16	7	6	51	63	69
Mozambique	30	22	19	34	43	47
Réunion	13	7	6	53	64	71
Rwanda	23	21	17	40	45	49
Somalia	31	23	20	33	41	45
Uganda	25	19	16	40	47	51
Tanzania	27	19	14	37	47	53
Zambia	26	18	14	38	47	53
Zimbabwe	23	15	10	42	52	58
Middle Africa	28	21	16	37	44	50

Table 5.3 (Continued)

Regions and Countries	Crude Death Rates				Life Expectancy		
	1950-55	1970-75	1985-90		1950-55	1970-75	1985-90
Angola	35	25	20		30	38	45
Cameroon	27	20	15		37	45	53
Central African Republic	29	22	18		34	43	49
Chad	32	25	20		33	39	46
Congo	25	19	15		36	47	53
Equatorial Guinea	32	24	20		34	41	46
Gabon	27	20	17		38	45	52
Zaire	26	19	14		41	46	52
Northern Africa	25	17	11		42	51	59
Algeria	24	15	8		43	55	64
Egypt	24	16	11		42	52	59
Libya	23	15	9		43	53	61
Morocco	26	16	10		43	53	61
Sudan	27	21	16		37	43	50
Tunisia	23	12	7		45	56	66
Southern Africa	21	14	10		44	53	60
Botswana	23	17	12		43	51	59
Lesotho	27	19	12		37	48	56
Namibia	25	18	12		39	49	56
South Africa	20	13	10		45	54	60
Swaziland	28	18	13		36	47	56
Western Africa	28	21	17		35	43	49
Benin	37	26	19		33	40	46

Table 5.3 (Continued)

Regions and Countries	Crude Death Rates			Life Expectancy		
	1950-55	1970-75	1985-90	1950-55	1970-75	1985-90
Burkina Faso	32	24	18	33	41	47
Cape Verde	19	12	8	49	58	66
Côte d'Ivoire	28	19	15	36	45	52
Gambia	34	27	21	30	37	43
Ghana	22	16	13	42	50	54
Guinea	34	27	22	31	37	43
Guinea Bissau	30	27	23	33	37	42
Liberia	27	20	16	38	48	53
Mali	32	25	21	33	39	44
Mauritania	31	24	19	33	40	46
Niger	32	25	20	33	39	45
Nigeria	27	20	16	37	45	51
Senegal	28	24	18	37	40	47
Sierra Leone	34	29	23	30	35	41
Togo	29	19	14	36	46	53

[1] Expressed in terms of per 1,000 population

Source: Compiled from *World Population Prospects 1990* (Sales No. E.91.XIII.4).

Table 5.4
Infant and Child Mortality, by Major Area, 1970-90

Major Area and Region	Probability of Dying Between Birth and Age 1				Probability of Dying Between Birth and Age 5			
	1970-75	1975-80	1980-85	1985-90	1970-75	1975-80	1980-85	1985-90
WORLD	94	86	79	71	144	131	118	105
Developed Regions	22	19	16	15	26	24	19	17
Developing Regions	106	97	89	79	164	150	135	119
Africa	140	126	116	106	233	203	186	167
Eastern Africa	138	130	125	116	228	218	207	191
Middle Africa	136	126	117	107	229	212	195	178
Northern Africa	138	117	99	86	219	183	152	129
Southern Africa	112	98	87	77	158	136	119	103
Western Africa	151	133	122	112	258	225	206	188
Latin America	80	70	63	56	115	99	88	78

Major Area and Region	Probability of Dying Between Birth and Age 1				Probability of Dying Between Birth and Age 5			
	1970-75	1975-80	1980-85	1985-90	1970-75	1975-80	1980-85	1985-90
Northern America	18	14	11	10	21	17	13	11
Asia	99	91	83	73	151	139	124	108
Europe	24	19	15	13	28	22	17	15
Oceania	40	36	31	26	53	48	41	33
Former Soviet Republics	26	28	26	24	36	38	36	32

Source: Compiled from United Nations, *World Population Monitoring 1989* (Sales No. E.89.XIII.12).

Table 5.5
Infant and Child Mortality of Selected African Countries

| COUNTRY | YEAR | Probability of Dying Between | |
		Birth and Age 1	Birth and Age 5
Algeria	1983	80	103
Benin	1977-81	108	204
Botswana	1979	80	112
Burkina Faso	1971	172	282
Burundi	1984	116	194
Cameroon	1974-78	106	195
Cape Verde	1983-85	68	---
Central African Republic	1970	141	239
Comoros	1976	94	154
Congo	1970	89	144
Côte d'Ivoire	1977-81	113	172
Egypt	1981	129	205
Gambia	1970	194	341
Ghana	1969	115	192
Kenya	1975	93	151
Liberia	1970-71	153	248
Libya	1969	120	186
Lesotho	1975	126	174
Malawi	1974	187	327
Mali	1980	180	350
Mauritania	1975	130	220
Mauritius	1984-86	25	31

Table 5.5 (Continued)

| COUNTRY | YEAR | Probability of Dying Between | |
		Birth and Age 1	Birth and Age 5
Morocco	1983	90	125
Mozambique	1975	164	281
Réunion	1986	11	16
Rwanda	1980	129	218
Senegal	1974-78	112	262
Sierra Leone	1971	206	364
South Africa	1980	80	---
Swaziland	1972	142	212
Tanzania	1975	129	217
Togo	1969	130	219
Tunisia	1981	74	102
Zambia	1970	105	173
Zimbabwe	1980	84	135
Zaire	1972	118	199

Source: United Nations, *World Population Monitoring, 1989* (Sales No. E.89.XIII.12),

Table 38.

Table 5.6
Maternal Mortality Rates for Developing Regions, around 1983 (per 100,000 live births)

Major Area and Region	Maternal Mortality Rate
WORLD	390
Developed Regions	30
Developing Regions	450
Africa	640
Eastern Africa	660
Middle Africa	690
Northern Africa	500
Southern Africa	570
Western Africa	700
Latin America	270
Caribbean	220
Central America	270
South America	280
Asia	420
Eastern Asia	55
South Eastern Asia	420
Southern Asia	650
Western Asia	340

Source: Compiled from World Health Organization, *Maternal Mortality Rates, Tabulation of Available Information*, 2nd Ed., Geneva, 1986.

Recently, a new method has been proposed to estimate maternal mortality from the proportion of sisters who have died during pregnancy, childbirth, or the puerperium, as reported by adult respondents in censuses or surveys (Graham, et al., 1988). The accuracy of this proposed technique is being tested to determine whether it can improve the current generally unreliable estimates in developing countries.

THE INFLUENCE OF ETHNICITY, KINSHIP, AND FAMILY PATTERNS ON CHILD MORTALITY

There is a direct relationship between stable family relationships and low levels of child mortality. Mothers have the primary responsibility for the care of their young children but often rely on other kin and children living at home to provide additional support. Child mortality is related to marital status, family, and household structure in a number of ways. First, children born to unmarried women have higher risks of death than to married women. Birth weights of illegitimate children are usually lower. Second, children of consensual unions have higher mortality than children of legal marriages, and infant mortality is higher among polygamous than monogamous unions (Caldwell, 1979). In addition, the attainment of small families results in child mortality declines. For example, in Ibadan, child mortality was lowest among women who had small families.

Ethnicity exerts a pronounced effect upon infant and child mortality differentials among the major ethnic groups in Ghana, Kenya, Liberia, Nigeria, Sierra Leone, and Sudan (UN, 1985). Child mortality differences were actually greater among rural ethnic than urban ethnic groups. Moreover, impressive ethnic variations were identified in the mortality of persons of all ages in Cameroon and the Central African Republic (UN, 1982a).

In rural Mali sharp differences were found in child mortality between different ethnic groups living in identical environmental circumstances, where the Fulani experienced twice the risk of dying as the Tamasheq (Hill, 1985). The higher child mortality was attributed to ecological and epidemiological (environmental) factors rather than to malnutrition or poverty.

There is a definite preference of sons in North Africa which results in excess female mortality. Throughout most of North Africa, the majority of Muslim women are secluded and exercise a minimum of autonomy and authority over their children's health (Caldwell, 1990). When mothers are given greater control over their children's health, declines in child mortality are accelerated.

SUMMARY AND IMPLICATIONS

Due to frequent epidemics, plagues, and strife in the early 1900s, death rates in Africa fluctuated from time to time. However, declines occurred after World

War II as biomedical discoveries effectively controlled various diseases.   The
crude death rate, for example, fell from 27 in 1950-55 to 15 in 1985-90, and
infant mortality dropped from 188 in 1950-55 to 103 in 1985-90.   Since birth
rates remained high during this period, the rapid declines in mortality resulted in
relatively large population increases.   Mortality levels will continue to improve
in Africa although droughts and famines are likely to affect nutritional standards
adversely.   With general improvements in sanitation, expanded hospital and clinic
facilities, and more trained health and medical personnel to administer health
care, health conditions should improve.

The major causes of death are closely related to a country's stage of
development.   The developing countries of the world, such as those in Africa,
have comparatively high death rates from infectious and parasitic diseases as well
as from respiratory diseases.   In contrast, they have relatively low death rates
from chronic degenerative diseases such as heart disease and cancer.   Deaths
from the first two major causes have declined in many African countries, whereas
deaths from degenerative diseases have increased.   Significantly, life expectancy
at birth has increased more than 10 years since 1950, going from an average of
38 years in 1950-55 to 52 years in 1985-90.

Many African governments have made firm commitments to supporting primary
health care programs, including immunization and rehydration programs for
young children.   These efforts will result in the saving of thousands of lives and
reduce the death rates of infants and children in early childhood.

REFERENCES

Ahmed, Ghyasuddin.   1988.   "Prospects of the Spread of AIDS and Models of
    Possible Initiation of the Disease and Intervention Measures to control it in
    Botswana and Other Countries of the Region."   Paper presented at the African
    Population Conference of the International Union for the Scientific Study of
    Population, Dakar, Senegal.

Anker, Richard and James C. Knowles.   1980.   "An Empirical Analysis of
    Mortality Differentials in Kenya at the Macro and Micro Levels." *Economic
    Development and Cultural Change* 29: 165-185.

Brass, William.   1975.   *Methods for Estimating Fertility and Mortality from
    Limited and Defective Data.*   Chapel Hill, NC: North Carolina Population
    Center Laboratories for Population Studies.

Brass, William et al.   1968.   *The Demography of Tropical Africa.*   Princeton, NJ:
    Princeton University Press.

Caldwell, J.C.   1979.   "Education as a Factor in Mortality Decline: an
    Examination of Nigerian Data." *Population Studies* 33: 395-413.

_____.   1990.   "Cultural and Social Factors Influencing Mortality Levels in
    Developing Countries."   In *World Population: Approaching The Year 2000*,
    edited by Samuel H. Preston, 44-59.   Newbury Park: Sage.

Carrier, Norman and John Hobcraft. 1971. *Demographic Estimation for Developing Societies*. London: Population Investigation Committee, London School of Economics.

Cipolla, Carlo M. 1965. "Four Centuries of Italian Demographic Development." In *Population in History*, edited by D.V. Glass and D.E.C. Eversley, 570-587. Chicago: Aldine Publishing Company.

Clavel, Francois et al. 1987. "Human Immunodeficiency Virus Type 2 Infection Associated with AIDS in West Africa." *New England Journal of Medicine* 316: 1180-1185.

Dawson, Marc H. 1981. "Disease and Population Decline of the Kikuyu of Kenya, 1890-1925." In *African Historical Demography*, edited by Christopher Fyfe and David McMaster, vol. 2, 121-138. Edinburgh, Scotland: University of Edinburgh.

Farah, Abdul-Aziz and Samuel H. Preston. 1982. "Child Mortality Differentials in Sudan." *Population and Development Review* 8: 365-383.

Ferembach, D. 1962. *La Nécropole Epipaléolithique de Taforalt études des Squelettes Humains*. Paris: Centre National de la Recherche Scientifique et la Ragat Mission Universitaire et Culturelle Francaise au Maroc.

Graham, W., William Brass, and R.W. Snow. 1988. *Indirect Estimation of Maternal Mortality: The Sisterhood Method*. Research Paper 88-1. London: London School of Hygiene and Tropical Medicine.

Graunt, John. 1939. *Natural and Political Observations Made Upon the Bills of Mortality*, edited by Walter F. Willcox. Baltimore, MD: Johns Hopkins Press. (Originally published in London, 1662.)

Halley, Edmond. 1693. "An Estimate of the Degree of Mortality of Mankind." *Philosophical Transactions of the Royal Society of London* 17: 596-610, 654-656.

Heligman, Larry and John H. Pollard. 1980. "The Age Pattern of Mortality." *The Journal of the Institute of Actuaries* 107: 49-80.

Hill, Allan G. ed. 1985. *Population, Health and Nutrition in the Sahel*. London: Routledge and Kegan Paul.

Kiser, Clyde V. 1944. "The Demographic Position of Egypt." *Milbank Memorial Fund uarterly* 22: 383-408.

Kumari, G. Suguna. 1974. *Complete Life Tables for the Island of Mauritius, 1971-73*. Rose Hill, Mauritius: Central Statistical Office.

_____. Undated. *Abridged Life Tables for Mauritian Males and Females, 1982-84*. Rose Hill, Mauritius: Central Statistical Office.

Kwast, Barbara E., Roger W. Rochat, and Widad Kidane-Mariam. 1986. "Maternal Mortality in Addis Ababa, Ethiopia." *Studies in Family Planning* 17: 288-301.

Lopez, A.D. and T.H. Hull. 1983. "A Note on Estimating the Cause of Death Structure in High Mortality Populations." *Population Bulletin of the United Nations 1982*, No. 14, 66-70, New York.

Patterson, K. David. 1981. "The Demographic Impact of the 1918-19 Influenza Pandemic in Sub-Saharan Africa: A Preliminary Assessment." In *African Historical Demography*, edited by Christopher Fyfe and David McMaster, vol. 2, 403-431. Edinburgh, Scotland: University of Edinburgh.

Pearson, Karl. 1901-02. "On the Change in Expectation of Life in Man During a Period Circa 2000 Years." *Biometrika* 1: 261-264.

Preston, Samuel. 1976. *Mortality Patterns in National Populations: With Special Reference to Recorded Causes of Death*. New York: Academic Press.

Ross, Robert. 1977. "Smallpox at the Cape of Good Hope in the Eighteenth Century." In *African Historical Demography*, edited by Christopher Fyfe and David McMaster, Vol. 1, 416-428. Edinburgh, Scotland: University of Edinburgh.

Russell, Josiah C. 1958. "Late Ancient and Medieval Population." *Transactions of the American Philosophical Society* 48: 3-152.

Rutstein, Shea O. 1983. *Infant and Child Mortality: Levels, Trends, and Demographic Differentials* (Senegal). Voorburg and London: World Fertility Survey Comparative Studies: Cross National Summaries.

_____. 1984. *Infant and Child Mortality: Levels, Trends, and Demographic Differentials* (Cameroon), Voorburg and London: World Fertility Survey Comparative Studies: Cross National Summaries.

Simonsen, J. Neil et al. 1988. "Human Immunodeficiency Virus Among African Men with Sexually Transmitted Diseases." *New England Journal of Medicine* 319: 274-278.

Sullivan, Jeremiah M. 1972. "Models for the Estimation of the Probability of Dying Between Birth and exact Ages of Early Childhood." *Population Studies* 26: 79-97.

UNICEF. 1988. *The State of World's Children, 1988*. New York: Oxford University Press.

United Nations. 1982a. *Levels and Trends of Mortality Since 1950*. New York.

_____. 1982b. *Unabridged Model Life Tables Corresponding to the New United Nations Model Life Tables for Developing Countries*. New York.

_____. 1985. *Socio-Economic Differentials in Child Mortality in Developing Countries*. New York.

_____. 1988. *Mortality of Children under Age 5; World Estimates and Projections, 1950-2025*. New York.

_____. 1990. *Demographic Yearbook 1988*. New York.

United Nations. 1985. Economic Commission for Africa. *Mortality Levels, Patterns, Trends and Differentials in Africa*. Addis Ababa, Ethiopia.

World Health Organization. 1967. *Manual of the International Statistical Classification of Diseases, Injuries, and Causes of Death*, vol. 1. Geneva.

_____. 1986. *Maternal Mortality Rates. A Tabulation of Available Information.* 2nd ed. Geneva.

_____. 1990a. *Current and Future Dimensions of the HIV/AIDS Pandemic.* Geneva.

_____. 1990b. *Update: AIDS Cases Reported to Surveillance, Forecasting, and Impact Assessment Unit*, Geneva.

6

The Age-Sex Structure of the Population

Demographers study the age and sex composition of different populations, what factors influence age-sex structure, and why age-sex composition varies from one population to another. In addition, they consider why populations with certain age-sex characteristics are likely to encounter particular social and economic problems.

THE NATURE OF AGE-SEX COMPOSITION

Population pyramids are graphic representations of the age and sex distributions of inhabitants. Past fertility, mortality, and migration levels determine the age and sex composition of the populations of different countries, and give present age-sex pyramids their distinctive shape. In this chapter, population pyramids are constructed as bar graphs, using five-year age categories, with males plotted to the left and females to the right of the center vertical age axis. Infants are always depicted at the base of each pyramid, with progressively older populations plotted successively towards the top. Each bar indicates the proportion of the total population that each age group comprises.

The shape is seldom a perfect pyramid since mortality, fertility, and migration usually fluctuate from year to year, altering the population structure accordingly. Irregularities in pyramids usually continue each successive census throughout the life of the population, progressively moving upward, then finally disappearing upon the death of the particular cohorts. Population pyramids, therefore, reflect the demographic histories of countries through changes in their age-sex structure. For example, a pyramid with a relatively broad base indicates a population with a very high birth rate, those with a narrow, triangular shape from the base to the top indicate both high birth and death rates, such as in Rwanda, the country with the highest total fertility rate in Africa. In contrast, when fertility and mortality are both low, the age-sex pyramid resembles a barrel or rectangle in shape, with a slightly sloping top at the oldest ages, as in the age-sex structure of the white population of South Africa. (The age-sex structures of Rwanda and South Africa were chosen to reflect contrasting patterns. The age-sex structure of neither country is, of course, necessarily representative of the entire African continent.)

In demography, the sex ratio is defined as the number of males per 100 females. At birth, there are usually around 105 boys born for every 100 girls. Thus, the sex ratio at birth in this example is 105. Since males usually have higher death rates than females at every age throughout life, the relative number of females increases progressively with age. Thus, the sex ratio tends to decline with advancing age. However, in the past, African women had very high maternal mortality rates and their death rates in the childbearing ages were often higher than those for men in the same age brackets.

Irregular age-sex patterns observed in some pyramids can be attributed to sudden declines in births and increases in deaths. They can also be caused by temporary fluctuations in deaths due to epidemics. The shape of the age-sex pyramid of non-citizens in Botswana is a result of the selective age-sex composition of the immigrants. The majority who had moved into Botswana were males in the young working ages of 25 to 39 (Tarver and Miller, 1988).

The pyramids of transitional populations reflect demographic changes in process. For example, the age-sex distribution of Réunion shows populations in different stages of transition. This age-sex pyramid reflects a very large cohort of children 15-19 years old in 1982 (born between 1963 and 1967). In addition, it clearly indicates that the number of births in each five-year period since that time has become progressively smaller, implying a definite decline in fertility during the past 15 years. Réunion is one of the few African countries to experience a definite decline in fertility throughout this period. (The Botswana and Réunion examples shown here are not, of course, representative of the age-sex structure of the entire African continent.)

REGIONAL PATTERNS OF AGE COMPOSITION

Africa's age composition has remained more or less stable since 1950. The proportionate number of children has increased slightly during this time, while the proportionate population of working ages has declined.

With high birth rates and declining death rates, coupled with slightly increasing life expectancy, the rapid population growth in Africa has resulted in a distinctive age structure. The population is very young and grows very rapidly as children mature and have children of their own at an early age. Africa, for example, has the highest relative number of children of all major regions of the world, as nearly every other person (45 percent) is a child under 15 years of age (table 6.1). In contrast, Europe has less than half the proportionate number of children under 15 as Africa, only about 21 percent.

The regional distribution of the working-age population follows a totally different pattern, as Africa has the smallest relative number of persons in the working ages of 15-64, only 52 percent. By comparison, fully two-thirds of those in North America and the former Soviet republics are between 15 and 64 years of age (table 6.1). In the wealthy developed nations there are about three persons in the working ages for each dependent person under 15 years of age, so the burden of providing adequate care for children is much less than that in developing countries. Educational, health, and other costs of rearing children to productive adulthood make it extremely difficult for poor developing countries to provide adequate care for so many youngsters. It should be noted, too, that even though the task of caring for children is less demanding in developed countries, the burden of caring for the aged there is much greater than in developing countries.

Africa also has the smallest proportionate number of elderly persons of all regions of the world: a mere three percent are 65 years of age and older. In contrast, 13 percent of Europe's population is 65 and older. In the northern European countries, the aged are relatively five times as numerous as in Africa, 15 compared to three percent, respectively. Consequently, the costs of providing care for the elderly in northern Europe are much greater than in Africa. The great differences in the proportionate numbers of aged are basically due to the greater life expectancies and lower birth rates in the developed countries. For example, the inhabitants of developed countries live, on the average, about 15 to 20 years longer than those in developing countries and their crude birth rates are approximately a third as high as in developing countries.

The great preponderance of children and the relative scarcity of working-age persons in Africa mean that the burden of rearing and educating the large number of youngsters falls on a comparatively small number of persons in the economically active ages. This burden is greatly accentuated by the fact that Africa is a very poor, developing region with an estimated 1987 per capita income of $748 (in constant 1980 U.S. dollars) (UN, 1990). The burden of providing adequate care for children is substantially less in developed regions than in Africa, not only because of comparatively fewer children but also because of much greater wealth: the 1987 per capita income of developed countries was $7,966--nearly 11 times that of Africa (UN, 1990).

Clearly, developing countries face heavy burdens in supporting their dependent-age populations, especially their children. High dependency rates may seriously hinder economic growth in these countries (Coale and Hoover, 1958). In fact, the critical economic growth and development problems that lie ahead in the developing countries are compounded by the large projected population growth, for population growth and economic growth are closely related (Cassen, 1976; McNicoll, 1982; Ware, 1978).

Table 6.1
Age-Sex Composition of the Major Regions of the World, 1990

Regions	Percentage of Total Population in Each Age Group			
	Under 15 Years	15-64 Years	65 Years and Over	Sex Ratio
WORLD TOTAL	33	61	6	101
Developed Countries[1]	22	67	11	94
Developing Countries[1]	37	59	4	104
Africa	45	52	3	99
West Africa	47	50	3	99
East Africa	47	50	3	97
North Africa	41	55	4	102
Middle Africa	45	52	3	98
Southern Africa	38	58	4	98
North America	22	66	12	95
Latin America	36	59	5	100
Asia	33	62	5	105
Europe	20	67	13	95
Oceania	27	64	9	101
Former Soviet Republics	25	65	10	90

[1] Percentages for developed and developing countries apply to the year 1985.

Source: Compiled from United Nations, *Demographic Yearbook 1990*

(Sales No.E/F.91.XIII.1).

THE CHANGING AGE STRUCTURE OF AFRICAN COUNTRIES

The projected declines in fertility and mortality in Africa between 1950 and 2025 will, of course, result in definite changes in the age composition of the population. While the actual number of inhabitants in each of the three major age groups will continue to increase in this 75-year period, the relative number of youths under 15 years of age is expected to decline (UN, 1991). In contrast, the proportionate numbers in the working ages of 15 to 64 and the elderly 65 years of age and over are projected to increase. These projected changes in age composition will be reflected, of course, in the changing dependency ratios.

The Dobe !Kung tribe in the Kalahari Desert of northwestern Botswana maintain favorable dependency ratios by shifting and adjusting their inhabitants among their various camps (Lee, 1984). These Bushmen near the Namibian border live almost entirely from hunting and gathering. When a camp becomes overpopulated with too many young children to feed it becomes a burden upon the working adults. Some families with young children are encouraged to join other camps with more balanced dependency ratios. In contrast, camps with a scarcity of children often recruit families with youngsters, particularly relatives with children.

PATTERNS OF SEX COMPOSITION

Throughout the world men were slightly more numerous than women in 1990, and the overall sex ratio was estimated to be 101 men per 100 women (table 6.1). Mortality is generally higher among males than females in each year of life, and these differences progressively widen as age increases. Consequently, sex ratios tend to fall directly with increasing age. For example, since developing countries had comparatively younger populations than developed countries, they also had relatively more males than females, 104 compared to 94 (table 6.1).

In 1990 the former Soviet republics had the lowest sex ratio of all major regions, due to the deaths of an estimated 26 million Soviet soldiers and civilians killed in World War II and an equal number believed to have died in labor camps, forced collectivization, famines, and executions during Stalin's rule (Dyadkin, 1973; Rosefielde, 1983). The majority of these 50 million victims were males (Eason, 1959).

As a result of low levels of fertility and declining mortality, and higher male than female mortality in the advanced ages, Europe and North America have the next lowest ratios. Asia has the highest sex ratio of all regions. This is due mainly to the influence of China and India, the two most populous countries in the world, where males outnumber females. In China, male children generally have been given better care than female children. So, historically, life expectancy has been higher for males than for females, at least to the end of childbearing age. Before 1980, males in India tended to have longer life expectancies than

females. Also, it is believed that underenumeration has been higher among
females, thereby artificially inflating some of the high sex ratios.

Another reason for the relatively high sex ratios in Asia results from the
traditional practice of infanticide, which was almost universally the practice of
female infanticide along with the extinction of defective children. In the
traditional societies of China, India, and Japan, as well as those in medieval and
early modern Europe, infanticide was widely practiced. It was common in many
ancient Greek city-states and in Rome.

In 1990, females outnumbered males in Africa with a sex ratio of 99 (UN,
1992). In practically all African countries the ratios ranged between 95 and 105.
Females were somewhat more numerous than males in Botswana, Congo, Gabon,
and Swaziland. Males were somewhat more numerous than females in Libya and
the Côte d'Ivoire, where the sex ratios were nearly 110. São Tomé and Príncipe,
and Western Sahara were the only two countries with greatly distorted sex ratios,
as there were 125 men for each 100 women in São Tomé and Príncipe, and 136
men for each 100 women in Western Sahara. Both countries had small
populations of between 60,000 and 75,000 when they were last enumerated, and
it is possible that tabulation and enumeration errors may also account for some
of the differences. Moreover, Western Sahara is a frontier country with a
predominantly male population.

International migrant workers absent from their places of usual residence when
population censuses are taken are not normally counted by census takers in their
home countries. This practice distorts sex ratios, as the predominantly male
migrants are not enumerated at their usual places of residence. For instance,
nearly 300,000 men from Lesotho, Mozambique, Botswana, Malawi, and
Swaziland were employed in gold and coal mines in the Republic of South Africa
from 1974 to 1986 (One-Hundredth, 1989). A similar situation applies in
countries in the major labor market areas of the Côte d'Ivoire and Libya.

SUMMARY AND IMPLICATIONS

The continent of Africa has a very distinctive age structure. It has the largest
proportionate number of children, the smallest relative number of persons in the
economically active ages, and the smallest relative number of aged individuals of
all major regions of the world. Thus, African countries are saddled with huge
young, dependent-age populations to support, with very meager resources to
undertake this task. This unique age composition is a result of high birth and
death rates and comparatively short life expectancies as relatively few persons live
beyond 65 years of age. The regional distribution of males and females follows
a somewhat different pattern: Africa has the lowest sex ratio of the three
developing regions, which is also slightly lower than the world average. In this
respect, the sex composition of the population is a result of the sex ratio at birth
together with the differentials in mortality and migration.

Age-sex pyramids clearly reflect the fluctuations in the number of births, deaths, and migrants that occur during the lifetime of the population. Pyramids depict the age-sex composition of a population and may be considered as demographic histories of a lifetime of individuals living at any one time. Obviously, changes in fertility, mortality, and migration result in changes in age composition. In turn, age composition directly affects fertility and mortality levels. High fertility usually results in a very young age structure, and declining fertility makes the population older. Declining mortality, in contrast, usually results in a younger population, as the relatively highest declines in death rates usually occur among children and young adults. In addition, in-migration usually lowers the age of a population while out-migration tends to increase the age.

REFERENCES

Cassen, Robert H. 1976. "Population and Development: A Survey." *World Development* 4: 785-830.

Coale, Ansley J. and Edgar M. Hoover. 1958. *Population Growth and Economic Development in Low-Income Countries*. Princeton, NJ: Princeton University Press.

Dyadkin, Iosif G. 1973. *Unnatural Deaths in the USSR, 1928-1954*. New Brunswick, NJ: Transaction Books.

Eason, Warren W. 1959. "The Soviet Population Today: An Analysis of the First Results of the 1959 Census." *Foreign Affairs* 37: 598-606.

Lee, Richard B. 1984. *The Dobe !Kung*. New York: Holt, Rinehart, and Winston.

McNicoll, Geoffrey. 1982. "Population and Development." In *International Encyclopedia of Population*, edited by John A. Ross, 519-525. New York: Free Press.

One-Hundredth Annual Report. 1989. Johannesburg, South Africa: Chamber of Mines of South Africa.

Rosefielde, Steven. 1983. "Excess Mortality in the Soviet Union: A Reconsideration of the Demographic Consequences of Forced Industrialization, 1929-1949." *Soviet Studies* 35: 385-409.

Tarver, James D. and H. Max Miller. 1988. "Migration in Botswana." *African Urban Quarterly* 3: 278-284.

United Nations. 1990. *National Accounts Statistics: Analysis of Main Aggregates, 1987*. New York.

_____. 1991. *World Population Prospects 1990*. New York.

_____. 1992. *Demographic Yearbook 1990*. New York.

Ware, Helen. 1978. *Population and Development in Africa South of the Sahara: A Review of the Literature, 1970-1978*, Appendix 7A. Mexico City: El Colegio de Mexico.   International Review Group of Social Science Research on Population and Development.

7

Urbanization in Africa

Historically, urbanization is a relatively recent phenomenon in which people increasingly live in more and more densely populated areas. Urbanization appeared in the latter part of the fourth millennium B.C. in Mesopotamia. Shortly afterwards it emerged in the Nile Valley region, next in the Indus Valley (presently West Pakistan) where cities flourished between 2500 and 1500 B.C., then in the Huang Ho Valley (Yellow River), and among the Maya in the Yucatan peninsula of Meso-America (Sjoberg, 1960).

DEFINITIONS OF *RURAL* AND *URBAN*

Although the African countries use different criteria in defining urban populations, the two most commonly used are a minimum number of inhabitants in each population center and the proportionate number in nonagricultural employment (UN, 1992). For example, in Mauritius and Nigeria, a locality must have at least 20,000 inhabitants to qualify as urban; in Senegal localities must have at least 10,000 inhabitants; and in Botswana, Ghana, Madagascar, Mali, Somalia, Sudan, and Zambia, localities must have a minimum of 5,000 residents. In Angola, the Central African Republic, Egypt, Kenya, and Liberia, the minimum number required is 2,000. At the other extreme, settlements as small as trading centers of 100 inhabitants in Uganda are classified as urban. Therefore, the definition of urban centers in Africa ranges from a minimum size of 100 up to 20,000 inhabitants.

In addition to population size, the other criterion most commonly used in defining urban is the relative importance of nonagricultural activities. Botswana, Nigeria, Zambia, and Zaire consider nonagricultural employment. In Botswana, for instance, an urban center must have not only a minimum population of 5,000 but at least 75 percent of its labor force engaged in nonagricultural work.

Thus, after the urban population of each geographical and political subdivision is determined, the rural inhabitants residing in the outlying areas comprise the remaining population. Instead of using comparable definitions of rural-urban residence throughout the 56 countries of Africa, the national definitions of each country are employed here. The United Nations has never recommended a uniform rural-urban residence definition for all countries in the world.

URBAN DEVELOPMENTS

Apparently, urbanization in Africa began around 3300 to 3200 B.C. Abydos, the earliest known capital of Egypt, had about 20,000 inhabitants in 3200 B.C. and was probably the first city in Egypt. Memphis was founded by Pharaoh Menes in 3114 B.C. and had about 30,000 inhabitants in 3000 B.C., and was probably the largest city in the world at that time. Egypt soon became the most highly urbanized country in the world with the most populous cities at different times until the Christian era. Four different ancient Egyptian cities were thought to be the largest city in the world at various times: Memphis in 3000 B.C., which later attained a population of over 100,000 in 430 B.C. (Beloch, 1886); in 1650 B.C. Avaris had a population of more than 100,000; in 1160 B.C. a census showed over 86,000 persons in the Thebes estate (Breasted, 1906); and in 320 B.C. Alexandria surpassed 300,000 (Chandler, 1987).

For centuries after the beginning of urbanization cities grew very slowly (UN, 1980, 1991). As late as 1800 only five percent of the world's inhabitants lived in urban areas. Then, the Industrial Revolution was accompanied by large population movements to urban areas, as millions moved to rapidly growing industrial cities in response to expanding employment opportunities. By 1850 around 10 percent of all residents in developed countries lived in urban centers and by 1900 a quarter were urban dwellers.

Urbanization increased quite rapidly after 1900. By 1990 around 75 percent of those living in developed countries were urban residents and over a third of the inhabitants of developing countries lived in urban places (table 7.1). Projections indicate that the urban population will continue to increase rapidly throughout the world and the African countries are projected to have the highest urban growth rates of all (table 7.2).

URBANIZATION IN PRE-COLONIAL AFRICA

Egypt, the site of the rich Nile Valley, has been the location of Africa's largest population centers from the earliest days. Urbanization in the Nile region of Egypt and Sudan was followed by major urban developments along the western Mediterranean coastline in the Maghreb region of North Africa. Carthage was established by the Phoenicians on the Tunisian coast in 814 B.C. and became the dominant city of its time in that area, greatly prospering through trade, and was thought to be the richest city in the world. Despite treaties, Carthage and Rome were rivals for wealth, influence, and power. They lived in an uneasy coexistence until the First Punic War in 264 B.C.

It is likely that the total number of inhabitants of Carthage was somewhere around 200,000 before it was destroyed by the Romans in the Third Punic War in 146 B.C. (Charles-Picard, 1961). There were other African cities in that area of the Mediterranean region at that time, with some probably having populations of 5,000 to about 50,000. Estimates of more recent city populations indicate that the Maghreb region was highly urbanized in the pre-colonial period. Centuries later, when northwestern Africa was flourishing during the Almoravid empire, the city of Fez had an estimated population of 200,000 and Marrakesh probably had 150,000 in 1200 (Chandler, 1987). A 1634 population estimate for Algiers was 100,000; Meknes, Morocco likely had 200,000 inhabitants in 1727; and Tunis had about 65,000 in 1500.

West Africa became the third major region of pre-colonial urban development to emerge. Here urbanization resulted mainly from long-distance, trans-Saharan trading and the development of indigenous handicraft industries. Large medieval kingdoms appeared in two contiguous but distinct areas--the Sudan and the Guinea Coast (Bairoch, 1988). Prior to European colonization three major kingdoms were established in the grassland region of western Sudan (the Niger River Basin) and two in central Sudan. Below the Sudan, several kingdoms and empires stretching from Nigeria to Senegal were created in the forested Guinea Coast. The capital cities of these early kingdoms became the largest population centers--just as in the present-day African countries.

In Western Sudan, Ghana was the earliest major kingdom, succeeded by the somewhat larger Mali Empire which was, in turn, replaced by the much larger Songhay Empire. Koumbi-Saleh, the capital of Ghana, had an estimated 30,000 population when it was destroyed by the Almoravids in 1076 (Maquet, 1962). Niani, the capital of Mali, had about 60,000 inhabitants in 1324 (Chandler, 1987) and Gao, the capital of Songhay, had an estimated 75,000 inhabitants in 1585 (Mauny, 1961). Jenne, Timbuktu, and Walata were prominent trading centers in western Sudan, with Timbuktu having an estimated 45,000 inhabitants in 1510 (Africanus, 1896). This medieval civilization lasted until 1591 when it was destroyed by the Moors.

The Hausa states were in the northern grassland area of Nigeria in central Sudan east of the Western Sudan kingdoms (Mabogunje, 1968). Originally there were seven states, each having a capital city walled for protection. Of these capitals, Zaria had an estimated 60,000 inhabitants in 1600 and Kano probably had about 75,000 in 1585 (Mauny, 1961) but declined to 30,000 in 1851 (Barth, 1857).

The Kanem-Bornu Kingdom in central Sudan east of the Hausa states was originally two separate empires, with Kanem on the east and Bornu on the

Table 7.1
Urban Population Estimates and Projections of Developed and Developing Countries, 1800-2025 (in millions)

Year	World			Developed Regions			Developing Regions		
	Total	Urban	Percent Urban	Total	Urban	Percent Urban	Total	Urban	Percent Urban
1800	978	50	5	273	20	7	705	30	4
1850	1,262	80	6	352	40	11	910	40	4
1900	1,650	220	13	575	150	26	1,075	70	7
1925	1,950	400	21	715	285	40	1,235	115	9
1950	2,516	734	29	832	448	54	1,684	286	17
1990	5,292	2,390	45	1,207	875	73	4,086	1,515	37
2000	6,261	3,198	51	1,264	946	75	4,997	2,251	45
2025	8,504	5,493	65	1,354	1,117	83	7,150	4,376	61

Source: Compiled from United Nations, *Patterns of Urban and Rural Population Growth*, Population Studies No. 68 (Sales No. E.79.XIII.9) and *World Urbanization Prospects 1990* (Sales No. E.91.XIII.11).

Table 7.2
Percentage of the Population Living in Urban Areas by Region, 1950-2025

Region	1950	1980	1990	2000	2025
WORLD	29	40	45	51	65
Developed Regions	54	70	73	75	83
Developing Regions	17	29	37	45	61
Africa	15	28	34	41	57
Eastern Africa	5	15	22	29	47
Middle Africa	14	31	38	46	64
Northern Africa	25	40	45	51	66
Southern Africa	38	48	55	61	74
Western Africa	10	26	33	40	58
Latin America	42	65	72	76	84
North America	64	74	75	77	85
Asia	16	26	34	43	60
Europe	57	70	73	77	84
Oceania	61	71	71	71	77
Former Soviet Republics	39	63	66	68	78

Source: Computed from United Nations, *World Urbanization Prospects 1990*
(Sales No. E.91.XIII.11).

west side of Lake Chad. Ngazargamu, the Bornu capital, had about 60,000 inhabitants in 1600 (Chandler, 1987). Njimi, the small capital city of Kanem, was on the east side of Lake Chad.

Among the many upper and lower Guinea Kingdoms were the Yoruba in the Guinea Coast of western Nigeria, the Benin and Ibo empires in southern Nigeria, the Akan in central Ghana, and the Wolof in Senegal. In the forested Guinea Coast Yoruba cities were comparatively large, with Ibadan being the dominant one with about 70,000 inhabitants in 1850. Katunga, an Oyo capital, probably had 75,000 inhabitants in 1750.

The early capital cities of the major Sudanese and Guinea kingdoms were small urban centers compared to modern metropolitan centers and were about half the size of those in northwestern Africa. None ever reached a population of 100,000 in pre-colonial days. Pre-colonial urbanization continuously increased in Nigeria and Ghana, with the urban growth in Senegal and the Côte d'Ivoire being of more recent origin in the colonial period.

Other scattered pre-colonial urban settlements appeared at different times and flourished for varying periods but they did not result in sustained urban developments. The settlement Great Zimbabwe prospered for probably a thousand years before it reached its peak population of 40,000 after 1440 (Fagan, 1965). Kilwa, an important shipping center founded on the Tanzanian coast about 975, had around 30,000 inhabitants when the Portuguese arrived about 1500 (Garlake, 1973). Axum, an ancient capital of Ethiopia, had about 33,000 inhabitants before it was destroyed in 1500 (Chandler, 1987). Also, Mbanzo Congo, the capital of the old Congo kingdom, was a major Portuguese slave *entrepôt* with an estimated 50,000 inhabitants in 1543 (Balandier, 1968).

URBANIZATION DURING COLONIALISM

In all, 27 countries experienced definite urban development during the colonial period. The discovery of diamonds around 1870 and gold in 1886 ushered in a period of marked population growth and urbanization in South Africa. Rapid urbanization was well underway when South Africa obtained its independence from Great Britain in 1910.

In the 50 years that followed the other 26 countries began their major urbanization in the latter part of the colonial period. By 1950 Dakar and Addis Ababa had urban agglomerations (which are comprised of central cities on the surrounding urban areas) of approximately a quarter of a million population, the largest of the newly urbanized areas.

After independence the urban agglomerations of another 12 countries reached at least 50,000 inhabitants (Tarver and Miller, 1988). That leaves only eight African countries with urban agglomerations smaller than 50,000 inhabitants: Comoros, Equatorial Guinea, Lesotho, St. Helena, São Tomé and Príncipe, Seychelles, Swaziland, and Western Sahara.

URBAN POPULATION CHANGE IN POST-COLONIAL AFRICA

Near the end of colonialism only two African cities had reached a population of at least one million, the Egyptian cities of Cairo and Alexandria. Casablanca, Morocco was the next largest agglomeration with about 710,000 inhabitants, and Cape Town, South Africa was next with a population of 620,000.

During colonial days, the number of African laborers needed in the eastern and southern African municipalities fluctuated from one colony to another from time to time. Most African workers employed by municipal governments and private companies were housed in dormitory-like quarters in compounds and were considered as transients rather than permanent city dwellers (Muwonge, 1980). European pass laws excluded most other eastern and southern Africans from residing in cities during colonial days except in certain circumscribed areas. As a result of the relatively small rural-urban movement of blacks, Africa was the least urbanized region in the world in 1950, with just 15 percent of its inhabitants living in urban centers (table 7.2).

Obviously, the rural population had been relatively stable during colonial days as European pass laws kept the number of eastern and southern Africans in urban areas to a minimum. Actually, the eastern and southern African cities were considered "European cities" and regarded as "white man's country" in which Africans were told that they had no right to permanent settlement (O'Connor, 1983). In contrast, during the colonial period blacks in the indigenous West African cities purchased urban property, erected city homes, and migrated freely between rural and urban areas (Gugler and Flanagan, 1978).

When the African colonies obtained their independence urbanization was greatly accelerated by the movement of millions from the rapidly deteriorating agricultural sector, where most migrants lived in rural villages. Frequent droughts, coupled with overgrazing, soil erosion, and other conditions that adversely affected crop and livestock production were factors contributing to the urbanward movement. Many were attracted to cities chiefly because of amenities, not because of any immediate employment offers. Under the pressures of poverty and unemployment thousands established residences in substandard housing in such well-known squatter settlements as the Mathare Valley of Nairobi and Grand Yoff on the outskirts of Dakar. Estimates of the percentage of the population living in the slums of 20 major African cities ranged from 30 percent in Nairobi to 90 percent in Addis Ababa (Obudho and Mhlanga, 1988). These shantytowns are, of course, subject to many serious health and sanitation problems.

With the huge exodus out of agricultural areas, Africa had the highest rate of urban population growth of all major regions in the world after 1950. For example, the number of urban Africans increased from 32 million in 1950 to 217 million in 1990. By 1990 34 percent of all persons were living in urban areas (table 7.2). Around 35 million inhabitants were added to the city population of

Nigeria, 18 million to the cities of Egypt, 15 million to cities in South Africa, and 10 to 12 million each to the cities of Algeria, Morocco, and Zaire.

By 1990, there were 21 agglomerations with one million or more residents (table 7.3 gives the nine largest agglomerations). In addition to the metropolises with a million inhabitants there are about 150 other cities with at least 100,000 inhabitants. Obviously, urbanization occurred at a rapid pace, with the growth of all these large urban agglomerations of at least a 100,000 inhabitants. Many are capital cities situated on coasts with harbors. Approximately 185 million persons have been added to African cities since 1950, with 60 percent or more of the growth in the major metropolises being attribute to migration.

AFRICA'S CITY-SIZE PATTERNS

Numerous studies of the size and distribution of urban communities have been undertaken. For example, Auerbach (1913) was credited with developing the rank-size rule from a distribution of cities by size, and Pareto curves have been fitted to city-size distributions (Saibante, 1928). Zipf (1941) extended and modified Auerbach's formula, and Duncan (1957) later evaluated these different formulations. These studies showed that small places greatly outnumber large ones and that the size distribution is usually highly skewed.

In this chapter a tripartite topology of African cities was constructed to reflect the city-size patterns of population centers in the different countries. Specifically, the threefold configuration was based upon the sizes of the three most populous cities in each respective country. For example, when the largest city of a country had at least twice as many inhabitants as the second size city, this pattern was classified as primate (Jefferson, 1939). In countries where the three largest cities were of approximately equal size, the city-size distribution was considered to be trinary, since the three largest population centers did not differ greatly in size. Other countries without primate or trinary cities were classified as secondary-type. Then, this tripartite topology of city sizes was used to examine patterns of population change in the African countries.

Primate Cities

The disproportionately large, multifunctional primate cities are concentrated in North, West, Middle, and the northern part of East Africa. There is a tendency for primacy to develop in countries both small in area and in population. Some scholars have assumed that primacy increases as the level of development and the degree of urbanization increases. However, an exhaustive study revealed that primate city structure was not a function of the levels of economic development, industrialization, or urbanization (Mehta, 1964).

Of the three city-size configurations, the primate pattern is the most common in Africa. Thirty countries have comparatively large primate cities, with most being national capitals. In fact, in 50 of the 56 African countries capital cities are the most populous urban centers (Christopher, 1985). Of the countries with primate cities only in Morocco, Tanzania, Benin, and Malawi were the largest cities not national capitals--namely Casablanca, Dar es Salaam, Cotonou, and Blantyre, respectively. In Cameroon, a country with no primate city, Douala was larger than the national capital Yaoundé. In the future, the city-size patterns of Benin, Cameroon, and Malawi may very well change but those in Morocco and Tanzania are likely to persist for some time.

A country's city configurations can change over time, as in Botswana. The largest population centers there in 1964 were the three village centers of Serowe (33,502 inhabitants), Kanye (31,303), and Molepolole (27,633). Clearly, there was little difference in the population size of these three centers, which together displayed a trinary pattern. By 1981 the size distribution of the three largest cities closely resembled a secondary-type. The 1991 census will show a primate city pattern, for the population of Gaborone, the national capital, is growing rapidly.

The total urban population of the 30 African countries with primate cities increased 63 percent in 1980 to 1990, approximately the same average as all 44 countries included in the tripartite typology (table 7.4). Over 50 million inhabitants were added to their urban populations in this 10-year period.

Trinary Patterns

The major cities in each country with trinary patterns are not necessarily identical in size. They are, however, the three largest cities, which do not differ greatly in population size. In this tripartite classification it is assumed that whenever the population of the largest city in a country is no greater than 2.25 times the population of the third largest city, that the city-size configuration is trinary. These relative thresholds, of course, could vary.

The Republic of South Africa is highly urbanized and has a definite trinary city configuration based upon the 1985 population of its three largest cities. Nigeria, the most populous country in Africa, also has a trinary pattern based upon the 1963 official census figures. The other half dozen countries with trinary city patterns have relatively small populations and are widely scattered geographically.

The urban population of the eight countries with trinary city typologies increased 66 percent between 1980 and 1990, about the average for all 44 countries in the classification. Nearly 27 million inhabitants were added to the urban population of these eight countries.

Secondary-Size Patterns

Countries with considerable differences in the size of their three largest cities were classified as secondary-type configurations. By definition, the most

Table 7.3
Urban Agglomerations in Africa with Two Million or More Inhabitants in 1990 (in millions)

Urban Agglomeration	1950	1960	1970	1980	1985	1990	2000
Cairo/Giza (Egypt)	2.41	3.71	5.33	6.93	7.92	9.04	11.83
Lagos (Nigeria)	.29	.76	2.03	4.45	5.83	7.71	12.89
Alexandria (Egypt)	1.04	1.50	1.99	2.53	3.11	3.68	5.11
Casablanca (Morocco)	.71	1.10	1.51	2.21	2.66	3.21	4.56
Kinshasa (Zaire)	.17	.45	1.37	2.24	2.78	3.50	5.52
Alger (Algeria)	.44	.87	1.32	2.11	2.46	3.03	4.53
Cape Town (South Africa)	.62	.80	1.11	1.61	1.93	2.31	3.18
Abidjan (Côte d'Ivoire)	.06	.18	.55	1.26	1.65	2.17	3.53
Tripoli (Libya)	.11	.17	.40	1.06	1.54	2.06	3.16

Source: Computed from United Nations, *World Urbanization Prospects 1990*

(Sales No. E.91.XIII.11).

Table 7.4
Urban Population Changes of African Countries Classified by a Tripartite
City-Size Typology, 1980-90

City-Size Pattern	Number of Countries	Urban Population 1980 1990 (millions)		Change	Percentage Change
Primate	30	84,191	137,297	53,106	63
Secondary	6	5,355	9,648	4,293	80
Trinary	8	40,215	66,808	26,593	66
Total	44	129,761	213,753	83,992	65

Source: Compiled from United Nations, *Demographic Yearbook 1990*

(Sales No. E/F.91.XIII.1).

populous city with a secondary-size pattern cannot be disproportionately large enough to be a primate city. For example, in Gambia the most populous city was not a primate city, even though it had over eight times as many inhabitants as the third largest city.

There were only six countries with secondary-type city patterns but they had the highest relative urban population gains of countries of all three different types of cities. These countries (Burkina Faso, Cameroon, Gambia, Swaziland, Seychelles, and Zimbabwe) nearly doubled the size of their urban populations between 1980 and 1990. In fact, the urban population of Swaziland more than doubled and that for Cameroon grew 86 percent.

THE URBAN INFORMAL SECTOR

In the past the informal sector accounted for about 60 percent of the urban labor force and a quarter to a third of the total urban income in Africa (ILO, 1985). For example, about 50 percent of the labor force in the Lagos and Senegal urban areas were informal sector workers (Trager, 1987). Informal sector workers engage mainly in labor-intensive enterprises such as selling cigarettes and matches, street vending of food, and brewing beer, all of which are very small enterprises. It is a poor man's sector and highly dependent upon family labor.

Those in the informal sector have low educational levels and obviously lack training and vocational skills for well-paid formal urban employment. Many who farm also moonlight in the urban informal sector.

SUMMARY AND IMPLICATIONS

Plato thought that the ideal Greek city size was about 5,040 citizens, small enough for its members to maintain personal contact with one another to make local democracy possible (Wycherley, 1949). Most ancient Hellenic *Polises* (cities) in Plato's time were rather small by modern standards but present-day city sizes in neither Greece nor Africa conform to Plato's principles of optimum size. By the year 2000 the megacities of Cairo/Giza and Lagos are each likely to have 12 to 13 million inhabitants, and several other large African metropolises may have at least four or five million residents.

The rapid population growth of African cities has greatly multiplied the demands for such social services as housing, water and sewer facilities, waste disposal, schools, hospitals, police and fire protection, public transportation, garbage collection, and various other related services. For example, Lagos has a very acute housing shortage, severe traffic congestion, and inadequate public utilities, classrooms, and hospitals (Oyekanmi, 1985). With rapidly mounting population pressures the availability and quality of urban social services are progressively deteriorating even for small metropolises as Bamako (World Bank, 1979).

Africa's future urbanization raises many pressing issues. In the past, for example, rapid urban population growth was not accompanied by comparable increases in development and expansions in industry.   Rather, industrial employment lagged behind urban population growth, creating a situation known in the western world as *over-urbanization*.   In addition, the relative scarcity of secondary and tertiary industries, as well as labor-intensive policies, have tended to perpetuate low levels of development and economic stagnation.   Quite often rapid urbanization was accompanied by shantytowns, squalor, and greatly magnified social, economic, and health problems.   With a continuation of the high rates of urbanization, per capita incomes and levels of living may drop even further unless development is greatly accelerated.

REFERENCES

Africanus, Leo. 1896. *The History and Description of Africa.* vol. 3. London: Haluyt Society.

Auerbach, Felix.   1913.   "Das Gesetz der Bevölkerungskonzentration." *Petermanns Mitteilungen* 54: 74-76.

Bairoch, Paul. 1988. *Cities and Economic Development.* Chicago: University of Chicago Press.

Balandier, Georges. 1968. *Daily Life in the Kingdom of the Kongo: from the Sixteenth to the Eighteenth Century.* London: Allen & Unwin.

Barth, Heinrich. 1857. *Travels and Discoveries in North and Central Africa,* vol. 1. New York: Harper.

Beloch, Julius.   1886.   *Die Bevölkerung der griechisch-Römischen Welt.* Leipzig, Germany: Duncker and Humblot (Reprinted, New York: Arno Press, 1979.)

Breasted, James H. 1906. *Ancient Records of Egypt,* vol. 4. Chicago: University of Chicago Press.

Chandler, Tertius. 1987. *Four Thousand Years of Urban Growth.* Lewiston, NY: St. David's University Press.

Charles-Picard, Gilbert and Colette Charles-Picard.   1961.   *Daily Life in Carthage at the Time of Hannibal.* New York: Macmillan.

Christopher, A.J. 1985. "Continuity and Change of African Capitals." *The Geographical Review* 75: 44-57.

Duncan, Otis Dudley. 1957. "The Measurement of Population Distribution." *Population Studies* 11: 27-45.

Fagan, Brian. 1965. *Southern Africa During the Iron Age.* New York: Praeger.

Garlake, Peter S. 1973. *Great Zimbabwe.* London: Thames and Hudson.

Gugler, Josef and William C. Flanagan. 1978. *Urbanization and Social Change in West Africa.* Cambridge: Cambridge University Press.

International Labour Organization. 1985. *The Informal Sector in Africa: Jobs and Skills Programmes For Africa.* Addis Ababa, Ethiopia.

Jefferson, Mark. 1939. "The law of the primate city." *Geographical Review* 2: 226-232.

Mabogunje, Akin L. 1968. *Urbanization in Nigeria.* New York: Africana Publishing Corporation.

Maquet, Jacques J. 1962. *Afrique les Civilizations Noires.* Paris: Horizons de France.

Mauny, Raymond A. 1961. "au Géographique de l'Ouest Africain au Moyen Age d'Apres les Sources Ecrites, la Tradition et l'Archéologie." In *Mémoires de l'Institut Francais d'Afrique Noire.* No. 61. Dakar, Senegal: Ifan.

Mehta, Surinder K. 1964. "Some demographic and economic correlates of primate cities: A case for reevaluation." *Demography* 1: 136-147.

Muwonge, Joe Wamala. 1980. "Urban Policy and Patterns of Low-Income Settlement in Nairobi, Kenya." *Population and Development Review* 6: 595-613.

Obudho, Robert A. and Constance Mhlanga. 1988. *Slum and Squatter Settlements in Sub-Saharan Africa.* New York: Praeger.

O'Connor, Anthony. 1983. *The African City.* New York: Africana Publishing Company.

Oyekanmi, Felicia Durojaiye. 1985. "Population Pressure and Housing Conditions in Lagos, Nigeria." Paper presented at the International Population Conference, International Union for the Scientific Study of Population, Florence, Italy.

Saibante, Mario. 1928. "La Concentrazione della Popolazione." *Merton* 7: 53-99.

Sjoberg, Gideon. *The Preindustrial City.* 1960. Glencoe, Illinois: Free Press.

Tarver, James D. and H. Max Miller. 1988. "Migration in Botswana." *African Urban Quarterly* 3: 278-284.

Trager, Lillian. 1987. "A re-examination of the Urban Informal Sector in West Africa." *Canadian Journal of African Studies* 21: 238-255.

United Nations. 1980. *Patterns of Urban and Rural Population Growth.* New York.

_____. 1991. *World Urbanization Prospects 1990.* New York.

_____. 1992. *1990 Demographic Yearbook.* New York.

World Bank. 1979. *Urban Growth and Economic Development in the Sahel.* Washington, DC: World Bank.

Wycherley, Richard E. 1949. *How the Greeks Built Cities.* London: Macmillan.

Zipf, George Kingsley. 1941. *National Unity and Disunity.* Bloomington, IN: Principia Press.

8

The Rural Population of Africa

Agriculture made its appearance in the Nile region around 10,000 years ago, and there is evidence of domesticated animals in Kenya and Tanzania in the sixth millennium B.C. (Bairoch, 1988). These early origins of sedentary rural people continue to be reflected in the dominant role played by rural society in Africa since that time.

Even though urbanization began around 3500 B.C., the total population of the world until recent times has been predominantly rural (UN, 1980). For example, 95 percent of the world's inhabitants lived in rural areas even as late as 1800 (table 8.1).

The Industrial Revolution, which began in England in the latter half of the eighteenth century and spread to other developed countries, was accompanied by rapid agricultural mechanization. Millions of rural residents moved to rapidly growing industrial cities in response to expanding employment opportunities. As a result, depopulation in the rural areas began and is continuing in most developed countries today. However, in Africa and other developing regions a technological revolution in the rural areas has not yet occurred. Rather, rural areas have continued to absorb more and more people. For instance, the rural population of Africa has increased steadily since 1950, the first year for which reliable estimates exist for the 56 individual countries (UN, 1991b).

WORLD RURAL POPULATION TRENDS

The relative size of the world's rural population declined very slowly, from 95 percent in 1800 to 87 percent by 1900 (table 8.1). Thereafter, the decline was somewhat more rapid, to about 70 percent in 1950, and 55 percent in 1990, and is projected to drop further to 35 percent by 2025. While the proportionate number of rural residents in the world steadily declined after 1800, their actual numbers continue to increase. By 2025, the rural population is projected to number 3.0 billion, more than three times its size in 1800.

In the developed countries the actual numbers of rural people increased from 1800 to 1925, when they reached an all time high, but have declined since (table 8.1). In fact, there has been a steady decline in the proportionate number of rural residents in the industrialized nations from 95 percent in 1800, to 60 in 1925, to 27 in 1990, and the percentage is likely to drop further to less than 20 by 2025.

Since 1800 the number of rural people in developing countries has consistently increased, more than tripling during that time. However, the proportionate number has declined, falling from 96 percent in 1800 to 63 percent in 1990. By 2025, rural inhabitants are projected to makeup about 40 percent of the total population of developing countries, but they will account for 92 percent of the total rural population worldwide.

Overall, rural residents outnumbered urban residents in the entire world in 1990 as they did before that time. But the preponderance of rural inhabitants in 1990, as in every other year since 1950, was due to their heavy concentration in developing countries (table 8.1). However, the projections indicate that urban residents worldwide will outnumber rural residents by 2000, as the rate of urban population growth will be much higher than rural population growth in both the developed and developing regions. At that time the world will have been transformed from a historically rural world to a predominantly urban world.

RURAL POPULATION GROWTH IN AFRICA

Africa was the most rural region in the world in 1950, with 85 percent of its people residing in rural areas and rural inhabitants outnumbered urban inhabitants in 54 of the 56 countries (table 8.2). In about 30 countries the rural population comprised at least 90 percent of the total population. However, there will be a gradual decline in the proportionate number of rural inhabitants during 1950-2025, dropping from 85 percent of the total population in 1950 to 43 percent in 2025 (Tarver and Miller, 1987). Every country is projected to follow a consistent decline in the relative number of its rural residents.

The number of rural inhabitants in Africa increased from almost 192 million in 1950 to 425 million in 1990, which was the highest relative rural population growth of all major regions in the world (table 8.2). Africa's rural population is projected to increase throughout 1990 to 2025 to approximately 685 million, about 60 percent since 1990. The number of rural inhabitants in Eastern and Western Africa together in 2025 is likely to be nearly four times as numerous as in 1950. In the other three regions the rural population will more than double.

Table 8.1
Rural Populations of Developed and Developing Regions, 1800-2025 (in millions)

Year	World			Developed Regions			Developing Regions		
	Total	Rural	Percentage Rural	Total	Rural	Percentage Rural	Total	Rural	Percentage Rural
1800	978	928	95	273	253	93	705	675	96
1850	1,262	1,182	94	352	312	89	910	870	96
1900	1,650	1,430	87	575	425	74	1,075	1,005	94
1925	1,950	1,550	79	715	430	60	1,235	1,120	91
1950	2,516	1,782	71	832	385	46	1,684	1,397	83
1990	5,292	2,902	55	1,207	330	27	4,086	2,572	63
2000	6,261	3,054	49	1,264	317	25	4,997	2,738	55
2025	8,504	2,974	35	1,354	235	17	7,150	2,739	39

Source: Compiled from United Nations, *Patterns of Urban and Rural Population Growth* (Sales No. E.79.XIII.9) and *World Urbanization Prospects 1990* (Sales No.E.91.XIII.11).

By 2025 rural residents are likely to be more numerous than urban residents in only 15 of the 56 countries. The smaller relative increase in the rural population is due to the higher projected rate of urban than rural population growth, resulting mainly from rural to urban migration. In any event, the number of rural inhabitants will continue to increase. By 2025, there are likely to be nearly four times as many living in rural Africa as in 1950, greatly increasing population pressures along with rising demands for more schools, hospitals, and all other community facilities needed in the villages of rural areas.

Between 1950 and 1990 Nigeria had, by far, the largest rural population growth of all countries in Africa, with an increase of 44 million. Ethiopia, the next highest, had a rural population gain of more than 22 million. Each of the 55 African countries had actual gains in the number of rural inhabitants between 1950 and 1990.

From 1990 to 2025 rural population increases of over 40 million persons are expected in Nigeria and Ethiopia, about 20 million in Kenya and Uganda, and about 12 million in Egypt and Tanzania. Mauritius, Tunisia, Réunion, and Seychelles are the only countries projected to have rural population losses.

SOME ADVERSE FEATURES OF AGRICULTURE IN AFRICA

Efforts to expand and diversify agricultural production were unfavorably affected by the 1979-80 oil price increases and by the world recession of the early 1980s, which reduced the prices of African exports. In addition, drought devastated about half of the countries in 1982 and 1985, resulting in great suffering and hardship. Many countries continue to experience severe difficulties. Calorie consumption declined and inadequate nutrition increased the susceptibility to disease, and indirectly led to higher mortality levels (FAO, 1986).

These and other factors, such as civil strife and low official prices for agricultural products, have been largely responsible for the present agricultural crisis in Africa. For example, agricultural production increased very slowly after 1970, at a rate of 1.3 percent annually in volume, whereas the annual population growth rate was 2.7 to 3.0 percent. While agricultural exports declined sharply, the importation of rice and wheat rose. As a result, Africa's share of world trade dropped for most commodities. In view of this severe situation the Food and Agriculture Organization developed a Regional Food Plan for Africa designed to accelerate agricultural production, particularly among small producers (Ghosh, 1984).

Most African farmers and farm workers are outside the cash economy in the informal sector. Millions are engaged in subsistence agriculture on family-held or communally-held lands, where farming is carried on by traditional methods with little technology and mechanization.

Table 8.2
Rural Population of the Major Regions of the World, 1950-2025 (in millions)

Region	1950		1990		2000		2025	
	Number/Percent		Number/Percent		Number/Percent		Number/Percent	
WORLD	1,782	71	2,902	55	3,054	49	2,974	35
Developed Regions	385	46	330	27	317	25	235	17
Developing Regions	1,397	83	2,572	63	2,738	55	2,739	39
Africa	190	85	425	66	514	59	685	43
Eastern Africa	62	95	154	78	194	71	288	53
Middle Africa	23	86	44	62	52	54	70	36
Northern Africa	39	75	78	55	87	49	92	34
Southern Africa	10	62	18	45	20	39	21	26
Western Africa	57	90	130	67	161	60	213	42
Latin America	97	58	128	28	127	24	120	16
North America	60	36	68	25	67	27	51	15
Asia	1,151	84	2,042	66	2,127	57	1,989	40
Europe	171	43	133	27	119	23	80	16
Oceania	5	39	8	29	9	29	9	23
Former Soviet Republics	109	61	99	34	100	32	78	22

Source: Compiled from United Nations, *World Urbanization Prospects 1990*

(Sales No. E.91.XIII.11).

PROSPECTS FOR THE FUTURE RURAL POPULATION OF AFRICA

East and West Africa are the most highly rural regions on the continent, and are expected to experience the largest numerical and relative rural population increases between 1990 and 2025, with gains of 60 to 80 percent. In fact, about 85 percent of all African rural population gains are projected to occur in these two regions and they are likely to face the most critical rural population pressures. Practically all of the projected rural population increases will, of course, occur in villages rather than on dispersed farms, and those villages near rapidly expanding urban centers are likely to experience major population gains.

Africa's rural population densities are expected to increase to 23 inhabitants per square kilometer in 2025 (table 8.3), with the greatest increases occurring in East Africa, where a few countries are likely to have 200 to 400 rural persons per square kilometer by 2025 (UN, 1982). Rapidly increasing rural population concentrations are quite likely to occur in many countries, intensifying both underemployment and unemployment, and resulting in declining per capita incomes (Gosling, 1979). With the present low level of development, productivity is likely to drop even further, creating economic stagnation. Almost always, rising population densities are accompanied by growing clamors for greater public services and facilities, which will be very difficult to finance.

In the future, rural to urban migration will undoubtedly continue at high levels but is unlikely to have an appreciable effect in reducing mounting population pressures in the African villages. The majority of the rural youths will probably continue to enter family agriculture on ethnic lands in the informal sector as in the past.

Some rural residents are reluctant to move to cities because of the relatively high unemployment in cities, the slums, the crime, and the widespread unserviced shantytown areas, which all serve as deterrents to many potential migrants from rural areas. In certain rural areas it is thought that strong extended family and kinship ties in the villages with an ethnic system of social organization reduces out-migration. However, in the Senegal River Valley such ethnic social organization has not slowed migration (Lacombe, 1969, et al., 1977). In any event, the patterns of rural-urban migration are not likely to change until major advancements in agricultural development occur or conditions in major cities improve. Certainly, it seems impossible to absorb the projected 260 million additional persons into Africa's present rural population by 2025 without greatly intensifying rural labor in many East and West African countries.

The major changes in store for Africa's economy by 2025 will undoubtedly follow rather closely the modernization experiences of the presently developed countries of the world (Schutjer, 1978). Historically, as development progressed in the industrialized countries the relative number of agricultural workers declined with advancing technology, while employment in secondary and tertiary industries such as manufacturing, construction, finance, transportation, and services increased. This development embodied not only a shift in the industrial structure of the labor force but also increased productivity and rising per capita incomes.

In Africa similar development is retarded not only by the huge informal subsistence sector but also by the relative scarcity of secondary and tertiary industries. For example, developed countries usually have a third or more of their workers engaged in manufacturing and industry. Many African countries, such as Rwanda and Niger, have fewer than five percent of their workers employed in industry (manufacturing, construction, mining and quarrying, and public utilities). For instance, the relative number of African workers in industry was estimated to be seven percent in 1950 and 12 percent in 1980. However, Tunisia, Egypt, Libya, Congo, and Algeria each had 25 percent or more of their 1981 workers employed in this activity. South Africa, with 29 percent of its workers in industry, has been classified as a developed country by the United Nations, and is the most advanced industrially.

RURAL AND URBAN CHANGE SINCE COLONIAL DAYS

Slave trade was the principal activity of Europeans in Africa until the early 1800s, when it was replaced by trade in gold, ivory, hides, gum, and beeswax. The production of maize, tobacco, peanuts, rubber, cocoa, and palm products expanded, and a number of chartered European trading companies began to conduct import and export business with the Africans along the coast and navigable rivers. By 1900 colonial governments had built over 100,000 kilometers of railroads to transport crops and other commodities from the interior. Both population and national output grew slowly at approximately the same rate (Reynolds, 1985). Very little urbanization actually occurred even though the Europeans had established some colonial cities.

In contrast to the European industrial revolution economic growth in Africa was due mainly to agricultural cash crop production, not to manufacturing (Duignan and Gann, 1975). However, two economic depressions and two world wars in the twentieth century curtailed agricultural output somewhat. Nevertheless, there was a rapid expansion in agricultural exports between 1938 and 1955-58, when the value of agricultural exports from the major African countries and territories increased from 44 million U.S. dollars to 161 million dollars (Neumark, 1964).

The rate of population growth began to accelerate after World War II and rapid population gains in the segregated colonial cities soon followed. The comparatively higher wage rates in cities attracted thousands of rural males even though most of this urbanization occurred without major economic development or industrialization.

Table 8.3
Rural Population Densities in Africa, by Regions and Countries, 1950-2025

Region and Country	Surface Area in Kilometers 1982	Number of Rural Residents perSquare Kilometer of Area			
		1950	1980	2000	2025
AFRICA	30,230,956	6	11	17	23
Eastern Africa	6,356,813	10	19	31	45
Burundi	27,834	87	142	245	384
Comoros	2,171	77	139	240	364
Djibouti	22,000	2	4	4	5
Ethiopia	1,221,900	15	28	45	69
Kenya	582,646	10	24	41	66
Madagascar	587,041	7	12	20	29
Malawi	118,484	23	47	89	143
Mauritius	2,045	172	272	343	293
Mozambique	801,590	8	13	15	17
Réunion	2,510	78	91	83	69
Rwanda	26,338	79	186	343	532
Seychelles	280	89	129	82	61
Somalia	637,657	3	6	8	11
Tanzania	945,087	8	17	22	32
Uganda	236,036	20	51	98	159
Zambia	752,614	3	5	7	9
Zimbabwe	390,580	6	14	22	27
Middle Africa	6,613,217	3	5	8	11
Angola	1,246,700	3	5	7	9
Cameroon	475,442	8	12	17	25
Central African Republic	622,984	2	2	3	4

112

Table 8.3 (Continued)

Region and Country	Surface Area in Kilometers 1982	Number of Rural Residents per Square Kilometer of Area			
		1950	1980	2000	2025
Chad	1,284,000	2	3	3	4
Congo	342,000	2	3	5	7
Equatorial Guinea	28,051	7	6	11	14
Gabon	267,667	2	2	3	3
São Tomé & Príncipe	964	56	66	78	80
Zaire	2,345,409	4	7	11	15
Northern Africa	8,524,703	5	8	10	11
Algeria	2,381,741	3	4	6	6
Egypt	1,001,449	14	23	29	27
Libya	1,759,540	1	1	1	1
Morocco	446,550	15	26	32	30
Sudan	2,505,813	3	6	10	13
Tunisia	163,610	15	19	25	23
Western Sahara	266,000	-	-	1	1
Southern Africa	2,693,415	4	6	7	8
Botswana	600,372	1	1	2	2
Lesotho	30,355	22	38	56	76
Namibia	824,292	1	1	1	1
South Africa	1,221,037	6	11	12	12
Swaziland	17,363	15	26	36	48
Western Africa	6,042,808	9	17	27	35
Benin	112,622	17	21	31	42
Burkina Faso	274,200	13	24	39	63
Cape Verde	4,033	33	55	82	103

113

Table 8.3 (Continued)

Region and Country	Surface Area in Kilometers 1982	Number of Rural Residents per Square Kilometer of Area			
		1950	1980	2000	2025
Côte d'Ivoire	322,463	7	17	29	44
Gambia	11,295	23	46	70	83
Ghana	238,537	18	31	54	65
Guinea	245,857	10	15	21	29
Guinea-Bissau	36,125	13	18	25	29
Liberia	111,369	6	11	14	18
Mali	1,240,000	3	5	8	12
Mauritania	1,030,700	1	1	1	1
Niger	1,267,000	2	4	6	9
Nigeria	923,768	32	62	100	117
St. Helena	122	33	33	66	98
Senegal	196,192	9	18	27	32
Sierra Leone	71,740	25	34	45	57
Togo	56,785	22	37	57	64

Source: Computed from United Nations, *Demographic Yearbook, 1982* (Sales No. E/F.83.XIII.1)

and *World Urbanization Prospects 1990* (Sales No. E.91.XIII.11).

Those Africans who obtained accommodations provided them in the cities were indeed fortunate. The overflow population was forced into shantytowns, which grew very rapidly. In marked contrast, urban population growth in developed countries occurred in response to industrialization and economic development (Bairoch, 1988).

SUMMARY AND IMPLICATIONS

A gradual transformation from a rural to an urban society in Africa is likely to occur between now and 2025. By 2025 Africa will have become a predominantly urban continent, with the urban population increasing from a mere 15 percent in 1950 to an expected 58 percent in 2025. Correspondingly, there will be a decline in the rural population, in the number of agricultural workers, and the number of informal sector workers (UN, 1988). Obviously, these projected changes imply greater modernization and development, and increases in mechanization and technology requiring relatively less rural manpower in agricultural production.

REFERENCES

Bairoch, Paul. 1988. *Cities and Economic Development*. Chicago: University of Chicago Press.

Duignan, Peter and L.H. Gann, eds. 1969-75. *Colonialism in Africa, 1870-1960*. 5 vols. Cambridge: Cambridge University Press.

Food and Agriculture Organization. 1986. *The State of Food and Agriculture, 1985*. Rome.

Ghosh, Pradip K. ed. 1984. *Developing Africa: A Modernization Perspective*. Westport, CT: Greenwood Press.

Gosling, L.A. Peter. 1979. "Population Redistribution: Patterns, Policies and Prospects." In *World Population and Development: Challenges and Prospects*, edited by Philip M. Hauser, 403-439. Syracuse, NY: Syracuse University Press.

Lacombe, Bernard. 1969. "Mobilité et Migration: Quelques Résultats de L'enquête du Sine-Saloum, Sénégal." *Cahiers Orstom serie sciences humaines* 6: 11-42.

Lacombe, Bernard, et al. 1977. *Exode Rural Et Urbanization Au Sénégal*. Paris: Orstom.

Neumark, S. Daniel. 1964. *Foreign Trade and Economic Development in Africa: A Historical Perspective*. Stanford, CA: Food Research Institute.

Reynolds, Lloyd G. 1985. *Economic Growth in the Third World, 1850-1980*. New Haven, CT: Yale University Press.

Schutjer, Wayne A. 1978. "Agricultural Development Policy and the Demographic Transition." *The Journal of Developing Areas* 12: 269-280.

Tarver, James D. and H. Max Miller. 1987. "The Rural Population of Africa."
   Rural Africana Issue no. 27: 47-60.
United Nations. 1980. *Patterns of Urban and Rural Population Growth.* New York.
_____. 1983. *Demographic Yearbook 1982.* New York.
_____. 1988. *World Demographic Estimates and Projections, 1950-2025.*
   New York.
_____. 1991a. *World Population Prospects 1990.* New York.
_____. 1991b. *World Urbanization Prospects 1990.* New York.

9

Internal Migration in Africa

Population censuses publish the basic concepts and definitions of internal migration as well as internal migration figures based upon questions about place of previous residence and place of birth. This chapter discusses the role of internal migration in the rapid urbanization of Africa. Also, it makes net migration estimates of African countries by residual methods for illustrative purposes when census counts of actual migrants are unavailable.

CONCEPTS AND DEFINITIONS OF MIGRATION

The concept of "migrant" has often been surrounded with a great deal of ambiguity. People in many different situations may or may not be migrants, depending upon the accepted definition. For example, it is customary to classify persons who move within a political or administrative unit or jurisdiction as *local movers*, but not as migrants. According to this definition, a *migrant* must actually move across definite area boundaries within that country, even if he only moves across a street or a road. However, a local mover may go a hundred miles or more within the same large local district and still not be classified as a migrant.

Some types of mobile persons who frequently present classification difficulties are seasonal or temporary migrants, contract migrants or guest workers, forced migrants, commuters, and internal refugees. How long must a person be absent from home before he qualifies as a migrant? How far must he travel from home? Also, are migrants to be classified on a *de jure* or a *de facto* residence basis? Many Africans have been allocated to the ethnic group of their allegiance for residence purposes rather than to their place of usual residence. Thus, many previously used definitions of migrants have been somewhat arbitrary.

Obviously, geographic mobility involves changes in the residences of people and may or may not involve social mobility. Regardless, political and administrative units of countries provide a basis for classifying residential movers. A person whose move is within a census district is identified as a local mover, whereas one who moves from one district to another within that country is classified as an internal migrant, not a local mover.

The practice is to count as movers only those persons whose residences are different at the beginning and end of the period. Movers who died during the period are excluded as well as those who moved and then returned to their previous residence.

A number of factors, of course, affect the rates of internal movement, including the numbers, sizes, and shapes of the political units in each country. For example, countries with relatively few districts, reasonably square in shape, tend to have comparatively small numbers of internal migrants, other things being equal. In contrast, countries with numerous districts, narrow and elongated in shape, usually have relatively large numbers of internal migrants.

The number of internal migrants for a geographic area always refers to movement during a specified period of time. For example, population censuses and surveys sometime ask a question for a person's residence one year ago, five years ago, or perhaps even the place of birth of individuals. In any event, as the duration of residence lengthens both the number of migrants and the rate of migration increases.

Most internal migration data for African countries come from population censuses and surveys, being based upon questions either about place of previous residence or place of birth. In addition, net migration estimates of provinces, districts, and other local governmental units of African countries are frequently made by indirect, residual methods in the absence of actual enumerations, as will be discussed later.

INTERNAL MIGRATION CLASSIFIED BY FORMER COLONIAL AREAS

The internal migration patterns will be examined for selected former British, French, and Portuguese colonies, as well as the former Belgian and Spanish colonies. Internal migration will be measured both by previous residence and lifetime migration based upon place of birth.

British Africa: Internal Migration Based Upon Previous Residence Questions

Anglophone countries such as Kenya, Zambia, Malawi, and Botswana asked for the place of residence one year ago in their population censuses. Based upon the 1979 population census, the rate of internal migration among inhabitants of the eight Kenyan provinces between 1978 and 1979 was 4.0 percent (Kenya,

1981, 1985). For Nairobi, the capital city, the rate was nearly 12 percent. Three of the eight provinces had substantial net migration gains and the other five had losses.

According to the 1977 census nearly 280,000 persons in Malawi moved from one census district to another between 1976 and 1977 (Malawi, 1980). This represents an annual internal migration rate of slightly more than five percent, with the rates of the 24 districts ranging from three to 10 percent. As a result of the various population movements the Central Region gained through migration while the Northern and Southern Regions lost.

Internal migration rates for the nine large provinces and 57 census districts in Zambia declined slightly, with the overall average rate dropping from six percent in 1968-69 to five percent in 1979-80 (*1980 Pop.*, Zambia, 1985). In the census year of 1969 Zambia was experiencing a post-independence boom and internal population movements were relatively high. However, the Copperbelt Province, particularly, suffered an economic recession in the 1970s, reducing the net migration gains about half by 1979-80 in that province. Now, Zambia's major area of in-migration is Lusaka, the national capital.

Information on internal movement in Botswana was for the year preceding the August, 1981 census for persons one year of age and over on that date (*Census*, Botswana, 1983). Urban residents were much more likely to be internal migrants between census districts than rural residents, as about 18 percent of the urban but only about six percent of the rural inhabitants moved from one district to another (Tarver, 1984). For Botswana as a whole about eight percent of the individuals one year of age and over in 1981 were internal migrants (table 9.1). Urban migrants were mainly long-distance migrants, as over 85 percent moved to noncontiguous census districts. Due to drought and related conditions rural to urban migration apparently was greatly accelerated urbanization (Tarver and Miller, 1987).

In each of the above four countries place of residence questions for one-year periods were used to measure internal migration. Botswana had the highest annual rate of internal migration at eight percent, Zambia was second with six percent in 1968-69 (which dropped to five percent in 1979-80), Malawi was next with five percent, and Kenya was last with four percent. These rates are for one-year periods but are not precisely comparable due to the varying sizes and shapes of the political subdivisions, as these factors affect the number of internal migrants. Moreover, internal migration varies greatly with changing social and economic conditions within a country and may differ significantly from one period to another, such as in Zambia.

Lifetime Migration Estimates

Lifetime migrants usually have different patterns of movement and different characteristics than recent migrants. For example, the distance of movement of lifetime migrants tends to be much greater than for recent migrants. As compared to nonmigrants, migrants are highly selective. Migrants have relatively few children, proportionately large numbers are in the working ages, disproportionately large numbers are males, and they have comparatively high educational levels.

Zimbabwe, Somalia, Gambia, Lesotho, and Liberia used place of birth questions in their population censuses to determine lifetime migration. Kenya and Zambia employed both place of previous residence as well as place of birth questions to measure internal migration.

According to the 1982 population census of Zimbabwe, 24 percent were not living in the province in which they were born (*Main*, Zimbabwe, 1985). In many respects the patterns of lifetime movement in Zimbabwe follow the predominant rural-urban population shifts of other African countries. For example, Harare, the national capital, has depended upon migration from outlying areas for most of its population growth. In 1982, only a third of all Harare residents had been born in the city. In Bulawayo, the second largest city in Zimbabwe, native-born residents made up only 35 percent of the total population. Therefore, the overwhelming proportion of the population gains in these two major cities came from migrants born elsewhere.

Place of birth information was obtained for residents of each of the 15 regions and 78 districts in Somalia's 1975 census (*Census*, Somalia, 1984). An average of 82 percent of all individuals were born in the region of their residence. Yet, the capital city of Mogadishu grew largely from migration, as 47 percent of its inhabitants were born outside the region.

Lifetime migration in Lesotho has been relatively small in magnitude. It is still quite rural and is a very small, compact country with only nine census districts. Slightly over a tenth of all native-born persons enumerated in the 1976 census of Lesotho lived in different districts than the one in which they were born (*1976*, Lesotho, 1981). Lifetime migration was more frequent among females than males, with 12 percent of the females and nine percent of the males living in districts other than the one of their birth. Maseru, the district containing the capital city, attracted the largest relative number of lifetime migrants, with 16 percent of the females and 12 percent of the males being born in other districts.

According to the 1973 census of Gambia, approximately 70 percent of all individuals lived in the local government area of their birth (*Pop. 73*, Gambia, 1976). Also, in 1974 about 73 percent of the inhabitants of Liberia lived in the county of their birth (*1974*, Liberia, 1977). However, only 40 percent of the residents of Montserrado, the county containing the capital city of Monrovia, were native born.

In the 1979 census of Kenya nearly two million persons, or about one out of every eight, were born in provinces outside the one of their birth (Kenya, 1981, 1985). Fully three-fourths of the 1979 residents of Nairobi were born elsewhere. Furthermore, Nairobi and the Rift Valley attracted about half a million lifetime migrants each.

Lifetime migration in the Zambia provinces increased slightly between 1969 and 1980 (1980 Pop., Zambia, 1985). In 1969, for instance, 20 percent of the residents lived outside the province of their birth and by 1980 about 22 percent lived in other provinces. Less than half of the residents of Lusaka had been born in the city itself.

The 1981 demographic survey of rural Ethiopia showed that women were more mobile than men. Eighty-six percent of the males but only 72 percent of the females had lived continuously in the same region in which they were born (Report, Ethiopia, 1985). Many women moved to the region of residence of their husbands after marriage. Clearly, African women migrate for educational, employment, marriage, and other opportunities (Thadani and Todaro, 1979). Women move because of their dissatisfaction with marriage prospects in their own rural villages, because of broken marriages, to marry upwardly mobile men, and for various other economic, personal, and social reasons (Little, 1972, 1973). In Cameroon where exogamy is practiced, wives usually move to the villages of their husband's clan (Podlewski, 1975).

French Africa

In the Maghreb countries of northwestern Africa around 1.75 million French nationals left during the years these three African countries were obtaining their independence. The French citizens were concentrated in the large coastal cities, so after their departure, the North Africans in the outlying rural areas and towns moved into the large cities which the French vacated. Population movements in the provinces of Morocco, the *Wilayas* of Algeria, and the *gouvernates* of Egypt and Tunisia, as well as the *Muqataas* of Libya, reflect major rural to urban population shifts and increasing urbanization (Cairo, 1973).

The population policies of the French government had a profound effect upon Francophone Africa. In the colonial days of 1954 to 1962, for example, the French's *regroupement* policy resulted in the forced movement of about 3.5 million residents of remote villages off their lands into urban areas (Cairo, 1973).

In the French-speaking countries of West Africa, practically all of the population gains from internal migration occurred in the capital cities and their suburbs, and the dominant direction of movement was to the coastal areas (Amin, 1974; Zachariah and Condé, 1981). The cityward movement in Burkina Faso and Togo was comparatively less than in the other Francophone countries of West Africa (Coulibaly, et al., 1980). The internal migration patterns of the Francophone countries of West Africa and the Maghreb countries of northwest Africa are similar to those in the other areas of Africa. Dakar and Abidjan have become primate cities in West Africa, exercising somewhat the same type of dominant influence that Algiers, Casablanca, and Tunis do in the Maghreb.

Table 9.1
Internal Migration Between Census Districts, Botswana, 1980-81

Census District by Residence	Population 1981	Internal Migrants Number	Internal Migrants Percent	Local Movers Number	Local Movers Percent	Total Movers Number	Total Movers Percent
		Urban Census Districts					
Gaborone	59,657	10,226	17.1	247	0.4	10,473	17.6
Francistown	31,065	5,736	18.5	94	0.3	5,830	18.8
Lobatse	19,034	4,107	21.6	67	0.4	4,174	21.9
Selebe-Phikwe	29,469	5,713	19.4	78	0.3	5,791	20.0
Orapa	5,229	915	17.5	2	0.0	917	17.5
Jwaneng	5,567	867	15.6	6	0.1	873	15.7
Total Urban	150,021	27,564	18.4	494	0.3	28,058	18.7
		Rural Census Districts					
Ngwaketse	104,182	6,295	6.0	10,589	10.2	16,884	16.2
Barolong	15,471	1,101	7.1	322	2.1	1,423	9.2
South East	30,649	2,060	6.7	832	2.7	2,892	9.4
Kweneng	117,127	4,373	3.7	12,699	10.8	17,072	14.6
Kgatleng	44,461	3,389	7.6	3,931	8.8	7,320	16.5
Central Serowe	92,227	8,397	9.1	8,817	9.6	17,214	18.7
Central Mahalapye & Tuli	82,982	5,132	6.2	8,977	10.8	14,109	17.0
Central Bobonong	46,436	4,058	8.7	4,724	10.2	8,782	18.9
Central Boteti	26,406	2,155	8.2	3,536	13.4	5,691	21.6
Central Tutume	75,227	6,842	9.1	3,546	4.7	10,388	13.8
North East	36,636	3,123	8.5	1,215	3.3	4,338	11.8
Ngamiland	68,063	2,128	3.1	10,534	15.5	12,662	18.6
Chobe	7,934	482	6.1	1,083	13.7	1,565	19.7
Ghanzi	19,096	721	3.8	3,794	19.9	4,515	23.6
Kgalagadi	24,059	1,154	4.8	2,255	9.4	3,409	14.2
Total Rural	791,006	51,410	6.5	76,854	9.7	128,264	16.2
Botswana Total	941,027	78,974	8.4	77,348	8.2	156,322	16.6

Source: Compiled from the Central Statistics Office, *Census Administrative/Technical Report and National Statistical Tables, 1981 Population and Housing Census*, Gaborone.

Portuguese Africa

The civil war that continued in Angola after the 1975 withdrawal of the Portuguese resulted in large-scale internal relocations of the population. There was a movement from cities to the rural areas as strife, famine, and disease were responsible for thousands of deaths. By early 1981, around half a million internal refugees had been relocated in settlements once occupied by the Portuguese. Mozambique and Guinea-Bissau faced similar internal relocations after the withdrawal of the Portuguese. In recent years the population of Mozambique has been quite mobile due to the civil war, drought, and violence.

The major internal population movements in the Lusophone countries are reflected by recent changes in the urban populations. The five former Portuguese colonies experienced major rural to urban population shifts and relatively large urban population increases that have added more than 6.8 million inhabitants to the urban areas since 1950.

Mozambique, for example, had only 147,000 urban inhabitants in 1950 but nearly 4.2 million in 1990. Angola had about 300,000 living in the urban centers in 1950 but more than 2.8 million in 1990. Another indication of the large rural-urban internal migration is the rapid increase in the population of the two dominant Lusophone urban agglomerations, each with a population of more than one million inhabitants. Luanda, Angola went from nearly 140,000 inhabitants in 1950 to over 1.7 million in 1990. During the same period, the population of Maputo grew from less than 100,000 to over 1.5 million, despite the instability in Mozambique.

Belgian Africa

Both Burundi and Zaire are former Belgian colonies. They are French-speaking and have experienced considerable unrest and guerrilla activities after independence, resulting in major dislocations of the African populations. Thus, there have been large internal population movements during these conflicts. Large increases in the urban populations reflect very large rural to urban migration. For example, the urban population of both countries numbered about 2.5 million in 1950. However, there were 14.3 million urban inhabitants by 1990, an increase of 12 million. Bujumbura's population advanced from 50,000 in 1950 to 246,000 in 1990, whereas Kinshasa's population went from 170,000 to 3.5 million in 1990. Now, the Kinshasa agglomeration is the fourth largest in Africa, slightly larger than Casablanca.

Spanish Africa

The two former Spanish colonies of Equatorial Guinea and Western Sahara experienced great unrest and instability since their independence. Most of

Equatorial Guinea's unrest resulted from the resistance to a corrupt government and Western Sahara has been plagued by conflicts over its sovereignty as an independent nation. Consequently, major internal dislocations and population movements have occurred.

Although both former Spanish colonies have fairly small populations they are nevertheless highly urbanized in terms of African standards, with 50 to 60 percent of the inhabitants residing in urban areas. The urban population of Equatorial Guinea grew from 36,000 in 1950 to 101,000 in 1990, whereas the urban population of Western Sahara went from 9,000 to 101,000 during the same period. Overall, there was a gain of about 157,000 urban inhabitants in both countries, which obviously reflects major rural to urban population shifts in these sparsely populated countries.

INTERNAL MIGRATION AND URBANIZATION

Internal migration has exerted a profound influence upon urbanization in Africa, greatly increasing the number of city residents. In fact, more than 185 million inhabitants have been added to African cities since 1950 (UN, 1991). Probably 60-70 percent of this rapid urban population growth has been the result of internal migration from outlying areas, mainly rural to urban migration within each country. The lifetime migration estimates to six African cities clearly document the great impact of migration upon urbanization. These large African cities reflect this modern urbanization process rather clearly as they dramatize the importance of migration in making rapid urban population growth possible. For example, in the 1979 census of Kenya nearly 830,000 inhabitants were enumerated in Nairobi, with only 26 percent having been born in the city. The other 600,000 residents, or 74 percent, had been born outside the city and then moved there later in their lives, turning Nairobi into a bustling, primate city. Approximately half of the 300,000 lifetime migrants to the Lusaka province in 1980 originated in outlying rural areas and in 1980-81 over 80 percent of the migrants to Botswana's urban centers were from rural areas. In the six major African cities, migration accounted for an average of 64 percent of the total city populations. In other words, two out of every three inhabitants were migrants attracted chiefly by employment opportunities and social services.

NET MIGRATION ESTIMATES BY RESIDUAL METHODS

Migration figures based on place of previous residence and place of birth are unavailable for some countries. It is possible, however, to estimate net migration by indirect methods without such data. Several different techniques are available for this purpose. Three different residual methods will be used here to illustrate intercensal net migration estimates for African countries: the vital statistics method, the life table survival rate method, and the census survival rate method.

Vital Statistics Method

This method requires the complete registration of births and deaths during an intercensal period.   This situation is rare in Africa, for few countries have sufficiently accurate civil registration statistics to use this method.   This computational procedure will be used here to estimate the net migration of the total population of the largest political subdivision in the Republic of Mauritius, the Island of Mauritius, which is assumed to have complete registration.

This method is usually used to estimate the net migration of the total population of an area during an intercensal period.   However, it may also be employed to estimate net migration by age, sex, nativity, and any other characteristic, provided that the appropriate population figures and vital statistics are published for the particular groups during the intercensal period (Hamilton, 1967). Seldom will it be possible to use this method in Africa because deaths, by age, sex, and other characteristics, are rarely tabulated for local administrative units.

The most recent population census of Mauritius was taken in 1983 and the previous census was taken in 1972.   The enumerated population of the Island of Mauritius was 826,199 in 1972 and 968,609 in 1983.   Birth and death statistics were considered to be fully registered.   A total of 247,812 births and 72,408 deaths were compiled for the intercensal period (Mauritius, 1984). Then, the following vital statistics method formula was used to estimate net intercensal migration:

$$M = P_1 - P_0 - B + D$$

where M is the estimated number of net migrants, P_1 is the 1983 population, Po the 1972 population, B is the number of births during 1972-83, and D is the number of deaths during the same period. The vital statistics method shows a total net out-migration of almost 33,000 persons during this 11-year period, an average of approximately 3,000 persons per year.

Life Table Survival Rate Method

In developing countries where complete vital statistics data are unavailable, survival rate methods are commonly used in estimating intercensal net migration. These techniques do not require accurate civil registration statistics. Moreover, they provide net migration estimates by age and sex. Two types of survival rates are used: one set is derived from life tables and the other is computed from censuses. For illustrative purposes, life table survival rates will be applied to males in Banjul, Gambia and census survival rates will be applied to males in the city of Nairobi to demonstrate the computational procedures of each method.

Data from the 1973 and 1983 Gambia population censuses were used to illustrate the computational procedures for estimating intercensal net migration of males, by age groups. Ten-year survival rates were taken from Model General Pattern UN life tables, with 35 years life expectancy at birth (UN, 1982). These life tables seem to be the most appropriate set available for Gambia in this period, for they reflect the high mortality rates at that time.

Forward life table survival rates are used here to estimate the net migration of the male population in the Banjul Local Government Area of Gambia between 1973 and 1983. Then, the estimated number of net migrants (table 9.2, column 7) were obtained by subtracting the 1983 population (column 6) from the expected 1983 population (column 5), and the net migration rates (column 8) were obtained by dividing the intercensal net migrants (column 7) by the corresponding 1973 population (column 3).

This computational method provides net migration estimates separately by five-year age groups for the male population of all ages in the first census and 10 years of age and over in the second population census, with children born during the period being excluded. There was an overall net migration of only about 250 males, with losses in ages 30 to 65 (column 7). During 1973-83 there was a net migration loss of 225 females aged 10 years and over in 1983 (the calculations for females are not shown here but were carried out as shown in table 9.2). Thus, there was a very small net migration gain for the capital city of Gambia during 1973 to 1983 (*Pop.*, Gambia 1976, 1986). Banjul was a small city of approximately 40,000 inhabitants and had a total population gain of only 5,000 residents in the 10 years, most of which was a result of an excess of births over deaths. Moreover, Gambia's inhabitants appear to be comparatively immobile, for in 1983 approximately 80 percent of all individuals lived in one of the eight major local government areas in which they had been born.

Census Survival Rate Method

Of all residual methods, the census survival rate method is usually preferred in estimating intercensal net migration. These rates are derived from national population censuses, using native populations, if possible, to obtain closed populations unaffected by emigration and immigration. After computing national census survival rates, they are then applied to the population of local administrative areas to estimate intercensal net migration. Census survival rates not only allow for mortality but also correct for the relative coverage and reporting errors in the two successive population censuses. Since the census survival rates have a built-in technique which corrects for net census undercounts by age, including underenumeration and misstatements of age, they have certain technical advantages over life table survival rates.

Table 9.2
Net Migration Estimates of the Male Population of the Local Government Area of Banjul,
The Gambia, By Life Table Survival Rates, 1973-83

Age 1973	1983	Population 1973	Life Table Survival Rates	Expected Population in 1983	Population in 1983	Net Migration 1973-83	Rate of Net Migration
0-4	10-14	2,977	.8596	2,559	2,107	-452	-15
5-9	15-19	2,445	.9347	2,285	2,417	132	5
10-14	20-24	1,838	.9263	1,703	2,983	1,280	70
15-19	25-29	1,933	.9035	1,746	2,710	964	50
20-24	30-34	2,490	.8868	2,208	1,675	-533	-21
25-29	35-39	2,272	.8694	1,975	1,340	-635	-28
30-34	40-44	1,567	.8464	1,326	961	-365	-23
35-39	45-49	1,108	.8175	906	805	-101	-9
40-44	50-54	889	.7799	693	607	-86	-10
45-49	55-59	730	.7314	534	461	-73	-10

Table 9.2 (Continued)

Age 1973	1983	Population 1973	Life Table Survival Rates	Expected Population in 1983	Population in 1983	Net Migration 1973-83	Rate of Net Migration
50-54	60-64	602	.6667	401	379	- 22	- 4
55+	65+	1,457	.4152	605	747	142	10
Total		20,308		16,941	17,192	251	1

1. Ten-year life table survival rates for males were taken from the "General Pattern" UN model life tables with 35-year life expectancy at birth.

Source: Compiled from United Nations, *Model Life Tables for Developing Countries* (Sales No. E.81.XIII.7); *Population Census 1973, Statistics for Local Government Areas and Districts*, Volume 3, Banjul, 1976; and Republic of the Gambia, *Population and Housing Census, 1983*, Banjul, 1986.

Table 9.3
Net Migration Estimates of the Male Population of Nairobi, Kenya, by Census Survival Rates, 1969-79

Age 1969	1979	Population 1969	Forward Census Survival Rates	Expected Population in 1979	Population in 1979	Net Migration 1969-79	Rate of Net Migration
0-4	10-14	39,107	.9932	38,841	31,170	-7,671	-20
5-9	15-19	29,166	.9318	27,177	40,108	12,931	48
10-14	20-24	19,694	.8974	17,673	80,084	62,411	353
15-19	25-29	24,748	.9184	22,729	69,136	46,407	204
20-24	30-34	44,247	.9471	41,906	50,788	8,882	21
25-29	35-39	38,155	.8302	31,676	31,109	- 567	- 2
30-39	40-49	56,787	.9012	51,176	43,258	-7,918	-15
40-49	50-59	30,758	.8833	27,169	18,989	-8,180	-30
50-59	60-69	13,309	.8401	11,181	6,119	-5,062	-45
60+	70+	7,248	.5503	3,989	3,673	- 316	- 8
		303,219		273,517	374,434	100,917	37

Total, All Ages, 1969

Totals, 10 Years of Age and Over in 1979

Source: Computed from the *Kenya Population Census*, Vols. 1 and 2, 1981 and 1985, respectively.

129

The census survival rate method is used here to estimate the net intercensal migration of the male population of Nairobi between the 1969 and 1979 censuses. The 1969-79 census survival rates shown in table 9.3, column 4, were derived from the 1969 and 1979 Kenya male populations, by age. These 10-year survival rates are appropriate for use in computing the 1969-79 net migration of males in every subdivision of Kenya. There was a net migration of approximately 100,000 males into Nairobi during 1969-79 (table 9.3). Gains occurred in the ages of 15 to 35 in 1979 and net losses in the other ages. The net migration gains for females were approximately half that of males and in the same age groups (the computations for females are not shown here). Thus, for Nairobi there was a total net migration of 150,000 inhabitants 10 years of age and over in 1979. Nairobi's population increased by more than 300,000 inhabitants in this decade. Therefore, migration accounted for approximately half of the increase and a natural increase in the population accounted for the rest.

SUMMARY AND IMPLICATIONS

Internal migration is a very important factor in population change and redistribution in Africa. In fact, between two-thirds and three-fourths of the residents of many large African cities are internal migrants born elsewhere. The evidence suggests that at least half are rural-urban migrants. The prospects are for the continued acceleration of urbanization and rural-urban migration in Africa. Rural areas with rapidly growing populations have large reservoirs of potential migrants.

Most African countries have secured internal migration figures from their population censuses by asking questions about place of prior residence and place of birth. When internal migration data are unavailable from these published sources one may make net migration estimates by one of the three residual methods presented in this chapter.

REFERENCES

Amin, Samir, ed. 1974. *Modern Migrations in Western Africa*. London: Oxford University Press.

Cairo Demographic Centre. 1973. *Urbanization and Migration in Some Arab and African Countries*. Research Monograph Series no. 4. Cairo: CDC Centre.

Census Administrative/Technical Report and National Statistical Tables, 1981 Population and Housing Census. 1983. Gaborone, Botswana: Ministry of Finance and Development Planning, Central Statistics Office.

Census of Population. 1984. Analytical Volume, 1975. Mogadishu, Somalia: Ministry of National Planning, Central Statistical Department.

Coulibaly, Sidiki P., Joel Gregory, and Victor Piche. 1980. *Les Migrations Voltaïques*. 2 vols. Ouagadougou, Haute-Volta: Institut National de la Statistique et de la Démographie.

Hamilton, C. Horace. 1967. "The Vital Statistics Method of Estimating Net Migration by Age Cohorts." *Demography* 4: 464-478.

Kenya Population Census. 1981. vol. 1, 1979. Nairobi, Kenya: Ministry of Economic Planning and Development, Central Bureau of Statistics.

Kenya Population Census. 1985. Analytical Report, vol. 2, 1979. Nairobi, Kenya: Ministry of Finance and Planning, Central Bureau of Statistics.

Little, Kenneth. 1972. "Voluntary Associations and Social Mobility Among West African Women." *Canadian Journal of African Studies* 6: 275-288.

_____. 1973. *African Women in Towns*. London: Cambridge University Press.

Main Demographic Features of the Population of Zimbabwe, 1982 Population Census. 1985. Harare, Zimbabwe: Central Statistical Office.

Malawi Population Census 1977. 1980. Final Report, vol. 1. Zomba, Malawi: National Statistical Office.

Mauritius Annual Digest of Statistics. 1984. Rose Hill, Mauritius: Central Statistical Office.

Podlewski, André. 1975. "Cameroon." In *Population Growth and Socioeconomic Change in West Africa*, edited by John C. Caldwell, 543-564. New York: Columbia University Press.

Population and Housing Census, 1983. 1986. Provisional Report. Banjul, Gambia: Central Statistics Office, Republic of The Gambia.

Population Census 1973. 1976. Statistics for Local Government Areas and Districts, General Report, vol. 3. Banjul, Gambia: Central Statistics Office, Republic of The Gambia.

Report on the Results of the 1981 Demographic Survey. 1985. Statistical Bulletin 46, Addis Ababa, Ethiopia.

Tarver, James D. 1984. "Migration of the Population of Botswana." *Pula* 4: 80-94.

Tarver, James D. and H. Max Miller. 1987. "Rural-urban migration in a developing country: Botswana, Africa." *Africa Quarterly* 24: 22-33.

Thadani, Veena N. and Michael P. Todaro. 1979. *Female Migration in Developing Countries: A Framework for Analysis*. New York: The Population Council.

United Nations. 1982. *Model Life Tables for Developing Countries*. New York.

_____. 1991. *World Urbanization Prospects 1990*. New York.

Zachariah, K. C. and Julien Condé. 1981. *Migration in West Africa: Demographic Aspects*. New York: Oxford University Press.

1974 Population and Housing Census of Liberia. 1977. Population Characteristics of Major Areas. Monrovia, Liberia: Major Political Divisions, PC-1.

1976 Population Census. 1981. Analytical Report, vol. 4.Maseru, Lesotho: Kingdom of Lesotho. The Bureau of Statistics Maseru.

1980 Census of Population and Housing of Zambia. 1985. 2 vols. Lusaka, Zambia: Central Statistical Office.

10

International Migration in Africa

Migration has played an important role in the distribution of the population in many areas throughout the world. For example, at least 65 million emigrants left Europe between 1820 and 1930, and 54 million came to the Americas (Woytinsky and Woytinsky, 1953). Migration not only affected the growth and decline of the total population of the areas of origin and destination but also altered their demographic characteristics.

The two major types of migration are international migration and internal migration. International migration involves the movement across national boundaries and internal migration, which was discussed in Chapter 9, involves movement within the boundaries of a country.

IMMIGRATION INTO AFRICA

North Africa

North Africans are descendants of various groups of immigrants from southwest Asia, some of whom probably entered Africa during the Paleolithic period which began about two and a half million years ago and lasted for more than two million years. For example, the Berbers, Phoenicians, Greeks, Romans, Arabs, and other groups came to North Africa centuries ago.

The Berbers, the earliest known residents of the western Mediterranean coast of Africa, probably came to the Maghreb region from Canaan, Syria, or Yemen thousands of years ago through Egypt and Ethiopia en route to northwestern Africa. These Berber tribes spoke a Hamitic-Semitic language, and maintained their identity and independence until they were assimilated by the Arabs after the latters' invasions of North Africa beginning in the seventh century.

The Berbers arrived in North Africa when the Sahara Desert was receiving at least twice as much rainfall as today and they expanded into the Sahara before desiccation set in around 2000 B.C. From time to time they wielded considerable economic and political power. Now, most Berbers throughout North Africa have intermarried with the Arabs, become Muslims, and adopted the Arabic language.

North Africa was an easy prey for armed aggressors. Consequently, a succession of conquests and invasions profoundly influenced the language, religion, and other aspects of the region's culture. For instance, Greek culture and philosophy were introduced into Egypt in 332 B.C. during the conquest of Alexander the Great. Greek civilization thrived in Alexandria, which also maintained a large Jewish population, until the Roman conquest. At that time, Alexandria had both the largest Jewish and the largest Greek populations of any city in the world.

The Romans occupied North Africa during the first and second centuries B.C. They were followed by the Vandals, an ancient Germanic tribe that migrated through south Spain, and invaded northwest Africa in A.D. 429. By 435 they controlled nearly all of the Roman province of northwest Africa and in 439 they took Carthage. The Byzantines captured Carthage in 533 and the Vandals were defeated.

In A.D. 639 the Arabs entered Egypt and soon occupied North Africa, and in the eleventh century they began to colonize North Africa. However, the historian Ibn Khaldûn doubted that all of the alleged Arab invasions actually occurred. Rather, he suspected that many of the invasions were fabrications of the Berbers (Khaldûn, 1969).

Sub-Saharan Africa

The black inhabitants of Africa who originated below the Sahara are descendants of the natives there. However, major emigrations from Asia occurred on the East Coast in the eighth and ninth centuries (Oliver and Fage, 1975). Shi'ite Muslim refugees from Oman, on the Arabian peninsula, and Sunni Muslims from Shiraz in Persia's gulf settled in different places from Mozambique to Somalia. The Shirazi were credited with building Kilwa and Mogadishu. The Shirazi, Omani, and Bantus lived peacefully and harmoniously in the coastal towns of East Africa, and both the Shi'ite from Oman and the Shirazi contributed substantially to the development of the area (Chittick, 1965). Later the Shirazi became very active politically in Zanzibar, where an armed uprising by the Afro-Shirazi party in January, 1964 deposed the sultan and led to the establishment of the Tanzanian Republic.

There were earlier migrations from Asia to Ethiopia and to the island of Madagascar. The Merina are thought to have migrated from Borneo to Madagascar in the first millennium B.C. (Murdock, 1959). Also, the origins of the Ethiopian Kingdom go back to the first millennium B.C. by settlers from South Arabia and Yemen (Shinnie, 1978).   Much later, East Indians were recruited to work in eastern Africa to replace slave labor, which had been abolished. They worked as laborers, clerks, and traders, but later many became businessmen and professionals.

European nations established trading posts in West Africa during 1400 to 1500, and Portugal established colonies. Portugal's search for a direct maritime trade route to India to obtain spices resulted in profitable gold dust, ivory, and slave trade in West Africa beginning in the fifteenth century. For example, it colonized the Cape Verde Islands in 1462 and São Tomé and Príncipe in 1483, and Bartholomeu Dias circumnavigated the Cape of Good Hope in 1487-88 (Ravenstein, 1900).

The Dutch established the first settlement in southern Africa at the Cape of Good Hope in 1652 to provide a stop-over for ships traveling to the Indian Ocean. Later, King Leopold of Belgium established a settlement in the Congo. By 1914 European colonies occupied the entire continent except Liberia and Ethiopia. Liberia was founded as an independent country in 1847 to resettle free blacks from the United States and was never a European colony. Ethiopia was invaded by Italy in 1935 and was occupied for about six years.

At the 1884 Treaty of Berlin, Africa was partitioned by the major European nations and the boundaries of the African colonies were established.   Few European settlers migrated to their African colonies as they had done in North and South America. For example, one British demographer estimated that there were no more than 135,000 Europeans in Africa in 1835 (Kuczynski, 1936).

In the late nineteenth century the discovery of diamonds and gold brought thousands of fortune seekers to South Africa.   Diamonds were discovered at Kimberley in different places during 1869-71 and gold was discovered shortly thereafter in the Transvaal in 1886. The huge profits from diamond mining were, in turn, used as capital in developing the gold mines in the Witwatersrand region of the Transvaal. Mining camps sprang up wherever gold was found and most mining centers grew rapidly (Callinicos, 1980). Soon Johannesburg, founded in 1886, was the largest city in the Transvaal, surpassing Pretoria, one of the national capitals, in size. By 1904 Johannesburg had more than four times as many inhabitants as Pretoria, about 156,000 compared to 37,000.

After liberation by the British forces in 1941 and the defeat of the Axis Powers in North Africa in 1943, nearly 225,000 Italians left their former colonies in Africa. At the same time, there was an immigration of British, French, and Portuguese into Africa. By 1960, more than two million Britons were in Africa. Just over a million were in South Africa and were in 200,000 in Zimbabwe, with smaller numbers in Kenya, Tanzania, Uganda, Zambia, and other English-speaking countries (UN, 1965). Also, nearly two million French citizens were in Africa, with around one million in Algeria, about 450,000 in Morocco, and 300,000 in Tunisia, and smaller numbers in the Côte d'Ivoire, Senegal, and other

French-speaking countries. In addition, about one million Portuguese were in Angola, Guinea-Bissau, and Mozambique. After the colonies obtained their independence most Europeans returned home.

EMIGRATION FROM AFRICA

Exportation of Slaves

The first major emigrant groups from sub-Saharan Africa were slaves. Traffic in African slaves was an old tradition, for black Africans had been exported to Arabia and the Persian Gulf area from the coastal region of East Africa since the beginning of the Christian era. Also, thousands of men, women, children, and eunuchs from West Africa were traded in the early commerce across the Sahara to North Africa. In the Americas African slaves were wanted primarily as laborers for the production of agricultural crops. For example, Brazil needed labor for its sugar and coffee estates, and imported the largest number of slaves of all New World countries. Also, tobacco, cocoa, and cotton were grown on a fairly large scale there.

Nearly 12 million African slaves were exported to the Americas between 1450 and 1900 (Lovejoy, 1982, 1983). About half were shipped from Africa in the eighteenth century, with English ships transporting about 40 percent of all slaves. Almost five million went to the various Caribbean Islands, which were colonies of a half dozen European countries (Curtin, 1969). Nearly as many were exported to the Portuguese colony of Brazil and less than two million to Central America. Around a half million were exported to North America.

Arab slave traders incorporated African slaves into their societies north of the Sahara and along the Indian coasts, and used them in military, administrative, and domestic service. Women and children were highly prized. Estimates of the magnitude of the Islamic slave trade in Africa vary considerably. According to Lovejoy (1982, 1983) there were 3.1 million slaves traded to the Arabs from 1500 to 1800. However, the Arabs may have traded as many or even more than were shipped across the Atlantic to the Americas. Austen, for example, estimated that more than 7.2 million slaves were traded to the Muslims prior to 1600. Of all slaves traded to them, 60 percent were part of the North African Saharan commerce and were exported from the Red Sea and East African ports to Arabia and India (Austen, 1979).

Various scholars have analyzed the impacts of African slave emigration upon the demographic changes in Africa. For example, the Portuguese took approximately two million slaves from Angola. According to one author, Angolan slave trading had only a nominal effect upon the total number of people living in the affected areas, even though it altered the age-sex composition of the population (Thornton, 1980, 1981).

Table 10.1
Refugees in the African Countries, 1989

Country of Asylum	Country of Origin	Number from Each Country	Total Refugees
Angola	Namibia	69,000	91,150
	Zaire	12,150	
	South Africa	10,000	
Benin	Chad	868	868
Botswana	Zimbabwe	624	2,092
	Others--Africa	1,468	
Burkina Faso	Chad	362	362
Burundi	Mostly Rwanda and Zaire	-----	267,500
Cameroon	Mostly Chad	51,000	51,000
Central African Republic	Chad	2,900	3,100
	Others--Africa	200	
Chad	Africa	3,695	3,695
Côte d'Ivoire	Vietnamese	300	465
	Others--Africa	165	
Djibouti	Ethiopia	1,550	1,550

Table 10.1 (Continued)

Country of Asylum	Country of Origin	Number from Each Country	Total Refugees
Ethiopia	Sudan	330,224	680,724
	Somalia	350,000	
	Others--Africa	500	
Ghana	Namibia	66	206
	Others--Africa	140	
Kenya	Uganda	6,400	12,500
	Ethiopia	2,800	
	Rwanda	2,000	
	Others--Africa	1,300	
Lesotho	South Africa	4,000	4,000
Liberia	Others--Africa	250	250
Malawi	Mozambique	720,000	720,000
Mozambique	Others--Africa	385	385
Namibia	Others--Africa	41,000	41,000
Nigeria	Chad	7,700	7,700
Rwanda	Burundi	60,000	60,000

Country	Origin		Total
Senegal	Guinea-Bissau	4,800	56,000
	Others--Africa	200	
	Mauritania	51,000	
Sierra Leone	Namibia	60	60
Somalia	Ethiopia	834,000	834,000
Sudan	Ethiopia	350,000	745,000
	Uganda	5,000	
	Chad	24,000	
	Others--Africa	366,000	
Swaziland	South Africa	6,000	27,915
	Mozambique	8,201	
	Others--Africa	13,714	
Tanzania	Burundi	154,700	266,500
	Rwanda	22,300	
	Zaire	16,000	
	Mozambique	72,000	
	Others--Africa	1,500	
Togo	Ghana	3,400	3,400
Uganda	Rwanda	75,000	126,300
	Sudan	50,000	
	Zaire	1,300	

139

Table 10.1 (Continued)

Country of Asylum	Country of Origin	Number from Each Country	Total Refugees
Zaire	Angola	344,909	344,909
Zambia	Angola	98,000	136,500
	Mozambique	20,000	
	Zaire	9,000	
	Others--Africa	9,500	
Zimbabwe	Mozambique	100,000	100,000
Total			4,589,131

Source: Compiled from the United Nations High Commissioner for Refugees, *Fact Sheets*,

Vol. 3 No. 2, Vol. 4 No. 1, Geneva, 1989, 1990.

In Dahomey (Benin) approximately the same number were exported as from Angola. An average of 8,500 Aja slaves were exported annually for 50 years between 1690 and 1740, leading to a marked depopulation because birth rates were not high enough to offset the great emigration losses. The loss and dislocation of the population as a result of the slave trade was clearly detrimental to the economy of Dahomey (Manning, 1982). According to some slave, trading had a much more adverse impact on the population of Benin than on the population of Angola.

Permanent Emigration From Africa to Europe

About four million French and British citizens departed for home when the colonies obtained their independence. Also, several thousand Spanish and Belgian colonists returned home. Apparently, the evacuation of these colonists went rather smoothly. The Lusophone colonies in Africa were not as fortunate.

Of all the European powers, Portugal stayed the longest in Africa. Also, it was the most authoritarian and oppressive, putting many Africans to work as slaves or at forced labor. The Portuguese dictator Antonio Salazar and his successor Marcello Caetano not only had armies in the rebellious colonies but also secret police with orders to jail, beat, and torture anyone active in the independence movements.

In the early 1970s Portugal was spending large sums in its five African colonies and trying to recover these expenditures. Furthermore, Portugal was the only European power that refused to grant independence to its colonies. Zimbabwe was the only non-Portuguese colony that had a protracted disagreement over the terms of its independence but its situation was quite different--it was a British colony.

In the early 1960s Africans in the Portuguese colonies became restless and started independence movements. Strife and unrest progressively intensified until April, 1974 when a military coup overthrew Marcello Caetano in Portugal. Attitudes toward granting independence to the African colonies changed quickly. Guinea-Bissau obtained its independence in September, 1974, and the other four colonies were given their independence in 1975.

While the Portuguese government encouraged the emigration of more than 400,000 to its African colonies between 1960 and 1973, the 1974 coup effectively ended further settlements (Christopher, 1984). Various estimates of the number of Portuguese in the five African colonies have been made (Bender, 1978; Middlemas, 1979). In all, there were 750,000 to one million Portuguese by 1974-75, and more than 150,000 Portuguese troops were stationed in Africa to keep order. By the end of 1977, more than one million Portuguese were thought to have returned from Africa (ICMC, 1977b).

Of the five Portuguese African colonies, Cape Verde had an emigration of nearly 50,000 to Portugal by 1970 to fill the vacant jobs of Portuguese who had migrated to other European countries for higher wages (ICMC, 1977a). After the 1974 revolution in Portugal, tensions, conflicts, and hostilities mounted as unemployment increased and economic conditions greatly deteriorated. Droughts, unproductive soils, and the rapid population growth in the Cape Verde Islands resulted in an emigration to nearby West African countries, as well as to Angola and Mozambique. Persistent poverty and periodic famines also prompted thousands to emigrate to the United States. Today an estimated 300,000 Cape Verdean descendants live in the United States, chiefly in Massachusetts and Rhode Island. Many others live in Portugal, the Netherlands, and São Tomé and Príncipe (Mango, 1984).

Permanent Emigration from Africa to Non-European Countries

An annual average of 1,700 Africans came to the United States in the 1950s. The number rose sharply thereafter to 3,300 in the 1960s, to 8,600 in the 1970s, and then to 15,500 in the 1980s (*Stat. Yearbook*, 1985).

By 1955 an annual average of 4,000 Africans were emigrating to the United States, Canada, Australia, and New Zealand, the four developed countries which accepted the largest number of immigrants during the last 20 years. By 1985 nearly 21,000 were emigrating annually. In contrast, the permanent movement of Jews from Africa to Israel declined from an annual average of 17,000 in 1955 to 2,000 in 1976-80.

Emigrant Guest Workers to Europe and Asia

Although the European labor markets were closed to Africans in the 1970s large numbers from the Maghreb countries returned there in the 1980s. By 1982, 796,000 Algerian, 431,000 Moroccan, and 189,000 Tunisian workers were in France for a total of more than 1.4 million North Africans (OECD, 1988). In all, there were nearly 1.8 million North African workers in Europe in the mid-1980s: 815,000 Algerians, 731,000 Moroccans, and 225,000 Tunisians (Costa-Lascoux and Temime, 1985).

Egypt is the largest supplier of migrant labor of all African countries, with at least one million workers abroad. The Asian countries that are the primary recipients of Egyptian labor are Saudi Arabia, Kuwait, the United Arab Emirates, Yemen, and Jordan. Sudan is the second largest African supplier of migrants, with most workers going to Saudi Arabia.

INTRACONTINENTAL MIGRATION

The great Bantu migration of the past and the current movements of temporary workers reflect two major types of intracontinental migration. Historically, one of the most widely known population movements in sub-Saharan Africa was the migration thousands of years ago of Bantu-speaking inhabitants (Oliver, 1970). In modern times, the movement of immigrant laborers among African countries involves several million workers to three major labor markets.

Bantu Migration

The original homeland of the Bantu language family was in the modern-day area of Nigeria and Cameroon (Guthrie, 1970). Their large-scale migrations into eastern, western, and southern Africa probably began thousands of years ago, creating many different dialects, physical types, and social customs through their assimilation of various groups along their migration routes.

In the region of their origin, they lived on the margin of forests, were pastoralists, and possessed knowledge of the cultivation of indigenous African plants. Later, they acquired knowledge of southeast root and tree crops. In addition, they had acquired the techniques of iron smelting, as they made both weapons and tools used in cultivation. Their hoe cultivation of millet and different varieties of sorghum later spread to central and eastern Africa, and then gradually southward.

By the beginning of the Christian era the Bantus had established villages as far south as present-day Zimbabwe and Zambia. Around the fifth century they pushed into South Africa, settling stable communities that spoke the southern Bantu dialects of Sotho, Venda, and Xhosa, as well as into Botswana, Swaziland, and Lesotho (Greenberg, 1972).

Today, the people of the Bantu language family occupy most of Africa south of the Equator, except for certain parts of the Republic of South Africa. Moreover, they number some 400 million inhabitants on the mainland of Africa and probably speak at least 300 different dialects.

Immigrant Laborers

There are three major centers of attraction for intracontinental temporary or seasonal migrants in Africa. The only major labor-importing country in North Africa is Libya. There are approximately half a million foreign workers there currently--a substantial reduction from previous years, particularly of workers from Egypt.

South Africa is the second major labor-importing country, where more than 200,000 blacks from Lesotho, Botswana, Swaziland, Mozambique, and Malawi work in the gold mines (Tarver and Miller, 1990). These international migrants are restricted to the mines and mining camps of South Africa, and are not permitted to have their families live with them (Callinicos, 1980). Regardless, the miners endure the isolation because of the lack of employment opportunities in their home countries (Wilson, 1972).

The Côte d'Ivoire is the largest importer of immigrant labor in West Africa, receiving about 1.5 million workers annually from Burkina Faso, Mali, Togo, and other neighboring countries, as well as from France. Foreigners comprise about a third of Côte d'Ivoire's labor force.

REFUGEES

Domestic strife involving ethnic, religious, racial, and ideological conflicts, as well as natural disasters such as drought and famine, have created immense refugee problems in Africa in recent years. The numbers have progressively grown from one million in 1973 to 2.25 million in 1978, to nearly 4.6 million in 1989 and 6.2 million in 1994--the highest of all major regions in the world (UNHCR, 1989, 1990). The countries with the largest number were Zaire, Tanzania, and Uganda in 1973; Somalia, Zaire, Angola, and Sudan in 1978; Somalia, Sudan, and Angola in 1981; and Somalia, Sudan, Malawi, and Ethiopia in 1989 (table 10.1). Since then, Somalia, Sudan, and Mozambique have had increasing numbers.

Approximately a million and a half refugees from Ethiopia and Sudan were in Somalia, Sudan, and Ethiopia in 1989. This represented a third of all refugees in Africa. The Eritrean conflicts of 1962 and 1978 in Ethiopia sent nearly a million fleeing to Somalia and Sudan. Also, the Ogaden conflict in Ethiopia in 1977-78 sent refugees into Djibouti as well as Somalia. In turn, Ethiopia has provided refuge for about 700,000 from Sudan and Somalia.

British Africa

One of the most infamous cases of refugees in Anglophone Africa was due to tyranny in Uganda where General Idi Amin seized power in a coup in 1971. In 1972 the UN Commission for Refugees assisted 35,000 Asians expelled from Uganda. Thousands of Asians in Kenya, Tanzania, and other East African countries also fled Africa to avoid persecution.

Then, in 1979, a combined force of Tanzanian army units and Ugandan exiles ended Amin's dictatorship. Between 350,000 to 400,000 sought asylum, with 300,000 going to Sudan and Zaire. Others sought haven in Kenya and Tanzania. In 1989, over 10,000 refugees from Uganda remained in Sudan and Kenya.

French Africa

The self-crowned emperor of the Central African Empire, Jean-Bedel Bokassa, was overthrown by the military with French support in the same year that Amin was deposed in Uganda. Before his overthrow, thousands from the Central African Empire had fled, with about 50,000 going to Cameroon.

Elsewhere in French-speaking Africa, civil strife began in Chad in 1963 after its independence in 1960. This resulted in civil war between President Habré's forces and guerrilla commandos in southern Chad in late 1984. To escape the escalating violence, more than 50,000 Chadians fled to Sudan, the Central African Republic, and Cameroon.

Portuguese Africa

Portugal's refusal to grant independence to its five African colonies in the early 1960s resulted in rebellion and violence. According to reliable accounts, São Tomé and Príncipe served as the place of exile and detention for Portuguese political prisoners of Lusophone colonial governments.

Strife associated with independence movements in Angola, Mozambique, and Guinea-Bissau resulted in thousands fleeing their homes. By 1975, about 450,000 from Angola were in exile, mostly in Zaire. Approximately 80,000 from Guinea-Bissau sought asylum in Senegal, and nearly 60,000 from Mozambique were in Tanzania. By 1989 there were about 440,000 refugees from Angola, with most seeking asylum in Zaire and Zambia. In recent years insurrection greatly intensified in Mozambique and over one million are currently seeking asylum in nearby countries. In 1989 about 720,000 were in Malawi and around 100,000 in Zimbabwe.

Belgian Africa

Zaire and Burundi, both French-speaking countries, are former colonies of Belgium. In Zaire unrest and instability continued after it gained independence in 1960. Civil war over the secession of Katanza and South Kasai provinces resulted in thousands of refugees fleeing to the Central African Republic, Sudan, Uganda, and Angola. After 1973 about a half million from Zaire sought asylum outside the country. In turn, between 300,000 and 600,000 sought refuge in Zaire, with most coming from Angola.

In Burundi ethnic conflicts between the Hutus and Tutsis resulted in sporadic warfare for years. The Tutsi, an aristocratic minority group that controls the government and the army, has frequently resorted to genocide. In 1972, for example, they murdered 100,000 Hutus. By 1975, about 150,000 Hutus had sought asylum, with 110,000 in Tanzania. By 1987, the number of refugees from Burundi in Tanzania had increased to 150,000. The 1988 massacre by the Tutsis took at least 20,000 Hutu lives and displaced as many as 50,000 who are in squalid Rwanda refugee camps. Conflict and unrest continues.

Spanish Africa

Citizens of Equatorial Guinea suffered from a corrupt, murderous dictator who was responsible for the exile of about one-third of the population (Cronje, 1976). By 1978, around 90,000 persons had sought asylum in Gabon and Cameroon.

The regime was overthrown in 1979 with Spanish assistance and most refugees returned home, although 30,000 still remained in Gabon in 1981.

Western Sahara also suffered instability and a territorial dispute with neighboring countries. The fighting following the partition of this country resulted in 50,000 refugees seeking asylum in Algeria. Morocco annexed Western Sahara and it was included in its 1982 population census. Now, the United Nations is attempting to resolve the sovereignty of this country and still recognizes Western Sahara.

POPULATION PRESSURES AND IMMIGRATION

Countries with rapidly increasing populations and deteriorating social and economic conditions eventually face serious population pressures. Such pressures, in turn, are likely to stimulate emigration to other countries offering greater economic opportunities. For example, the East African country of Rwanda is comparatively small, with a population density of 275 persons per square kilometer in 1990. Beginning in 1978 its government began encouraging its citizens to emigrate to reduce population pressures and to improve the level of living of its inhabitants. Apparently, the Rwanda governmental policy in favor of emigration also involved a policy of genocide towards the Hutus who live both in Rwanda and in Burundi. Some of the Rwanda's Hutus were resettled in Tanzania in the early 1960s but periodic massacres by the hostile Tutsis in neighboring Burundi continue to result in thousands of Hutu refugees in Rwanda. Therefore, the emigration of a sufficiently large number of Hutus might possibly relieve population pressures and perhaps some strife in Rwanda.

The Republic of Mauritius is another country faced with serious population pressures and the government has encouraged emigration to reduce unemployment.

Immigration often has a profound influence upon the demographic characteristics of the population of the countries of origin and destination. For example, some rather marked changes in the composition of emigrants from Mauritius occurred during 1960 to 1974. It faced serious population pressures and encouraged emigration. In 1960-64 most emigrants were males 20-29 years of age with male emigrants outnumbering female emigrants almost two to one. In 1965-69 there was an emigration of comparatively large numbers of families, as proportionately more women and children emigrated from Mauritius. By 1970-74 a disproportionate number of women 15-29 years of age emigrated with relatively few children leaving Mauritius. Within 15 years the predominant pattern of emigration shifted from one of young males to families, then to young females.

The age-sex composition of the foreign-born population of some African countries reveal unique characteristics. For example, practically all foreign-born in South Africa in 1970 were men under 35 years of age. Most were skilled workers and others recruited from different countries to work in the gold mines.

The age-sex structure of foreign-born residents of Zambia in 1969 differed from those in South Africa. There was a substantial immigration of families into Zambia and the pyramid indicates that family immigration was relatively greater among recent than among earlier immigrants.

SUMMARY AND IMPLICATIONS

Various groups of immigrants, some of whose origins are still obscure, settled in North Africa in prehistoric times. Berbers, Phoenicians, Persians, Greeks, Romans, Arabs, and others came in ancient and medieval times. The earliest immigrants into sub-Saharan Africa came from South Arabia to Ethiopia in the first millennium B.C. Merina immigrants from Borneo arrived in Madagascar about the same time. Later in the eighth and ninth centuries migrants from Oman and Shirazi from the Asian continent settled on the East Coast. Between five and six million Europeans came to Africa during colonialism but most left after the colonies obtained their independence.

The first major group of emigrants from Africa were slaves. Some 20 million were taken across the Atlantic and the Sahara. Current intercontinental emigration is comparatively small, with around 40,000 to 50,000 leaving Africa annually. Many guest workers in Europe have chosen to remain there. Political and social strife and unrest have led to three to four million African refugees who have sought security outside their home countries, a form of short-distance temporary forced migration. Refugees tend to move very rapidly and in relatively large numbers but travel fairly short distances. Their numbers change rather quickly from time to time. Most are either repatriated or resettled in the country of their first asylum. Based upon recent experiences in Somalia, Sudan, and Mozambique, it seems likely that large refugee movements will probably continue in the future.

Rapidly increasing population growth in Africa will exert strong pressures for greater emigration in the future to other areas of the world. Since most African countries are likely to have relatively large population increases, it is unlikely that many emigrants will seek new homes in nearby countries because they, too will offer only limited opportunities. Regardless, strict immigration restrictions and quotas in most developed countries will continue to serve as constraints on intercontinental movement.

REFERENCES

Austen, Ralph A. 1979. "The Trans-Saharan Slave Trade: A Tentative Census." In *The Uncommon Market: Essays in the Economic History of the Atlantic Slave Trade*, edited by H.A. Gemery and J.S. Hogendorn, 23-76. New York: Academic Press.

Bender, Gerald J. 1978. *Angola Under the Portuguese: The Myth and the Reality*. London: Heinemann.

Callinicos, Luli. 1980. *A People's History of South Africa: Gold and Workers, 1886-1924*. Johannesburg, South Africa: Ravan Press.

Chittick, Neville. 1965. "The Shirazi colonization of East Africa." *Journal of African History* 6: 275-294.

Christopher, A. J. 1984. *Colonial Africa*. London: Croom Helm.

Costa-Lascoux, Jacqueline and Emile Temime. 1985. *Les Algériens en France*. Paris: Publisud.

Cronje, Suzanne. 1976. *Equatorial Guinea--The Forgotten Dictatorship*. London: Trade Printing Company.

Curtin, Philip D. 1969. *The Atlantic Slave Trade: A Census*. Madison, WI: University of Wisconsin Press.

Greenberg, J. H. 1972. "Linguistic Evidence Regarding Bantu Origins." *Journal of African History* 13: 189-216.

Guthrie, Malcolm. 1970. "Some Developments in the Prehistory of the Bantu Languages." In *Papers in African Prehistory*, edited by J.D. Fage and R. A. Oliver, 131-140. Cambridge: Cambridge University Press.

International Catholic Migration Commission. 1977a. "Cape Verde Immigrants in Portugal." *Migration News* 26th year, no. 3, 32-34.

_____. 1977b. "Returnees to Portugal." *Migration News*, 26th Year, no. 4, 19-23.

Khaldûn, Ibn. 1969. *The Muqaddimah: An Introduction to History*, translated by Franz Rosenthal. Princeton, NJ: Princeton University Press.

Kuczynski, Robert R. 1936. *Population Movements*. London: Oxford University Press.

Lovejoy, Paul E. 1983. *Transformations in Slavery*. Cambridge: Cambridge University Press.

Lovejoy, Paul E. 1982. "The Volume of the Atlantic Slave Trade: A Synthesis." *Journal of African History* 23: 473-501.

Mango, Cecily. 1984. *Cape Verde: A Country Profile*. Washington, DC: U.S. Agency for International Development.

Manning, Patrick. 1982. *Slavery, Colonialism and Economic Growth in Dahomey, 1640-1960*. Cambridge: Cambridge University Press.

Middlemas, K. 1979. "Twentieth Century White Society in Mocambique." *Tarikh* 6: 30-45.

Murdock, George P. 1959. *Africa: Its Peoples and Their Culture History*. New York: McGraw-Hill.

Oliver, Roland. 1970. "The Problem of the Bantu Expansion." In *Papers in African Prehistory*, edited by J.D. Fage and R.A. Oliver, 141-156. Cambridge: Cambridge University Press.

Oliver, Roland and J.D. Fage. 1972. *A Short History of Africa*. Middlesex, England: Penguin Books.

Organization for Economic Co-operation and Development. 1988. *Continuous Reporting System on Migration, 1987*. Paris.

Ravenstein, E.G. 1900. "The Voyages of Diogo Cão and Bartholomeu Dias, 1482-1488." *The Geographical Journal* 16: 625-654.

Shinnie, P.L. 1978. "The Nilotic Sudan and Ethiopia, 660 B.C. to A.D. 600." In *The Cambridge History of Africa*, edited by J.D. Fage, vol. 2., 210-271. Cambridge: Cambridge University Press.

Tarver, James D., and H. Max Miller. 1990. "International Migration in Botswana." In *Handbook on International Migration*, edited by William J. Serow et al., 25-36. Westport, CT: Greenwood Press.

Thornton, John. 1980. "The Slave Trade in Eighteenth Century Angola: Effects on Demographic Structures." *Canadian Journal of African Studies* 14: 417-427.

Thornton, John. 1981. "The Demographic Effect of the Slave Trade on Western Africa 1500-1850." In *African Historical Demography*, edited by Christopher Fyfe and David McMaster, vol. 2, 691-720. Edinburgh, Scotland: University of Edinburgh.

United Nations. 1965. *Demographic Yearbook, 1964*. New York.

United Nations High Commissioner for Refugees. 1989,1990. *Fact Sheets*, vol. 3, no. 2 and vol. 4, no. 1, Geneva.

U.S. Department of Justice, Immigration and Naturalization Service. 1985. *Statistical Yearbook*. Washington, DC.

Wilson, Francis. 1972. *Labour in the South African Gold Mines, 1911-1969*. Cambridge: Cambridge University Press.

Woytinsky, Wladimir S. and Emma S. Woytinsky. 1953. *World Population and Production: Trends and Outlook*. New York: Twentieth Century Fund.

11

The Economically Active Population

The social and economic status of a country largely depends upon the number and characteristics of its workers. The size, structure, and composition of the labor force, along with its age, sex, education, and skills, greatly determine a country's income and level of living.

THE CONCEPT OF ECONOMIC ACTIVITY

Information on labor force participation has been collected in national censuses of population, labor force sample surveys, and related field studies conducted in the African countries over time. *Economically active* persons are defined as those supplying labor for the production of goods and services during a specified reference period or at some specified date. All persons actually engaged in productive work or actively seeking work are classified as economically active. This concept conforms to the standard definition of economically active populations (ILO, 1976). In some countries the minimum age to qualify as economically active may be as young as six years of age. In other African countries it may be as high as 16 years of age, but usually ranges between six and 16 years.

Difficulties often arise in the measurement of economic activity in censuses and surveys, particularly in the collection of employment data from unpaid family workers in the informal sector and from females in the subsistence agricultural sector. The underenumeration of female members of the labor force is much greater among seasonal workers and the International Labour Office economic activity rates reflect these underenumerations.

FORMAL AND INFORMAL SECTOR WORKERS

Economically active persons who are employers, self-employed, or wage employees are cash-earning members of the formal sector of the labor force. Non-cash workers in family agriculture, itinerant vendors of everyday goods, and operators of other petty enterprises are classified as informal sector workers. The informal sector, of course, includes any income-producing activities outside of formal sector wages. When formal sector workers begin to appear in progressively greater numbers the traditional informal structures of countries are being transformed into nonagricultural economies.

In 1970 formal sector workers probably comprised 30 to 40 percent of Africa's total labor force. The International Labour Office estimated that by the mid-1970s the informal sector accounted for about 60 percent of the urban labor force (ILO, 1985). For example, the relative importance of the informal sector in the urban areas of about a dozen African countries ranges from 95 percent in Benin to less than 40 percent in the Congo (table 11.1). In West Africa the informal sector is very diverse and is relatively larger in the cities there than in the cities of Asia and Latin America (Trager, 1987).

Between five and ten percent of all members of the agricultural labor force are probably cash-earning formal sector workers. Generally, the subsistence agricultural workers live on communal lands and use traditional methods of crop production involving a minimum of mechanization and scientific agriculture. As the African economies modernize the number of informal workers decline.

There is a large concentration of teenagers in the African cities because of the prevailing patterns of large scale rural-urban migration. Many of these youths are unemployed in the formal sector but are working in the informal sector assisting their parents and other relatives in petty trading, gardening, raising poultry, caring for donkeys and other livestock, gathering water and wood, and performing a host of chores which contribute to the livelihood of the family. Other family members also play significant roles in the informal employment structure of urban areas by selling cigarettes and matches, and street food vending.

Impressive gains are likely to occur in the modernization of the African economies in the future. The United Nations, for example, has classified the Republic of South Africa as a developed country and other such designations may follow in the future. The relative number of formal sector workers will continue to increase and may even approach 75 percent by 2025. Such a sizable expansion in the cash-earning sector will represent a significant gain in formal employment.

ACTIVITY RATES BY AGE AND SEX

Of all persons in the economically active ages in Africa, around 40 percent have been members of the labor force since 1950. About 50 percent of the men and 28 percent of the women are economically active (tables 11.2, 11.3, 11.4). Between the ages of 25 and 55 about 95 percent of all males are in the labor force, whereas about half of all women of this age are economically active. In those ages of peak work activity, relatively twice as many men as women are in the labor force. Childbearing, school attendance, and infirmities at older ages curtails the economic activity of many. In fact, most of those of working ages not in the labor force were either homemakers or students (ILO, 1986).

Age-specific economic activity rates, defined as the number of economically active persons in the different age groups per 100 persons in these age groups, vary significantly from one age to another (tables 11.2, 11.3, and 11.4). For males, they begin from a low of 27 percent among those 10-14 years of age in 1990. Then, they rise sharply to peak levels in the 30-34 age group but decline to less than 40 percent in the ages of 65 and over in 1980 and 1990.

The age-specific activity rates of women differ from men. Women begin work at relatively young ages but rise much more rapidly to reach their peak levels at earlier ages than men. Also, their highest rates are much lower than for men. For example, in 1980 women reached their maximum level of labor force participation at 35-39 years of age with 51 percent. After age 55 their activity rates decline (table 11.4). Unlike males, females in developing countries exhibit highly variable activity rates from one population group to another within the same country. For instance, married and unmarried women, mothers and childless women, and educated and uneducated females have quite diverse activity patterns (Standing, 1978).

Family agriculture is the principal activity of most young members of the African labor force. The majority of the remaining youths are in school while the oldest members of the labor force tend to be in family agriculture. Thus, cash employment is the main activity only of persons in the prime working ages. This pattern of economic activity has generally been characteristic of developing countries (Durand, 1975).

The labor force participation rates of African workers have consistently fallen since 1950 and are likely to reach their lowest levels around 2000 to 2010, then gradually increase thereafter. The labor force participation rates of males in each of the five major regions are projected to decline between 1950 and 2025 but the activity rates of females in northern and southern Africa will probably increase.

Indeed, there is a wide range in the relative number of economically active persons in the different countries. For example, the percentage of males in the labor force varies from about 40 percent to between 55 and 60 percent. The range for women is even greater, varying from four percent to over 50 percent. Overall, the total labor force participation rates ranged from a low of 22 percent in Algeria to 55 percent in Mozambique. Nearly two-thirds of those in the African labor force were men.

Table 11.1
Percentage of the Labor Force in Selected Countries Engaged in Informal Sector Employment, mid-1970s

Areas	Percent
Abidjan (Côte d'Ivoire)	44
Nairobi (Kenya)	44
Kumasi (Ghana)	65
Urban Areas (Senegal)	50
Lagos (Nigeria)	50
Urban Areas (Burkina Faso)	73
Banjul (The Gambia)	42
Lome (Togo)	50
Urban Areas (Benin)	95
Brazzaville (Congo)	37
Urban Areas (Niger)	65

Source: Compiled from International Labour Organization, *The Informal Sector in Africa: Jobs and Skills Programme for Africa*, Addis Ababa, 1985.

Women in South Africa had slightly lower activity rates than women for Africa as a whole. One of the most distinctive labor force patterns of African women is among the Muslims in the countries of North Africa. Here women are discouraged from working outside the home. Accordingly, less than 10 percent of the North African women were members of the labor force. In Algeria, Libya, and Egypt about five percent of the women were members of the labor force. Morocco, Sudan, and Tunisia were somewhat more westernized in this respect with relatively twice as many females in the labor force.

OCCUPATIONAL AND INDUSTRIAL STRUCTURE

Censuses and surveys usually obtain information on the occupational and industrial characteristics of members of the labor force. However, these characteristics are usually gathered only for members of the formal labor force sector.

The total economically active populations for Africa by major occupational and industry groups are not published. Thus, it is necessary to add the figures of those countries published in the annual *Yearbooks of Labour Statistics* (ILO, 1985, 1988) and in the *Demographic Yearbooks* to obtain estimates in each classification for all countries. The percentages in tables 11.5 and 11.6 correspond fairly closely with the 1980 estimates of the percentage economically active in agriculture in table 11.7 and are used here to reflect the approximate occupational and industrial structure of Africa for that date. Comparable figures published in the *1988 Yearbook of Labour Statistics* understate the relative number of economically active persons in agriculture for Africa by 20 percent (ILO, 1988). Consequently, they are not representative of Africa as a whole in 1980 and are not shown here.

Occupational Characteristics

Occupational classifications are based upon the type of work a person in the labor force performs, regardless of the industry in which he works. Occupational attachments are frequently used in assessing the supply and demand of specific types of workers. Each economically active person is assigned to both an occupational and an industrial category. Both the United Nations and the International Labour Office classify workers into seven major occupations (table 11.5).

By far the largest number of workers are in the broad occupational category of the agricultural sector, which includes agriculture, animal husbandry, forestry, fishing, and hunting. Females are relatively more numerous than males, with 78 percent of their economically active workers in this category to only 57 percent of the males. Crop production in Africa is usually considered to be a woman's job and there are more women than men in family agriculture. In addition, women carry water for household consumption, gather firewood, cook, wash, and perform other household duties, as well as care for children. The husbands in family agriculture usually care for cattle and other livestock, and some may have informal sector jobs.

Production workers, transport equipment operators, and laborers comprise the second largest occupational group and are considered to be laborers. This occupational class manufacturing workers, miners, welders, food processors, weavers, and tanners, and accounts for almost 18 percent of all male workers but only four percent of all female workers. As a result, 82 percent of all female and 74 percent of all male workers are employed in the two broad agricultural and production groups. Cash-earning females are usually concentrated in agricultural, service, professional, and sales occupations, and are underrepresented in production, construction, transport, and management occupations.

Industrial Characteristics

Clearly, the male and female labor force members are highly concentrated in four industries. Agricultural production occupies the efforts of no less than 87 percent of all women and over 62 percent of all men. This preponderance of agricultural workers is, of course, a distinctive feature of developing countries.

Usually developing countries are noted for their relative paucity of industrial activity. Only 10 percent of the economically active males in the 12 countries included in table 11.6 were engaged in manufacturing. In contrast, most developed countries have between 30 and 40 percent of their labor force in industry.

Community, social, and personal services made up around 10 percent of the labor force, and half that many worked in wholesale and retail trade. The other five industrial groups attracted a total of less than 10 percent of all workers. However, table 11.6 clearly indicates that the industrial structure of the labor force has not changed greatly from dominant agricultural industries to secondary and tertiary industries as in the developed countries.

Economically active females had somewhat different industrial attachments than males. For example, there were 24 percent more females than males working in agriculture, five percent fewer in community, social, and personal services, eight percent fewer in manufacturing, and four percent fewer in wholesale and retail trade (table 11.6).

Historically, the economy of nearly every African country was almost completely devoted to agriculture. Millions were engaged in traditional subsistence farming in the informal sector. The size of this huge informal sector has, of course, dwindled even though few technological innovations have actually been introduced in agriculture. For example, a consistent, steady decline in the relative size of the agricultural labor force has occurred in each of the African countries since 1950. Even so, over 80 percent of these countries still had the majority of their workers engaged in agricultural pursuits in 1980 (ILO, 1986). By 1990, 63 percent of the economically active were still engaged in agricultural work (table 11.7).

Generally, the relative size of the industrial labor force in each country has increased consistently as the size of the agricultural labor force declined. On the whole, however, gains in industrial employment have been comparatively small, for there were only a half dozen countries with 25 percent or more of their workers in industrial employment in 1980. For 1990, around 37 percent of the economically active were engaged in nonagricultural employment, with about a third being industrial workers (table 11.7).

EMPLOYMENT BY MAJOR ECONOMIC SECTORS

Between 1950 and 1990 the relative number of economically active workers in agriculture declined about 20 percent (table 11.7). Although agricultural employment has been steadily declining for years, it nevertheless occupied the efforts of nearly 75 percent of all women and 60 percent of all men in the labor force in 1990. In contrast, the number of workers in industry and services doubled between 1950 and 1990. As a result of these divergent trends nearly 65 percent of all economically active persons were in the agriculture sector in 1990, and about 35 percent in industry and services combined.

Technologically, Southern Africa is the most advanced region, with 80 percent of its economically active workers in industry and services combined. North Africa is next, with nearly 60 percent. On the other hand, East Africa is still the most traditional region, with less than 25 percent of its workers in both industry and services.

Africa's economy is likely to undergo considerable advancement by 2025. For instance, the nonagricultural labor force (both industry and services) is projected to expand by 2025 to 56 percent of the total labor force. By 2025 the size of the agricultural labor sector likely will be nearly twice that in 1990 (table 11.7). Nevertheless, the proportionate number of agricultural workers is projected to decline from 63 percent in 1990 to 44 percent in 2025 (UN, 1988). During this period, the number of informal sector workers is projected to decline in somewhat the same fashion. These projected changes in the structure of the labor force should greatly alter the present economy.

PROFESSIONAL AND GOVERNMENT EMPLOYMENT

African countries have relatively few administrators and managers, with only one percent working in this major occupation (ILO, 1985). Other professional workers are also greatly underrepresented (UN, 1986). On the other hand, Africa has the largest relative number of government workers in the nonagricultural sector of all major regions of the world (Heller and Tait, 1984). Slightly more than 30 percent of all nonagricultural employees in selected African countries were civil servants in central government, compared to 21 percent in Latin America, and 14 percent in Asia.

In several African countries central government employment is exceptionally high. For example, over half of Liberia's nonagricultural workers are central government employees. In Tanzania, Benin, Togo, and Zambia, over 40 percent are civil servants in central government. The African governments are characteristically highly centralized, with the relative employment in local government in the nonagricultural sector amounting to only about two percent. In fact, countries such as Cameroon, Liberia, Senegal, Swaziland, Tanzania, and Togo have no local government structures.

Government employment was generally modest in size in the colonial days, except perhaps for a few countries such as Kenya and Tanzania. Some have assumed that the African governments simply inherited the large bureaucracies from their European colonial powers. This is not the case, however, because the colonial civil services were rather small in size when the African countries attained their independence. It was not the bulging bureaucracies that the African governments inherited from the Europeans but rather small dual civil services for Europeans and Africans (and in most of East Africa Indians constituted a third separate group), each with its own pay structure (Miller, et al., 1991).

Rapid increases in government employment occurred in the newly independent countries, particularly in Kenya and Nigeria. There are several different reasons for the expansion in the number of African civil servants after independence.

First, part of the growth was in response to rising demands for greater public services, especially in education and health care. Most colonial governments had neglected the educational systems.

Second, increases in the total incomes of the African countries led to increases in government expenditures which, in turn, resulted in hiring more civil servants and increasing their salaries.

Third, African governments generally assumed the responsibility for providing employment, especially under conditions of high unemployment and high underemployment. For example, many countries greatly expanded public service employment, trying to reduce high levels of urban unemployment.

Fourth, an expansion in the number of civil servants occurred due to the policy in some countries of guaranteeing university graduates government employment.

Fifth, socialism has been responsible for major increases in public service employment in some countries. Tanzania, for example, nationalized banking, commerce, transportation, and other industries, which resulted in large increases in the number of civil servants.

EMPLOYMENT STATUS AND THE ECONOMICALLY INACTIVE

Status in employment and the working-age population outside of the labor force are two other important aspects and concepts of the working-age population.

Status in Employment

Another way of examining the economically active population is to classify workers in terms of their status in employment. There are two major status categories of workers. The first combines employers and self-employed own-account workers. An employer is defined as a person who operates an economic enterprise or engages independently in a profession or trade and hires one or more employees. An own-account worker operates an economic enterprise or engages in a profession or trade but hires no employees.

The second status group is comprised of employees. An employee is a person working for a public or private employer, and may receive wages, salaries, commissions, tips, piece-rate pay, or pay in kind. The other status category is comprised of unpaid family workers, members of producers co-operatives, and persons not classified by status.

The most distinctive feature of the status of employment is that there were relatively three times as many female employers and own-account workers combined as female employees, 44 compared to 14 percent, respectively. Among male workers, however, there were slightly more employees than employers and self-employed workers, together.

Economically Inactive Population

The working-age population not in the labor force was reported for 14 countries. Most of those not in the labor force were either homemakers or students. Most of the males not working were students. On the other hand, nearly 70 percent of the women not in the labor force were homemakers and 20 percent were students.

SUMMARY AND IMPLICATIONS

The middle class has not developed fully in the African countries. Moreover, there are relatively few administrators and managers and professional workers. Also, Africa has a large proportion of civil servants in the nonagricultural sector, about 30 percent, which is the highest of all major regions in the world.

The African labor force is still concentrated in the dominant agricultural economy, carried on mainly by women. Approximately 90 to 95 percent of those who work in family agriculture are non-cash informal sector workers. Both the urban and rural informal sector workers probably comprise around 60 percent of the total labor force.

Table 11.2
Economic Activity Rates of the African Population, by Age, 1950-2025

Age Groups	1950	1960	1970	1980	1990	2000	2010	2020	2025
10-14	35	32	30	28	22	16	11	7	6
15-19	63	60	57	52	50	47	45	44	42
20-24	71	70	69	67	66	66	66	67	67
25-29	73	73	73	72	71	71	71	71	72
30-34	75	74	74	73	72	71	71	72	73
35-39	75	74	74	74	72	71	71	71	72
40-44	75	74	74	74	72	71	70	71	71
45-49	75	74	74	73	72	70	69	69	69
50-54	73	73	73	71	70	68	69	66	66
55-59	70	70	69	68	65	63	60	58	58
60-64	65	64	62	60	56	53	49	45	43
65+	50	46	63	39	37	33	29	24	21
All ages	44	43	41	39	38	37	37	39	40

Source: Compiled from International Labour Office, *Economically Active Population Estimates and Projections, 1950-2025*, Vol. 2, Geneva, 1986.

Table 11.3
Economic Activity Rates of the Male Population of Africa, by Age, 1950-2025

Age Groups	1950	1960	1970	1980	1990	2000	2010	2020	2025
10-14	44	40	37	34	27	21	15	10	8
15-19	79	75	70	64	61	59	57	54	53
20-24	93	92	90	87	87	87	86	86	86
25-29	97	97	97	96	96	96	95	95	95
30-34	98	98	98	97	97	97	97	97	97
35-39	98	98	98	98	98	98	97	97	97
40-44	98	98	98	97	97	97	97	97	97
45-49	98	97	97	97	97	96	96	96	96
50-54	97	96	96	96	95	94	94	93	93
55-59	95	95	94	93	91	90	88	87	86
60-64	92	90	88	84	81	77	73	69	67
65+	77	71	66	59	54	49	43	36	32
All ages	58	56	53	51	50	49	49	52	54

Source: Compiled from International Labour Office, *Economically Active Population Estimates and Projections, 1950-2025*, Vol. 2, Geneva, 1986.

161

Table 11.4
Economic Activity Rates of the Female Population of Africa, by Age, 1950-2025

Age Groups	1950	1960	1970	1980	1990	2000	2010	2020	2025
10-14	26	25	23	22	16	11	8	4	3
15-19	47	46	44	41	38	36	34	33	32
20-24	49	48	49	47	46	45	46	47	49
25-29	50	49	50	48	47	46	46	48	49
30-34	52	51	51	50	47	46	46	47	48
35-39	52	51	51	51	46	45	45	45	46
40-44	53	52	52	51	48	45	44	44	45
45-49	53	52	52	51	49	44	43	43	43
50-54	52	51	51	49	46	43	40	40	41
55-59	47	47	47	46	42	39	34	32	31
60-64	42	41	39	39	34	31	27	23	22
65+	28	26	24	23	22	19	17	14	12
All ages	31	30	29	28	26	24	24	25	27

Source: Compiled from International Labour Office, *Economically Active Population Estimates and Projections, 1950-2025*, Vol. 2, Geneva, 1986.

Table 11.5
Percentage of All Economically Active Persons Working in Each Major Occupational Group for Selected African Countries, by Sex, Early 1980s

Major Occupation	Male	Female	Total
Professional, technical, and related workers	5	5	5
Administrative and managerial workers	1	-	-
Clerical and related workers	5	4	5
Sales workers	5	2	4
Service workers	6	3	6
Agricultural sector: Agriculture, animal husbandry, forestry workers, and fishermen	57	78	62
Laborers: Production and related workers, transport equipment operators, and laborers	17	4	14
Workers not classified	4	4	4
Total	100	100	100

Source: Compiled from United Nations, *Demographic Yearbook 1984* (Sales No. E/F.85.XIII.1); and International Labour Office, *Yearbook of Labour Statistics*, Geneva, 1985.

Table 11.6
Percentage of All Economically Active Persons Working in Each Major Industrial Group for Selected African Countries, by Sex, Early 1980s

Major Industry	Male	Female	Total
Agriculture, hunting, forestry, and fishing	63	87	70
Mining and quarrying	1	--	--
Manufacturing	10	2	7
Electricity, gas, and water	--	--	--
Construction	3	--	2
Wholesale and retail trade	6	2	5
Transport, storage and communications	3	1	3
Financing, insurance, real estate, and business services	--	--	--
Community, social and personal services	11	6	10
Activities not defined	3	2	3
Total	100	100	100

Source: Compiled from United Nations, *Demographic Yearbook 1984* (Sales No. E.85.XIII.1).

Table 11.7
The Economically Active Population in Agriculture, Africa, 1950-2025

| Year | Agricultural Workers | | | | |
| | Number in Millions | | Percent Economically Active in Agriculture | | |
	Male	Female	Total	Male	Female
1950	50,186	31,022	82	78	88
1960	57,320	36,335	78	75	86
1970	65,862	43,931	74	70	83
1980	77,516	52,432	69	64	78
1985	84,429	56,726	66	61	76
1990	92,222	61,205	63	58	73
2000	110,637	72,345	57	52	68
2010	133,325	87,391	52	47	62

Table 11.7 (Continued)

| Year | Agricultural Workers | | |
	Number in Millions		Percent Economically Active in Agriculture
2020	158,924	106,013	47	42	57
2025	171,678	117,229	44	40	54

Source: Compiled from United Nations, *World Demographic Estimates and Projections, 1950-2025,* (ST/ESA/SER.R/79).

Projections indicate that Africa's economy will undergo marked modernization by 2025. For example, the relative number in the nonagricultural labor force is likely to be 56 percent, whereas the proportionate number in agriculture will probably decline to 44 percent by 2025. In the meantime, the relative number of informal sector workers may fall as low as 25 percent. These major changes are likely to increase the number of service workers by 10 or 15 percent and somewhat less in industry.

REFERENCES

Durand, John D. 1975. *The Labor Force in Economic Development: An International Comparison of Census Statistics.* Princeton, NJ: Princeton University Press.

Heller, Peter S. and Alan A. Tait. 1984. *Government Employment and Pay: Some International Comparisons.* Occasional Paper 24. Washington, DC: International Monetary Fund.

International Labour Office. 1976. *International Recommendations on Labour Statistics*, Geneva.

_____. 1985,1988. *Yearbook of Labour Statistics.* Geneva.

_____. 1986. *Economically Active Population Estimates and Projections, 1950-2025* Africa, vol. 2. Geneva.

International Labour Organization. 1985. *The Informal Sector in Africa: Jobs and Skills Programme for Africa.* Addis Ababa, Ethiopia.

Miller, H. Max, Ram N. Singh, and James D. Tarver. 1991. "Government Employment in the English-speaking Countries of Africa." *African Population Studies* 5: 48-64.

Standing, Guy. 1978. *Labour Force Participation and Development.* Geneva: ILO.

Trager, Lillian. 1987. "A Re-examination of the Urban Informal Sector in West Africa." *Canadian Journal of African Studies* 21: 238-255.

United Nations. 1986. *Demographic Yearbook 1984.* New York.

_____.1988. *World Demographic Estimates and Projections, 1950-2025.* New York.

12

Income and Economic Welfare in Africa

The amount of income that individuals, families, and households receive is the most sensitive measure of their economic well-being, as income is essential to provide the necessities and amenities of life. The income of the various countries in the world is derived from many sources and each country's total income is based upon a different "basket" of goods and services. Income is a crucial subject in Africa because this continent has the lowest per capita income of all major regions in the world. Rapid population growth coupled with low rates of economic growth have resulted in declining per capita incomes in many African countries.

SOURCES OF INCOME

Total income includes both cash income and income in kind. The main sources of cash income include salaries, wages, self-employment earnings, business profits, rental income, interest and dividends, royalties, commissions, pensions, annuities, social security benefits, unemployment benefits, and other similar sources. To cash income must be added various types of income in kind. For example, workers in non-cash family agriculture produce their living in a subsistence, barter economy. The International Labour Organization (1985) estimates that from a quarter to a third of the total African urban income comes from the informal sector, comprised of petty, labor-intensive enterprises. For example, many women supplement their cash incomes with informal sector activities such as street food vending, beer brewing, and the sale of cigarettes and matches.

COLLECTION OF INCOME DATA

Two different methods are employed in the collection of income data. The first method uses a national accounts approach and the second obtains income data from individuals and households in censuses and surveys (UN, 1985).

National Accounts Statistics

National accounts statistics are collected annually for each country, and great uniformity and comparability has been achieved (UN, 1990). These statistics provide data for economic development measures expressed in rates of gross domestic product, economic structure expressed in terms of the shares of gross domestic product, and the measurement of capital formation by type of finance.

The United Nations (1985), the International Monetary Fund (1986), the Organization for Economic Co-operation and Development (1986), the World Bank (1984, 1986), and the United Nations Economic Commission for Africa (1987), as well as the statistical offices of the individual African countries (for example, Botswana: *Rural*, 1976 and *National*, 1984), have published various series of national accounts income data.

The United Nations system of national accounts uses Gross Domestic Product (GDP) per capita and the Gross National Product (GNP) per capita as measures of the average income of each country. The GDP includes the value of all production within a country both to residents and nonresidents. On the other hand, the GNP measures the total domestic and foreign production of the residents of a country. For example, it includes payments to residents from abroad, such as remittances to migrant workers. However, it excludes payments to foreigners, such as profits earned by foreign companies and the earnings of short-term expatriates. The essential difference is that the GDP of a country is equivalent to the GNP minus the gross product which originates outside the country.

The national accounts system also estimates the total private consumption of each country. Private consumption expressed in the GNP at factor cost (market price) is a measure of economic welfare and an indicator of spending power since it reflects personal disposable income.

Individual and Household Income Statistics

The second method of collecting income data uses censuses and surveys to obtain the figures (UN, 1985). From income data obtained in interviews it is possible to compute various averages and measures and display the figures in various distributions. For example, the percentage of individuals earning different amounts can be computed, the inequality of income may be determined, and the percentages living in poverty can be estimated. Moreover, the changing income distributions may be studied over time to determine whether certain gaps are narrowing or widening.

Income distribution statistics for individuals and households have been collected by the United Nations (1985), the International Labour Organization (1979), the Food and Agricultural Organization (1983), and World Bank (1986), and under the auspices of national governments and other agencies through sample surveys.

Income distribution statistics collected in censuses and surveys for individuals and households can be ranked into percentile groups by total household income. The extent of poverty and of affluence in each country depends, of course, not only upon the average level of income but also the extent of inequality in its distribution.

Both major methods of collecting income data provide important information about different aspects of the economic status of people. The collection of distribution-type income data for individuals and households has been neglected in recent years, making it impossible to calculate certain measures.

REGIONAL AND WORLD INCOME ESTIMATES

Per capita income estimates based upon population and total GDP statistics serve as the basis for examining income trends and differentials in the major regions of the world (table 12.1). These income estimates in constant prices between 1970 and 1987 were made in 1980 U.S. dollars.

Both the total GDP and the per capita GDP of most major regions experienced relatively large gains between 1970 and 1980. Then, the growth leveled off after 1980 due to a worldwide recession. Between 1980 and 1983 oil price increases contributed to the rising inflation and unemployment. A recovery followed the recession with declines in oil prices, real interest rates, and inflation, although unemployment remained relatively high throughout 1985.

Per capita GDP was about seven percent higher in 1987 than in 1980 in constant prices throughout the world except in Africa and Latin America. Africa had the lowest per capita GDP of all major regions in the world and was only 27 percent of the 1987 world average. In terms of constant prices Africa's per capita GDP income declined 11 percent between 1980 and 1987.

INCOMES OF THE AFRICAN COUNTRIES

Annual per capita GDP income estimates were made in constant 1980 U.S. dollars for 1970, 1975, 1980, 1985, and 1987 for 53 of the 56 African countries, all except St. Helena, Eritrea, and Western Sahara.

In Africa the per capita GDP income in constant 1980 U.S. dollars increased from $730 in 1970 to $798 in 1975, then to $844 in 1980. By 1987 the average GDP income fell to $748 in constant dollars, a decline of more than 10 percent since 1980 (table 12.2).

There were pronounced regional variations in the average per capita incomes during 1970 to 1987. The residents of Southern Africa, for example, had by far the highest per capita incomes throughout the period. In 1987, the average GDP per capita income of Southern Africa was $1,847 in constant 1980 U.S. dollars. The 1987 per capita income of the inhabitants of North Africa was about 70 percent as high, with an average of $1,285.

West Africa was next highest with an average of $626, and Middle Africa was next with an average of $404 in 1987. Finally, East Africa was the poorest with an average of only $341 in constant 1987 dollars (table 12.2).

The different regions experienced divergent trends in average incomes during 1970 to 1987. In Southern and North Africa the average 1987 per capita incomes were higher than in 1970. In contrast, the 1970 average incomes in the other three regions were higher than in 1987.

Southern Africa

The South region had the highest average per capita income of all regions throughout 1970 to 1987. For example, the 1987 GDP income of $1,847 in constant U.S. dollars was nearly two and one-half times that of the average for Africa as a whole.

Per capita income in the Republic of South Africa has been relatively high, ranging from $1,908 in 1970 to $1,978 in 1987. Since 90 percent of the total population of this five-country region lives in the Republic of South Africa, it exerts a dominant influence upon the average income for the southern region as a whole. As a result of sustained development, the United Nations now considers the Republic of South Africa as a developed country, the only developed nation in Africa.

Botswana's per capita income more than tripled, going from $546 in 1970 to $1,767 in 1987. Diamond mining has been mainly responsible for the major gains in income. Also, the average per capita income of Swaziland nearly doubled during this period. Per capita incomes generally increased in Lesotho but declined in Namibia.

Northern Africa

North Africa had the second highest average per capita income of all regions, with the incomes among its six countries varying considerably. Libya, an OPEC country, had the highest income of all African countries, with an average of $5,898 in 1987. In 1980 its per capita GDP rose to nearly $11,700 but then declined. Unlike the Republic of South Africa, Libya is the least populous country in its region, so its high income doesn't greatly affect the overall northern regional average.

Table 12.1
Total and Per Capita Gross Domestic Product in Constant 1980 U.S. Dollars, by Major Regions of the World, 1970-87

Major Region	In Billions of Dollars Total Gross Domestic Product/Net Material Product					Per Capita Gross Domestic Product/in Constant U.S. Dollars				
	1970	1975	1980	1985	1987	1970	1975	1980	1985	1987
WORLD	7,943	9,559	11,527	13,104	13,958	2,148	2,343	2,591	2,701	2,779
Africa	264	330	403	430	439	730	798	844	778	748
Europe	3,421	4,073	4,809	5,303	5,605	7,438	8,599	9,927	10,774	11,328
North America	2,220	2,509	2,952	3,398	3,627	9,802	10,506	11,718	12,833	13,463
Latin America	501	664	854	888	943	1,754	2,053	2,355	2,197	2,237
Asia	1,397	1,817	2,325	2,867	3,114	665	772	900	1,011	1,058
Oceania	140	166	186	217	231	7,243	7,845	8,158	8,826	9,116
Former Soviet Republics	427	560	700	833	889	1,759	2,201	2,636	3,001	3,151

Source: Computed from United Nations, National Accounts Statistics: Analysis of Main Aggregates, 1987 (Sales No. E.90.XVII.8).

Algeria, an OPEC member like Libya, had the second highest per capita GDP income of $2,433 in 1987. (Algeria, Tunisia, Egypt, and Libya are oil exporting countries, with Algeria and Libya being OPEC members.) Algeria's per capita income increased nearly 50 percent between 1970 and 1985. Tunisia had the third highest income, with a 1987 average of $1,461. Morocco and Egypt followed, with averages of approximately $900 to $1,000, and Sudan was lowest, with a 1987 per capita income of $457 in constant 1980 dollars. Sudan's per capita income declined about 20 percent in the 1970-87 period.

Western Africa

Inhabitants of the west region had the third highest per capita income in 1987, with an average of $626. The average GDP rose from $749 in 1970 to $847 in 1975, then declined to $626 in 1987. In fact, Senegal, Cape Verde, and Guinea-Bissau were the only West African countries to have higher per capita incomes in 1987 than in 1980 (table 12.2).

Residents of the Côte d'Ivoire had the highest GDP of all countries, with an average of slightly more than $1,000 in 1987. Nigeria (an OPEC member) was next highest, with a per capita income of $783 in 1987. Senegal and Cape Verde followed with 1987 per capita incomes of $500 to $550. Finally, Burkina Faso, Mali, Guinea, and Sierra Leone had the lowest incomes of the 17-country region, with 1987 averages of less than $300 in constant 1980 U.S. dollars.

Middle Africa

Middle Africa, with the fourth highest per capita GDP of the five regions, had an average income of $404 in 1987. Gabon, an OPEC member, consistently had high per capita incomes throughout the 1970-87 period. However, Gabon's 1987 per capita income was less than half its 1975 average. The Congo and Cameroon, both oil exporters, had substantial increases in their incomes during 1970-85 and ranked just below Gabon in 1987. Angola was next highest, with a 1987 per capita income of $405; the Central African Republic, São Tomé and Príncipe, Equatorial Guinea, Zaire, and Chad had per capita incomes of approximately $300 or less. During this 17-year period Angola and Chad experienced sizable declines in income due to unrest and instability.

Eastern Africa

This 18-country region had the lowest per capita income of the five regions, with an average of $341 in 1987. The region's income in constant U.S. dollars declined almost 20 percent after 1970, falling from $419 in 1970 to $341 in 1987.

Three small island countries in the Indian Ocean had relatively high per capita incomes. For example, Réunion, with a per capita income of $4,748 in 1987, was the second highest of all African countries. Réunion is a *departement* of France and receives substantial monies by virtue of this status. Seychelles, with a 1987 per capita income of $2,463, had the fourth highest income, and Mauritius, with a per capita income of $1,662, ranked eighth highest. In contrast, a half dozen East African countries had average 1987 incomes of less than $300.

POPULATION AND ECONOMIC GROWTH IN AFRICA

Studies of the impact of population change upon economic development have been inconclusive, since there are demographic influences on economic growth as well as the effects of economic growth on population change (McNicoll, 1982; Cassen, 1976). Investigations undertaken about 20 years ago indicated that high rates of population growth in the African countries were likely to hinder economic growth in the short run (UNECA, 1968, 1969, 1971). Since the association of the two variables has not been precisely established, the relationship will be examined here because the African countries not only have the highest rates of population growth of all countries in the world but also the lowest per capita income.

In analyzing the relationship of population growth and economic development, nonagricultural income at constant prices in each country's currency was used as the measure of economic growth. This measure excludes the entire agricultural subsistence sector, the income from which is practically impossible to estimate. Population growth was related to change in total nonagricultural income first, then to changes in per capita nonagricultural income. The significance of the relationship between population and economic growth was tested by computing simple coefficients of correlation for the time series of data reported for each country. Every correlation coefficient large enough to be significant at the five percent level was considered statistically significant.

It is impossible to estimate reliably the value of the total annual production of subsistence agriculture in the African countries. Usually an estimate of subsistence income per capita is multiplied by the estimated number of persons in subsistence agriculture to obtain an estimate of its total value in each country. When a large majority of the population in engaged in subsistence agriculture as in Africa, population data enter for a substantial proportion of the GDP. For this reason, nonagricultural income was selected as the index of economic growth.

Definite relationships were found between population growth and economic growth. For example, there was an increase in both population and total nonagricultural incomes in constant prices after 1950 in most of the 44 countries reporting nonagricultural income, although there were a few exceptions (table 12.3). In 39 of the countries population growth and total nonagricultural income were positively related, with 33 of the correlation coefficients significant. This direct association clearly indicates that population growth and economic growth occurred simultaneously. Nevertheless, this does not necessarily imply that growth in either produced the growth in the other in a strictly causal way.

Only five of the 44 countries did not conform to the overall direct relationships between income and population growth. For example, nonagricultural income in Angola reached its peak in 1973, fell to less than half in 1975, then remained somewhat constant due to instability and unrest. Also, Chad's nonagricultural income peaked in 1977, then fell to less than 40 percent of that value. In Angola, Chad, Uganda, São Tomé and Príncipe, and Zaire population growth was accompanied by declining nonagricultural income. However, only one of the negative coefficients of correlation was large enough to be significant, that for São Tomé and Príncipe.

Population growth and per capita nonagricultural income were positively associated in 30 of the 44 countries, with 27 of the correlation coefficients significant (table 12.3). Only in Malawi, Rwanda, and Zimbabwe were the positive relationships statistically insignificant. Per capita nonagricultural income was negatively related to population growth in 14 of Africa's 44 countries, with the following nine correlation coefficients being significant: Ghana, Zambia, Madagascar, Uganda, Zaire, Angola, Chad, Liberia, and São Tomé and Príncipe.

During 1950-81 rapid population growth generally occurred in the countries with relatively large increases in nonagricultural income. As a result, there tended to be a direct association between population growth and economic growth. There were a few exceptions, of course, especially in countries experiencing pronounced unrest and strife.

POPULATION AND ECONOMIC WELFARE IN AFRICA

The relationship of population growth and economic welfare was investigated to determine whether disposable income and spending power increased with population growth. Private consumption in constant prices was employed as the measure of economic welfare, as it is an indicator of the spending power of people and reflects their personal disposable income. The definition of economic welfare used is that of private consumption expressed in the GNP at factor cost in constant prices.

Population growth and total private consumption in constant dollars were positively related in 44 of the 47 countries studied (table 12.3). Only in Angola, Chad, and Guinea-Bissau did population growth occur while total private consumption declined, with Guinea-Bissau being the only country with a significant negative correlation coefficient. Both total nonagricultural income and total private consumption declined sharply in Angola and Chad, whereas Guinea-Bissau experienced a decline only in private consumption.

In 32 of the 47 countries per capita private consumption was positively related to population growth, with 22 of the correlation coefficients significant (table 12.3). Per capita consumption declined as population growth occurred in the other 15 countries, with the negative correlation coefficients being significant for Guinea-Bissau, Madagascar, Ghana, Angola, Mozambique, and the Congo.

During 1950-81 population growth was positively related to both increases in nonagricultural income and in private consumption (Tarver, 1986). In countries characterized by instability and unrest (such as Angola and Chad) these patterns were not apparent. Obviously, political strife, along with rapid population growth, has hindered economic development and contributed to declines in personal disposable income.

POVERTY AND INCOME DISTRIBUTION

Certainly, poverty is concentrated in countries with low per capita incomes such as Mozambique and Chad, each with 1987 per capita GDPs of less than $150 in constant 1980 U.S. dollars. Persons in poverty are those with incomes insufficient to meet the basic needs for food, clothing, shelter, medical care, and other necessities.

The International Labour Organization estimated that 205 million, or 68 percent, of the sub-Saharan Africans were living in poverty in 1974 (table 12.4). By 2000 probably 215 million will be in poverty. Several different estimates of poverty exist (International Confederation of Free Trade Unions, 1984). The United Nations (1990) estimated that one-third of the urban residents of sub-Saharan Africa were living below the poverty line and nearly two-thirds of the rural people were below the poverty line during 1977-87. The World Bank (1990) estimated that 47 percent of the 480 million inhabitants in sub-Saharan Africa were poor and two-thirds of them were in extreme poverty in 1985.

According to the ILO estimates Zambia had the greatest concentration of poverty of 10 selected countries, with 60 percent of its residents in poverty in 1980 (table 12.5). In eight of these countries rural residents experienced much higher poverty levels than urban residents. Only in Sierra Leone did the living conditions of rural residents compare favorably with urban inhabitants.

Historically, most Africans with high incomes were concentrated in cities which created marked rural-urban income differences (Jamal and Weeks, 1988). Although some scholars contend that the rural-urban income gap has narrowed, table 12.5 does not show that rural-urban poverty differentials have disappeared. Clearly, table 12.5 illustrates substantial rural-urban disparities in poverty levels in 1970-80 in several African countries. Some scholars have suggested that the income gap between the comparatively rich and the poor may have widened with rising incomes, since increasing income levels often help the poor very little.

Table 12.2
Per Capita Gross Domestic Product Income Estimates in Constant 1980 U.S. Dollars, by Countries and Regions, Africa, 1970-87

Country and Region	1970	1975	Per Capita Domestic Product 1980	1985	1987
AFRICA	730	798	844	778	748
Northern Africa	913	1,024	1,310	1,328	1,285
Algeria	1,647	1,791	2,259	2,477	2,433
Egypt	336	404	599	833	870
Libya	8,184	9,599	11,696	7,550	5,898
Morocco	687	788	980	979	976
Sudan	578	567	545	459	457
Tunisia	842	1,146	1,369	1,478	1,461
Eastern Africa	419	412	372	343	341
Burundi	208	205	230	255	261
Comoros	456	428	355	367	366
Djibouti	1,655	1,432	1,115	1,023	1,000
Ethiopia	104	106	106	94	198
Kenya	370	380	426	401	415
Madagascar	439	402	372	301	291

Malawi	130	172	200	187	177
Mauritius	762	1,061	1,172	1,394	1,662
Mozambique	283	229	200	110	114
Réunion	2,567	2,988	3,935	4,488	4,748
Rwanda	140	183	225	221	211
Seychelles	1,604	1,729	2,333	2,369	2,463
Somalia	619	647	515	538	537
Tanzania	266	281	272	234	341
Uganda	1,511	1,339	948	838	546
Zambia	825	804	677	567	527
Zimbabwe	775	834	751	783	757
Middle Africa	546	535	500	519	404
Angola	934	514	449	456	405
Cameroon	747	778	983	1,169	823
Central African Republic	453	399	384	365	312
Chad	296	323	224	160	144
Congo	989	1,040	1,022	1,475	1,042
Equatorial Guinea	643	516	253	202	187
Gabon	3,901	6,909	5,311	4,213	3,126
São Tomé & Príncipe	699	506	500	308	310

Table 12.2 (Continued)

Country and Region	1970	Per Capita Domestic Product			
		1975	1980	1985	1987
Zaire	308	300	234	218	184
Southern Africa	1,770	1,923	1,964	1,862	1,847
Botswana	546	779	1,127	1,681	1,767
Lesotho	171	203	285	260	277
Namibia	1,666	1,645	1,537	1,237	1,232
South Africa	1,908	2,069	2,109	1,996	1,978
Swaziland	516	923	964	911	914
Western Africa	749	847	843	668	626
Benin	352	378	336	303	309
Burkina Faso	158	177	185	176	180
Cape Verde	393	335	360	466	512
Côte d'Ivoire	980	1,090	1,242	1,070	1,022
Gambia	315	398	373	325	341
Ghana	522	465	446	365	375
Guinea	303	326	358	264	261
Guinea-Bissau	394	367	286	289	307
Liberia	536	518	489	383	342

Nigeria	1,004	1,170	1,125	856	783
Mali	213	214	243	216	238
Mauritania	572	591	534	495	493
Niger	389	345	454	374	353
Nigeria	1,004	1,170	1,125	856	783
Senegal	603	587	536	541	552
Sierra Leone	366	351	377	330	290
Togo	434	423	433	366	361

Source: United Nations, *National Accounts Statistics: Analysis of Main Aggregates, 1987* (Sales No. E.90.XVII.8).

Table 12.3
Correlation Coefficients of Population and Nonagricultural Income and Private Consumption, 1950-81

| | Simple Correlation Coefficients | | | |
| | Population and Nonagricultural Income | | Population and Private Consumption | |
Country	Total	Per Capita	Total	Per Capita
Algeria	.87	.68	.95	.92
Angola	-.27	-.56	-.27	-.68
Benin	.97	.77	.94	-.30
Botswana	.98	.99	.98	.97
Burkina Faso	.98	.98	.92	.76
Burundi	.95	.88	.96	.83
Cameroon	.93	.90	.93	.11
Cape Verde			.58	-.07
Central African Republic	.84	-.00	.77	.18
Chad	-.52	-.70	-.01	-.08
Congo	.95	.85	.68	-.60
Côte d'Ivoire	.99	.76	.98	.23

Egypt	.98	.92	.96	.95
Ethiopia	.88	.60	.99	.97
Gabon			.96	.97
Gambia	.94	.99	.80	.39
Ghana	.41	-.93	.78	-.79
Guinea	.99	.98	.33	-.36
Guinea-Bissau	.97	.91	-.73	-.96
Kenya	.98	.88	.97	.68
Lesotho	.87	.79	.95	.92
Liberia	.27	-.72	.76	-.29
Libya	.73	-.11	.99	.89
Madagascar	.30	-.87	.61	-.86
Malawi	.99	.00	.99	.97
Mali	.74	.57	.97	.84
Mauritania	.85	.51	.94	.42
Mauritius	.95	.92	.85	.73
Morocco	.97	.93	.99	.95
Mozambique	.15	-.46	.37	-.61

Table 12.3 (Continued)

	Simple Correlation Coefficients			
	Population and Nonagricultural Income		Population and Private Consumption	
Country	Total	Per Capita	Total	Per Capita
Niger	.91	.69	.54	-.48
Nigeria	.96	.93	.95	.85
Rwanda	.26	.22	.96	.52
São Tomé & Príncipe	-.38	-.54	.17	.11
Senegal	.90	-.38	.93	.15
Sierra Leone	.89	-.16	.98	.75
Somalia	.96	.79	.96	-.24
South Africa			.98	.50
Sudan	.93	.84	.93	.24
Swaziland	.98	.89	.89	.81
Tanzania	.97	.79	.99	.97
Togo	.97	.86	.89	.87
Tunisia	.99	.99	.99	.86
Uganda	-.38	-.86	.89	.26
Zaire	-.36	-.81	.11	-.21

Simple Correlation Coefficients

Country	Population and Nonagricultural Income		Population and Private Consumption	
	Total	Per Capita	Total	Per Capita
Zambia	.07	-.89	.93	.24
Zimbabwe	.78	.15	.61	-.14

1. Not significant at the five percent level.

Source: Computed from nonagricultural income and private consumption estimates from the World Bank, *World Tables* (Baltimore: Johns Hopkins University, 1983).

Table 12.4
Estimates of Poverty in Sub-Saharan Africa, 1974-2000

Year	Total Population (Millions)	Poverty of Food		Poverty of Basic Needs	
		Population (Millions)	Percent	Population (Millions)	Percent
1974	303	116	38	205	68
1982	370	124	34	200	54
1987	420	131	31	221	53
2000	583	147	25	215	37

Source: Compiled from the International Confederation of Free Trade Unions, *The African Worker and the World Economic Crisis*, Dakar, 1984.

Table 12.5
Poverty Estimates of the Rural and Urban Inhabitants of Selected African Countries

Country	Year	Entire Country	Urban Population	Rural Population
Botswana	1974-78	46	----	----
Gabon	1975	15	----	----
Ghana	1970	----	----	50
Kenya	1976	32	8	38
Lesotho	1978	30-40	33	30-40
Nigeria	1978	24	24	40
Rwanda	1975	39	30	60
Sierra Leone	1977	45	56	40
Tanzania	1980	30	19	33
Zambia	1980	60	25	80

Source: Compiled from the International Confederation of Free Trade Unions, *The African Worker and the World Economic Crisis*, Dakar, 1984.

Table 12.6
The Inequality of Income Distribution in Selected African Countries

Country	Year	Percentage of Total Household Income of the	
		Lowest 40 Percent	Highest 20 Percent
Malawi	1967-68	21.5	50.6
Tanzania	1969	16.0	50.4
Kenya	1976	8.9	60.4
Sierra Leone	1967-69	15.1	52.5
Sudan	1967-68	12.9	49.3
Zambia	1976	10.8	61.1
Egypt	1974	16.5	48.0
Mauritius	1980-81	11.5	60.5

Source: Compiled from the World Bank, *World Development Report 1984 and 1986*

(New York: Oxford University Press).

In the early stages of development countries tend to have relatively few persons in their middle classes. Evidence indicates that the initial inequality in income distribution usually increases in the early phases of development, levels off, then reverses itself in the advanced stages (Kuznets, 1955, 1963). In many cases, however, the poor in rural areas benefit little from economic growth at any stage of development.

Another set of poverty estimates for 15 African countries (five of which were also included in table 12.5) suggests that between 10 to 70 percent of the inhabitants of some countries were living in poverty in 1975 (Ahluwalia, et al., 1979). For example, over 60 percent of the residents of Ethiopia were estimated to be living below the poverty level, about half of those in Uganda, Zaire, Sudan, Tanzania, and Kenya, and approximately a third of those in Nigeria and Senegal. Four other countries had around a fifth to a fourth in poverty and a couple had only 10 percent, a comparatively low percentage for African countries.

Of the six African countries with half or more of their inhabitants below the poverty level in 1975, Ethiopia, Tanzania, and Kenya had experienced annual GDP per capita growth rates of 1.4 to 2.8 percent since 1960 (Ahluwalia et al., 1979). This economic growth brought few benefits to the poor in these countries, however.

World Bank estimates (1984, 1986) provide further evidence of the inequality of income distribution. For example, the income share of the poorest 40 percent of the households in eight countries was only about 10 to 15 percent of the total household income (table 12.6). The percentage of income received ranged from a low of nearly nine in Kenya households to nearly 22 in the Malawi households. In contrast, the wealthiest 20 percent of the households received about 50 to 60 percent of the total household income. The fairly high per capita incomes of a few African countries suggest that the inequality of income distribution between the rich and poor may have actually widened with increasing income, perpetuating widespread poverty.

SUMMARY AND IMPLICATIONS

Economic development in Africa will continue to progress very slowly as long as the population grows more rapidly than its income. For example, since 1980 the number of inhabitants increased about three times faster than the total GDP, resulting in a decline in per capita GDP income. Africa's per capita income has been the lowest of all major regions in the world since 1980. Oil exports have raised the incomes appreciably in only two countries, Gabon and Libya.

There are marked differences in the average incomes of the countries and regions of Africa. For example, the southern region had by far the highest income of all regions and North Africa had the next highest income. The other three regions had considerably lower incomes throughout 1970 to 1987.

190 The Demography of Africa

Population growth was positively related to economic growth and economic welfare during 1950-81. Since many factors stimulate population and economic growth, it is impossible to assign primary causes to any one variable. Certainly the policies of individual governments play crucial roles. The underlying importance of political stability in economic development has been widely observed (Reynolds, 1985). Certain African countries have had relatively stable political and social conditions since independence and economic growth and economic welfare were closely related to population growth. In contrast, some countries that experienced instability and unrest suffered declining per capita nonagricultural income and declining per capita private consumption. Political strife definitely hindered economic development and resulted in declines in per capita personal disposable income in a number of countries like Angola and Chad, although high rates of population growth continued.

REFERENCES

Ahluwalia, Montek S. et al. 1979. "Growth and Poverty in Developing Countries." *Journal of Development Economics* 6: 299-341.
Cassen, Robert H. 1976. "Population and Development: A Survey." *World Development* 4:785-830.
Food and Agricultural Organization. 1983. *An International Comparison of Household Income Distribution: A Provisional Report*. Rome.
International Confederation of Free Trade Unions. 1984. *The African Worker and the World Economic Crisis*. Dakar, Senegal.
International Labour Organization. 1979. *Household Income and Expenditure Statistics, 1968-1976*. Geneva.
_____. 1985. *The Informal Sector in Africa: Jobs and Skills Programme for Africa*. Addis Ababa, Ethiopia.
International Monetary Fund. 1986. *International Financial Statistics*. Washington, DC.
Jamal, Vali, and John Weeks. 1988. "The Vanishing Rural-Urban Gap in Sub-Saharan Africa." *International Labour Review* 127: 271-292.
Kuznets, Simon. 1955. "Economic Growth and Income Inequality." *American Economic Review* 49: 1-28.
_____. 1963. "Quantitative Aspects of the Economic Growth of Nations VIII: Distribution of Income by Size." *Economic Development and Cultural Change* 11: 1-80.
McNicoll, Geoffrey. 1982. "Population and Development." In *International Encyclopedia of Population*, edited by John A. Ross, 519-525. New York: Free Press.
National Accounts of Botswana 1981/82. 1984. Gaborone, Botswana: Ministry of Finance and Development Planning, Central Statistics Office.

Organization for Economic Co-operation and Development. 1986a. *National Accounts of OECD Countries Main Aggregates*, vol. 1. Paris.

_____. 1986b. *National Accounts of OECD Countries*. Detailed Tables, vol. 2. Paris.

Reynolds, Lloyd G. 1985. *Economic Growth in the Third World, 1850-1980*. New Haven: Yale University Press.

Rural Income Distribution Survey in Botswana 1974/75. 1976. Gaborone, Botswana: Government Printer.

Tarver, James D. 1986. "Population and Economic Growth and Welfare in Africa." *Africa Quarterly* 23: 43-58.

United Nations. 1990. *National Account Statistics: Analysis of Main Aggregates, 1987*. New York.

_____. 1985. *National Accounts Statistics: Compendium of Income Distribution Statistics*. New York.

_____. 1990. *Human Development Report, 1990*. New York: Oxford University Press.

United Nations. Economic Commission for Africa. 1968,1969,1971. *A Survey of Economic Conditions in Africa*. New York.

_____. Economic Commission for Africa. 1987. *Gross Domestic Product in Current Market and Constant Prices*. Addis Ababa.

The World Bank. 1984,1986,1990. *World Development Reports, 1984, 1986 and 1990*. New York: Oxford University Press.

13

Education of the Population

Literacy and education are indispensable for development and advancement, for there must be enough engineers, physicians, teachers, and various types of scientists and other professionals to manage the complex administration of each nation's economic and political structure. The educational level of a country is exceedingly important, as well-educated workers are increasingly essential for productive occupations and careers. A country with a high proportion of illiterates is poorly prepared to cope with modern technology. Yet, 178 million Africans 15 years of age and over were illiterate in 1990 (UNESCO, 1990). This means that over half (50.1 percent) of the adult population was unable to read and write. The number of illiterate adult Africans is projected to reach 186 million by 2000.

According to Duncan, Featherman, and Duncan (1972), educational attainment is a very significant socioeconomic variable. Education usually has a greater explanatory power of demographic characteristics than other measures of social status such as occupation and income. For example, as educational attainment increases the age at marriage also increases, and the average number of births per woman become progressively smaller (World Fertility Survey, 1983a, 1983b). Moreover, education is highly related to mortality, especially infant mortality (Caldwell, 1979).

For these and other related reasons, this chapter examines Africa's educational institutions, the changing school enrollments and educational attainment of its inhabitants, the major changes in teaching staffs, and expenditures on public education which support this important educational effort.

SCHOOL ENROLLMENT

In 1987 over 932 million children were attending school throughout the world, 51 percent more than in 1970 (tables 13.1, 13.2). Enrollments in developing countries accounted for three-fourths of all students in 1987. Moreover, the number of students in developing countries increased over 75 percent, whereas those in developed countries increased only five percent during 1970-87. Obviously, the much greater increase in the developing areas was due both to the relatively higher birth rates as well as to the larger increases in the proportions enrolled in school.

The largest relative enrollment increases of all major regions in the world occurred in Africa, especially in the sub-Saharan countries (table 13.2). Moreover, Africa experienced the largest proportionate increases in the number of students in each of primary, secondary, and university levels in 1970-87 (table 13.3), as many African countries implemented policies to raise the educational levels of their youths.   During this period total school enrollments in North America in the first and second levels actually declined, while Europe experienced a 15 percent decline in first-level enrollments. Between 1970 and 1987, the number of first-level students in developing countries increased about 50 percent, the number of second-level students increased nearly 150 percent, and the number of third-level students in universities and other institutions of higher education increased over 275 percent (table 13.2). Obviously, these relatively large gains reflect an increasing retention of youths in school and, of course, a higher educational attainment.

The proportionate number of children in school has risen at all levels since 1960 throughout the world (table 13.3). Nevertheless, the strides have been much greater in developing than in developed countries. In Africa, for example, the relative number of children attending school at all levels practically doubled between 1960 and 1987. Even so, developed countries had relatively twice as many attending second-level schools as developing countries in 1987 and also had about four times as many students, comparatively, attending third-level institutions.

In all regions of the world except Asia and Africa boys and girls attend schools at the primary, secondary, and university levels in approximately equal numbers. However, equality of educational opportunity does not exist for African and Asian girls, as they are underrepresented in schools at almost all levels (table 13.3). However, African female students in each level increased much more rapidly than male students even though the traditional patterns of giving preferences to educating boys was still evident. For example, the number of females in African schools almost tripled from 1960 to 1987, whereas the number of males in school just about doubled.

African girls have indeed made impressive gains in school attendance and enrollment since 1960. For example, in that year only 31 percent of the primary-level girls were in school. However, 68 percent were in school in 1987. Only three percent of the secondary-level girls were in school in 1960. By 1987 this proportion had risen to 23 percent. Overall, 38 percent of all African school-age girls were enrolled in 1987 compared to only 14 percent in 1960.

Moreover, the proportionate number of second and third-level students in the Arab countries of Africa have increased much more rapidly than in the non-Arab countries. Nearly three times as many African girls of school age were enrolled in 1987 as in 1960. Rapid educational advancements for young African females seem likely to continue.

EDUCATIONAL ATTAINMENT

Illiteracy is most highly concentrated in the developing regions of the world, mainly in Africa and Asia. It continues to handicap the 178 million adults in Africa unable to read and write (table 13.4). Educational facilities have been quite limited since the colonial period due to poverty, inaccessibility, and an inarticulated demand. For example, 27 African countries had illiteracy rates of 50 percent or more in 1990, with more than 75 percent of the inhabitants in Burkina Faso, Sierra Leone, Benin, Guinea, and Somalia being illiterate (UNESCO, 1990). Only five countries had illiteracy rates of less than 30 percent. Of these, St. Helena had the lowest rate, with less than five percent unable to read and write.

The ability to read and write is very important but certainly is not the most precise measure of educational level nor attainment. Rather, a much more appropriate index of educational level is the amount of formal education a person has completed.

Educational attainment is, of course, very low in the African countries. Of the 27 countries that reported school levels, the most highly educated were residents of South Africa. There, 54 percent of all white South African youths were enrolled in secondary school, 46 percent of the Asian students, 29 percent of the coloured students, and 19 percent of the African youths. Seychelles had nine percent with a secondary education. Mauritius, Swaziland, and Liberia ranked next highest. At the other extreme, in 10 of the 27 African countries 80 percent or more of the adult population had never attended school. In Mauritius, Seychelles, and Lesotho about a quarter to a third were without any schooling whatever. There are probably eight to 10 countries in which at least 75 percent of the adult population is unable to read and write.

Many government schools face serious problems such as inadequate staffing and lack of qualified teachers, shortage of teaching and learning materials, poor home environment, overcrowded classes, shortage of equipment and furniture, great distances from homes to schools, and serious socioeconomic problems for the unemployed parents.

Table 13.1
Total School Enrollment for the Major Regions of the World, by Level of Education, 1970-87

Major Region	Number Enrolled (In Thousands) By Level and Year							
	Total		First Level		Second Level		Third Level	
	1987	1970	1987	1970	1987	1970	1987	1970
WORLD TOTAL	932,066	615,944	582,767	430,147	289,982	157,700	59,316	28,097
Developed Countries	227,998	217,682	106,171	119,212	90,268	77,691	31,558	20,779
Developing Countries	704,068	398,262	476,596	310,935	199,714	80,009	27,758	7,318
Africa (total)	91,034	34,226	68,321	29,371	20,650	4,454	2,063	401
Africa (non-Arab States)	63,036	22,451	50,976	20,331	11,431	2,019	629	101
Africa (Arab States)	27,998	11,775	17,345	9,040	9,219	2,435	1,434	300
Asia	531,623	324,012	345,192	242,939	165,442	74,186	20,989	6,886
Latin America	101,443	56,286	71,816	46,576	22,769	8,070	6,859	1,640
Europe (incl. USSR)	142,694	135,396	64,549	76,226	63,099	49,364	15,046	9,806

Major Region	Total		First Level		Second Level		Third Level	
	1987	1970	1987	1970	1987	1970	1987	1970
North America	60,283	61,837	30,296	32,445	16,159	20,252	13,827	9,140
Oceania	4,989	4,188	2,594	2,590	1,863	1,374	533	224

Number Enrolled (In Thousands) By Level and Year

Source: Compiled from various editions of the *UNESCO Statistical Yearbook*.
As defined by the UNESCO in these tables the Arab states include the
following nine countries: Algeria, Djibouti, Egypt, Libya, Mauritania,
Morocco, Somalia, Sudan, and Tunisia.
The remaining 46 non-Arab countries are approximately equivalent to
sub-Saharan Africa.

Table 13.2
Percentage Changes in Total Enrollment for the Major Regions of the World, by Level of Education, 1970-87

Major Region	Total	First Level	Second Level	Third Level
WORLD TOTAL	51	35	84	111
Developed Countries	5	-11	16	52
Developing Countries	77	53	150	279
Africa (Total)	166	133	364	414
Africa (Non-Arab States)	181	151	466	523
Africa (Arab States)	138	92	279	378
ASIA	64	42	123	205
Latin America	80	54	182	318
Europe (Incl. USSR)	5	-15	28	53
North America	-2	-7	-20	51
Oceania	19	0	36	138

Source: Compiled from UNESCO, *Statistical Yearbook, 1989*, Paris.

Table 13.3
Adjusted Gross Enrollment Ratios of Youths for the Major Regions of the World,
by Level of Education and Sex, 1960-87 (percentage)

Major Region	Year	Percentage Enrolled by Level							
		Total		First Level		Second Level		Third Level	
		M	F	M	F	M	F	M	F
WORLD TOTAL	1960	51	39	95	73	31	24	7	4
	1980	60	50	100	88	50	39	13	10
	1987	61	51	100	93	54	43	14	11
Developed Countries	1960	69	65	100	100	62	60	17	10
	1980	74	74	100	100	83	86	31	29
	1987	77	77	100	100	91	92	34	34
Developing Countries	1960	44	29	90	61	20	11	3	1
	1980	56	44	100	85	42	29	7	4
	1987	57	46	100	91	47	33	9	6
Africa (Total)	1960	26	14	54	31	7	3	1	.3
	1980	49	36	90	69	29	17	5	2
	1987	51	38	84	68	39	23	6	3
Africa (Non-Arab States)	1960	24	13	51	30	5	2	1	.1
	1980	48	35	90	71	24	14	3	1
	1987	48	36	82	68	34	18	4	1
Asia	1960	50	32	100	68	26	15	4	1
	1980	57	44	100	86	45	31	8	4
	1987	58	45	100	95	49	35	9	5

Table 13.3 (Continued)

Major Region	Year	Percentage Enrolled by Level							
		Total		First Level		Second Level		Third Level	
		M	F	M	F	M	F	M	F
North America	1960	86	82	100	100	87	88	36	22
	1980	81	83	100	99	88	91	52	57
	1987	88	90	100	100	100	100	60	68
Europe (Incl. USSR)	1960	63	60	100	100	56	53	13	8
	1980	70	70	100	100	82	85	23	21
	1987	74	73	100	100	89	90	26	25
Oceania	1960	68	65	100	100	56	53	14	6
	1980	74	72	100	100	73	76	24	20
	1987	74	74	100	100	80	82	26	26
Latin America	1960	42	39	75	71	15	14	4	2
	1980	65	63	100	100	44	45	15	12
	1987	68	67	100	100	52	56	18	16

Source: Compiled from UNESCO, *Statistical Yearbook, 1989*, Paris. All ratios or percentages greater than 100 are due to late entry and repeated enrollments.

TEACHING STAFFS

Personnel in the teaching profession are another essential aspect of education. Worldwide, the number of teachers increased relatively faster than the number of students in 1970-87 (tables 13.2, 13.5). The total number of teachers increased 66 percent while the numbers of students increased about 50 percent, which decreased the class loads of many teachers, particularly at the first level. Most African countries have first-level pupil-teacher ratios of 30-50, with a few having smaller as well as larger ratios.

Proportionally, teaching staffs expanded nearly five times as rapidly in developing as in developed countries during 1970-87. Very small increases in teaching personnel occurred in Europe and North America, nearly all at the third educational level. Also, the number of teachers increased much more rapidly at every educational level in Africa than in any other major region of the world (table 13.5). The relative changes in the number of teachers in both North Africa and the sub-Saharan countries of Africa were equally high between 1970 and 1987.

In 1987 most teachers at the first educational level in developed countries were women, while in developing countries most were men. The same patterns existed at the second educational level, even though the proportionate number of female teachers dropped appreciably in both developed and developing regions (UNESCO, 1989, table 2.5). Thirty-five percent of Africa's first-level teachers were women, the lowest proportion of all regions in the world. Only about 30 percent of all second-level teachers in Africa and Asia were women, also the lowest proportion of all regions.

EDUCATIONAL EXPENDITURES

More than 925 billion dollars were spent worldwide on public education in 1987, nearly six times the amount in 1970 (table 13.6). Per capita educational expenditures rose over 300 percent, going from $45 in 1970 to $186 in 1987. Clearly, expenditures were disproportionately greater in developed than in developing areas. In 1987, for example, 88 percent of all expenditures were on schools in developed countries, whereas only 25 percent of all pupils lived in those countries. Expressed on a per capita basis, $680 was spent per capita on public education in developed regions in 1987 while only $29 was spent per capita in developing regions. Consequently, the per capita expenditures in developed countries were more than 23 times that in developing countries.

Africa and Asia had the lowest public education expenditures per capita of all major regions in the world throughout the 1970 to 1987 period. Even though the per capita public educational expenditures in Africa increased nearly 390 percent between 1970 and 1987, Africa had the lowest per capita public education expenditure of all regions, only $34 compared to $1,252 in North America.

Table 13.4
The Illiterate Population of the World 15 Years of Age and Over, by Sex
and Major Region, 1990 (in millions)

| | Total | | Male | Female |
	Number	Percent	Percent	Percent
WORLD TOTAL	948	27	19	34
Developed Countries	32	3	3	4
Developing Countries	917	35	25	45
Africa	178	50	38	62
Sub-Saharan Africa	139	53	41	64
Arab Africa	46	49	36	62
Asia	700	34	23	44
Latin America	44	15	14	17
Europe (incl. USSR)	19	3	2	4
Oceania	1	8	6	9
America	50	10	9	11

Source: Compiled from UNESCO, *Compendium of Statistics on Illiteracy*,
No. 31, Paris, 1990.

1. Published figures for the continent of America and the
percentages for Arab Africa apply to all Arab states.

Table 13.5
Changes in the Teaching Staffs of the Major Regions of the World, by Level of
Education, 1970-87

Major Region	Year	Teaching Staff (In Thousands)				Percentage Change in Teaching Staff, 1970-87			
		Total	First Level	Second Level	Third Level	Total	First Level	Second Level	Third Level
WORLD TOTAL	1970	25,924	14,837	8,957	2,130	66	45	95	94
	1987	43,075	21,528	17,427	4,118				
Developed Countries	1970	12,021	5,472	5,033	1,516	21	2	33	48
	1987	14,509	5,594	6,674	2,240				
Developing Countries	1970	13,903	9,365	3,924	614	105	70	174	206
	1987	28,566	15,934	10,753	1,878				
Africa (Total)	1970	967	735	202	29	208	159	372	345
	1987	2,982	1,900	953	129				
Africa (Non-Arab States)	1970	609	502	96	11	191	155	358	373
	1987	1,770	1,278	440	52				
Africa (Arab States)	1970	358	233	106	18	239	167	384	328
	1987	1,212	622	513	77				
Asia	1970	11,472	7,420	3,483	569	92	58	154	155
	1987	22,031	11,733	8,846	1,452				

Table 13.5 (Continued)

Major Region	Year	Teaching Staff (In Thousands)				Percentage Change in Teaching Staff, 1970-87			
		Total	First Level	Second Level	Third Level	Total	First Level	Second Level	Third Level
Latin America	1970	2,314	1,525	629	160				
	1987	4,729	2,703	1,486	539	104	77	136	237
Europe (Incl. USSR)	1970	7,849	3,658	3,449	742				
	1987	9,680	3,665	4,817	1,198	23	-	40	61
North America	1970	3,139	1,403	1,121	615				
	1987	3,343	1,394	1,185	764	6	-1	6	24
Oceania	1970	182	96	72	15				
	1987	310	133	140	37	70	39	94	147

Source: Compiled from UNESCO, *Statistical Yearbook, 1989*, Paris.

204

Table 13.6
Estimated Public Expenditures on Education in U.S. Dollars, by Major Region, 1970-87

Major Region	Public Expenditure on Education (In Millions of Dollars)			Per capita Public Expenditure on Education (In U.S. Dollars)		
	1987	1970	Percentage Change	1987	1970	Percentage Change
WORLD TOTAL	928,256	159,900	481	186	45	313
Developed Countries	818,238	145,444	463	680	142	337
Developing Countries	110,018	14,456	661	29	6	383
Africa (Total)	19,923	2,406	728	34	7	386
Africa (Non-Arab States)	5,918	1,151	414	13	5	160
Africa (Arab States)	14,005	1,255	1,016	99	14	607
Asia	177,010	13,389	1,222	61	7	771
Latin America	32,558	5,649	476	78	20	290
Europe (Incl. USSR)	347,565	64,098	442	447	92	386
North America	338,104	71,830	371	1,252	317	295
Oceania	13,096	1,984	560	524	103	409

Source: Compiled from UNESCO, Statistical Yearbook, 1989, Paris.

North African countries have been somewhat more generous in supporting public schools than have the sub-Saharan countries. In 1987, for example, the North African countries spent nearly eight times as much per capita on public education as did the sub-Saharan countries (table 13.6).

Relative increases in total public education expenditures in 1970-87 favored schools in developing regions comparatively more than those in developed regions, with the percentage increases being approximately 660 and 460 percent, respectively (table 13.6). Asia experienced the largest proportionate increase in total public education expenditures between 1970 and 1987 of all major regions. Africa was second highest, with total educational expenditure increases of over 700 percent. The smallest relative increases were in Europe and North America, where nearly 75 per cent of the total public educational expenditures in the world occur.

SUMMARY AND IMPLICATIONS

Educational attainment in Africa is the lowest in the world. Moreover, Africa has the lowest per capita public educational expenditure of all major regions. Despite these deficiencies, Africa has made rapid progress in its educational achievements, especially with the rapidly increasing enrollments of girls. Importantly, Africa experienced the most rapid increases in total enrollment and in the number of teachers of all major regions of the world in 1970-87. Should these developments continue they will substantially raise the future levels of educational attainment in Africa.

The increasing levels of educational attainment of African youths have many profound and interrelated implications for future African societies. The most highly educated will have greater skills than those in earlier generations and possess a higher degree of specialization that was previously lacking in the labor force. This, in turn, should increase productivity, and result in higher incomes and levels of living. The effects of raising the educational levels of African girls should prove to be one of the most significant of all in long-term effects, resulting in larger proportions of women entering the labor force. Moreover, raising the educational levels of women should result in the postponement of marriage, which in turn will reduce fertility and family size. In fact, education has been shown to be the most important socioeconomic status variable explaining family size.

More highly educated individuals result in greater mobility and advancement. Consequently, the various improvements in the African educational institutions should prove to be by far the most significant socioeconomic trend now underway.

REFERENCES

Caldwell, J.C.   1979. "Education as a Factor in Mortality Decline: An
   Examination of Nigerian Data." *Population Studies* 33: 395-413.
Duncan, Otis Dudley, David L. Featherman, and Beverly Duncan. 1972.
   Socioeconomic Background and Achievement. New York: Seminar Press.
UNESCO. 1989. *Statistical Yearbook 1989*. Paris.
_____. 1990. *Compendium of Statistics on Illiteracy*. Paris.
World Fertility Survey. 1983a. *The Egyptian Fertility Survey, 1980* Statistical
   Tables, vol. 4. Voorburg and London: International Statistical Institute.
_____. 1983b. *The Ghana Fertility Survey, 1979-80: A Summary of
   Findings*. Voorburg and London: International Statistical Institute.

14

Population Projections

Mathematical methods, component methods, methods which employ indicators of population change, and various combinations of these have been the principal methods used in projecting the populations of countries (Shryock, et al., 1971). Mathematical methods will be considered first here followed by component methods, as these are the two methods designed for national projections of the total population. Then, the projection of social and economic characteristics will be discussed and examples presented.

Around 20 African countries scheduled their first population censuses in the 1980 round. Although it is impossible to use the logistic curve or the method of fitting straight lines or polynomials in projecting the populations of these countries with just one or two population counts, the other projection methods are appropriate.

MATHEMATICAL METHODS

Various types of exponential formulas have been applied in projecting the total population of areas. One of the most frequently used mathematical methods for short-range projections is the geometric curve. The projection formula which assumes an annual constant rate of population growth is as follows:

$$P_t = P_o (1+r)^t, \qquad (14.1)$$

where P_t is the projected population at future time t, P_O is the population at the beginning of the projection period (usually the last census count or most recent estimate), r is the projected rate of population growth per year, and t stands for time (the number of years in the future from the base projection period). In order to apply Equation 14.1, it is necessary to use a previously derived annual rate of change (r). This number is an annual rate calculated from the last two censuses, a rate based upon a longer period, or an assumed rate.

For illustrative purposes, the projected 1991 population of the Republic of Botswana will be computed by Equation 14.1. The projected constant annual rate of population growth (r) will be based upon the total population change between the two most recent censuses taken in August, 1971 and August, 1981, where 574,094 and 941,027 inhabitants were enumerated in the two respective censuses (*Census*, Botswana, 1983). The computations required to calculate the rate of population growth per year (r) involve the use of common logarithms and are as follows:

$$\frac{P_2}{P_1} = (1+r)^t, \qquad (14.2)$$

which gives an annual growth rate of 5.1 percent between August, 1971 and August, 1981.

The population growth rate of 5.1 percent reflects a regular annual increase during 1971 to 1981 at a constant rate of growth. Using this calculated value of r to project the August, 1991 Botswana population, Equation 14.1 becomes:

$$P_{1991} = P_{1981} (1+.0506593)^{10},$$
$$= (941,027) (1.639151)$$
$$= 1,542,485.$$

These calculations provide an August, 1991 projected population of Botswana of slightly over 1.5 million, a gain of 601,458 inhabitants in the 10-year projection period since August, 1981.

Population growth, however, usually occurs as a continuous process and not by constant, regular, periodic changes. Equation 14.3 below considers r as an exponential rate of growth and not an annual geometric rate of growth:

$$P_t = P_o e^{rt}, \qquad (14.3)$$

where P_t is the projected population at future time t, P_o is the population at the beginning of the projection period, e is the base of the natural system of logarithms, r is the projected continuous rate of population growth, and t represents time (the number of years in the future from the base projection date). The continuous rate of growth (r) must be calculated before projecting the population by Equation 14.3.

For illustrative purposes, the exponential rate of population growth (r) will be calculated for the Republic of Botswana between the two most recent censuses, as follows:

$$\frac{P_2}{P_1} = e^{rt}, \qquad (14.4)$$

where P_1 is the number of inhabitants enumerated in the 1971 census (574,094), P_2 is the number of inhabitants enumerated in the 1981 census (941,027), e is the base of the natural system of logarithms, t is the exact number of years between the August, 1971 and August, 1981 censuses (10), and r is the continuous rate of growth. The calculations below give a value of r of 4.9 percent.

$$\frac{941,027}{574,094} = e^{rt}$$

By employing the continuous rate of population growth of 4.9 percent the following August, 1991 projected Botswana population is obtained:

$$P_{1991} = P_{1981} \, e^{(10)(.04941787)}$$
$$= (941,027)(1.6391514)$$
$$= 1,542,486.$$

For comparative purposes, the exponential rate of population growth calculated by Equation 14.4 is lower than the geometric rate of growth (5.1 percent) computed by Equation 14.2. However, the projected 1991 population calculated by Equation 14.3 is identical to the projected population computed by Equation 14.1. When making population projections by the use of growth rates, the exponential rate of growth in Equation 14.3 is preferred for it assumes a continuous rate of future population growth. In contrast, the geometric rate assumes a constant annual growth. Therefore, the exponential growth rate seems to be a more realistic and reasonable method to use in projecting population.

The total population of a country may be projected by fitting straight lines or higher-degree polynomials to its previous census figures. For instance, in the examples presented here, straight lines (first-degree polynomials) were fitted to the past census enumerations of Algeria (*Annuaire*, 1984), Egypt (*Central*, 1983), and Tunisia (*Recensement*, undated) to determine their suitability for projecting the future population of these countries. In all three countries population growth greatly accelerated in recent years. Consequently, the first-degree polynomials fail to project the future population of any of the three countries reasonably. One possible solution for countries with these types of growth patterns is to base the population projections only upon observations during the censuses after sustained population growth began.

Logistic curves may also be fitted to previous census data to project the population of countries with certain types of trends (Pearl, 1920, 1923; Pearl, et al., 1940). However, this curve has many limitations and requires several observations. Unfortunately it was falsely claimed to be a general law of population growth. Even so, only a few African countries, such as Seychelles, have taken as many as 20 different population censuses (d'Espaignet, 1984). For these reasons, the logistic curve was not used here.

COMPONENT METHODS

Projections are often made by the component method because it provides future populations classified by age and sex. This method may be used to project the populations of ethnic and racial groups and rural-urban areas as well. Projections can be made for any future date or dates but are usually made for every year or every fifth or tenth year following the last census. This method projects the components of future population change (fertility, mortality, and migration) separately and is unusually flexible in its procedures. Illustrative projections will be presented here for selected African countries to show the great flexibility of the component method in projecting for varying periods of time as well as selected socioeconomic characteristics of projected populations.

The illustrative population projections presented here do not involve complex assumptions that vary in different segments of the projection period. For instance, the example presented for Nigeria shows the procedures for calculating future populations for ten-year projection periods, using net migration as one of the components (Census of Nigeria, 1968). In the five-year projections for Mauritius and Réunion, a two-component method was employed by omitting net migration. These projections also show how model life tables may be used to project the number of survivors in developing countries with limited mortality data.

Population Projections for a Ten-Year Period

An application of Lotka's stable population theory (1907, 1956) is shown in the rural Nigerian population projections, by age and sex characteristics, from 1963 to 1973. When this procedure is followed one may use life table survival rates from Coale and Demeny's *Regional Model Life Tables* (1966) or the United Nations *Model Life Tables* (1982) to allow for mortality during the projection periods. In table 14.1, for example, 10-year survival rates were taken from the United Nations *Model Life Tables* of the general pattern with a life expectation at birth of 38 years for males and 39 years for females (UN, 1982). Since mortality rates are likely to decline for some time in the African countries, one may assume that life expectancy at birth will increase about one-half of a year during each year of the first projection period, then half as much in later periods.

Table 14.1
Projected Female Population of Mauritius, 1988

Age in 1983	Population 1983	5-Year Survival Rates	Expected Survivors, 1988	Age-Specific Birth Rates	Estimated Births 1983	Estimated Births 1988
Births 1983-88	49,822	.9336	46,514			
0-4	58,048	.9819	56,997			
5-9	54,187	.9943	53,878			
10-14	48,781	.9948	48,527			
15-19	58,284	.9924	57,841	40.1	2,337	2,319
20-24	53,769	.9902	53,242	132.6	7,130	7,060
25-29	45,838	.9880	45,288	131.0	6,005	5,933
30-34	39,478	.9850	38,886	85.7	3,383	3,333
35-39	28,590	.9808	28,041	40.8	1,166	1,144
40-44	21,258	.9743	20,712	13.6	289	282
45-49	20,151	.9639	19,424	1.9	38	37
50-54	16,486	.9471	15,614		20,348	20,108
55-59	17,916	.9209	16,499			

Table 14.1 (Continued)

Age in 1983	Population 1983	5-Year Survival Rates	Expected Survivors, 1988	Age-Specific Birth Rates	Estimated Births 1983 1988
60-64	13,005	.8795	11,438	Total Births in 5 Years:	
65-69	10,259	.8170	8,382		101,140
70-74	7,263	.7308	5,308	Males (.5074%) = 51,318	
75-79	4,695	.6168	2,896	Females (.4926%) = 49,822	
80 & Over	4,167	.4106	1,711		
TOTAL	502,175		531,198		

Source: Computed from Mauritius Central Statistics Office, *Annual Digest of Statistics* and *1983 Housing and Population Census of Mauritius*, Vol. 1, 2, and 5, Rose Hill, 1984 and from United Nations, *Model Life Tables for Developing Countries* (Sales No. E.81.XIII.7).

Table 14.2
Projected Male Population of Mauritius, 1988

Age in 1983	Population 1983	5-Year Survival Rates	Expected Survivors, 1988
Births, 1983-88	51,318	.9240	47,418
0-4	59,095	.9805	57,943
5-9	55,007	.9932	54,633
10-14	50,337	.9933	50,000
15-19	59,482	.9898	58,875
20-24	54,629	.9870	53,919
25-29	45,940	.9850	45,251
30-34	40,143	.9812	39,388
35-39	27,764	.9747	27,062
40-44	20,687	.9645	19,953
45-49	19,900	.9486	18,877
50-54	16,669	.9247	15,414
55-59	17,682	.8891	15,721
60-64	12,190	.8367	10,199

Table 14.2 (Continued)

Age in 1983	Population 1983	5-Year Survival Rates	Expected Survivors, 1988
65-69	8,893	.7651	6,804
70-74	5,382	.6749	3,632
75-79	2,800	.5678	1,590
80 & Over	1,657	.3925	650
TOTAL	498,257		527,329

Source: Computed from Mauritius Central Statistics Office, *Annual Digest of Statistics* and *1983 Housing and Population Census of Mauritius,* Vol. 1, 2, and 5, Rose Hill, 1984 and from United Nations, *Model Life Tables for Developing Countries* (Sales No. E.81.XIII.7).

Table 14.3
Projected Economically Active Persons, Réunion, by Age and Sex, 1987

Age in 1987	MALE			FEMALE		
	Projected Male Population Active 1987	Proportion Economically Active, 1982	Projected Number of Economically Active, 1987	Projected Female Population, 1987	Proportion Economically Active, 1982	Projected Number of Economically Active, 1987
16-19	28,541	35.3	10,075	27,881	25.9	7,221
20-24	23,671	76.3	18,061	24,796	56.7	14,059
25-29	18,621	92.3	17,187	20,386	50.3	10,254
30-34	16,442	93.1	15,308	16,964	46.9	7,956
35-39	13,734	92.6	12,718	13,998	43.7	6,117
40-44	12,378	89.9	11,128	12,666	40.4	5,117
45-49	10,794	86.3	9,315	11,433	37.0	4,230
50-54	8,438	80.3	6,776	8,986	32.4	2,911
55-59	7,152	69.6	4,978	8,098	25.9	2,097
60-64	4,978	30.9	1,538	5,995	11.9	713
65&Over	6,619	5.5	364	10,717	1.3	139
TOTAL	151,368		107,448	161,920		60,814

Source: Computed from *Resultats du recensement de la population dans les departments d'outre-mer, 1982*, Saint-Denis, 1983.

217

Age-specific birth rates for rural Nigerian females were assumed to remain constant throughout 1963 to 1973 (Nigeria, 1968). With a steadily declining number of rural women in the reproductive ages in the ten years, 51.8115 percent of all children were born in the first quinquennium of the decade. Accordingly, these different birth estimates, by sex, were made for each of the two separate five-year projection periods. Then, survival and net migration rates were applied to the children born in the decade to calculate their projected number on July 1, 1973. The 1973 rural female population of Nigeria was projected to be 28.4 million, about one-sixth fewer than in 1963 and a comparatively small loss for that time.

Population Projections for a Five-Year Period

In some countries emigration and immigration are rather small in volume and tend to offset each other. Consequently, population projections are often made by assuming no net immigration by the projection formula $P_1 = rP_0$. For example, the 1983-88 projections of the population of Mauritius (tables 14.1, 14.2) assume no net international migration during this five-year period and are computed on the basis of two components of population change. However, government estimates indicate an annual international migration loss of around 2,000 males and females each out of a total of about one million residents (Census of Mauritius, 1984). Thus, there may be around 20,000 net international migrants from Mauritius during the 1983-88 projection period, a comparatively small loss in any event.

An important demographic feature of Mauritius is that it is one of the few African countries with a relatively low rate of population growth, about half that of the continent of Africa as a whole. The 1983-88 population projections imply a population increase of only 5.8 percent in this five-year period.

PROJECTIONS OF SOCIOECONOMIC CHARACTERISTICS

Projections of such characteristics as school enrollment, families and households, and economic activity are essential for national planning purposes. Moreover, these projections are often based upon previously projected populations distributed by age and sex.

The country of Réunion will be used to illustrate the projection of one socioeconomic characteristic--that of economic activity. The latest census of population in Réunion was conducted in March, 1982 (Réunion, 1982) and the proportions of economically active, by age and sex, were computed for individuals 16 years of age and over (table 14.3). Next, the population of Réunion was projected to 1987, by age and sex. Then, the number of economically active males and females in 1987 was projected by assuming that the proportionate number of economically active individuals, by age and sex, would be the same in 1987 as in 1982. According to the 1987 projections there will be a small decline in the number of economically active individuals due to decreases in the number of persons of working age, even though there is likely to be a moderate overall population gain.

Of course, the economically active population of Réunion could have been projected to 1987 by much more elaborate procedures than the one used here. Also, it should be emphasized that the methods of projecting different socioeconomic characteristics vary somewhat from one projection to another. Nevertheless, in projecting various socioeconomic characteristics, the age-specific ratio method has been widely used.

PROJECTING POPULATIONS THROUGH SIMULTANEOUS EQUATION TECHNIQUES

Matrix algebra enables one to execute the computational steps of the cohort component method in a somewhat more elegant and efficient manner. Through the use of matrices it is possible to project simultaneously the three components of population change rather than compute each of the components individually (Tarver and Thompson, 1976). Mathematically, the procedure is to compute a population matrix by using projected birth rates, survival rates, net migration rates, and the percentages of projected births that are males and females. The product of the projection matrix (π) and the initial population vector (P_o) is the projected population vector P_1 at the end of a given projection period as shown in the following expression:

$$P_1 = \pi P_o. \qquad (14.5)$$

The population projections obtained by matrix algebra are identical with those obtained by the conventional three-component method which separately computes births, deaths, and net migrants.

SUMMARY AND IMPLICATIONS

One of the major concerns of development in the African countries is rapid population growth. Projections of future populations provide a basis for planning a wide range of activities at district, regional, and national levels. For example, the future needs for schools, hospitals, roads, housing, utilities, and many other facilities and services largely depend upon the size and composition of the future population.

Some commonly used projection techniques have been illustrated here. The component method is especially useful, for it provides age-sex distributions of projected populations. These projected age-sex populations, in turn, serve as the basis for projecting different socioeconomic characteristics.

No completely accurate method exists for projecting future populations. However, two fairly reliable rules apply to all types of population projections: first, the dependability of projections declines as the projection period lengthens, and second projections tend to be more accurate for large, heavily populated areas than for thinly populated ones.

REFERENCES

Annuaire Statistique De L'Algérie, 1982. 1984. Numero 11, edition. Algiers, Algeria: Office National Des Statistiques.

Census Administrative/Technical Report and National Statistical Tables, 1981 Population and Housing Census. 1983. Gaborone, Botswana: Ministry of Finance and Development Planning, Central Statistics Office.

Central Agency for Public Mobilization and Statistics. 1983. *National Statistics, 1952-1982*. Cairo: Campas.

Coale, Ansley J. and Paul Demeny. 1966. *Regional Model Life Tables and Stable Populations*. Princeton, NJ: Princeton University Press.

d'Espaignet, E.T. 1984. *The Population of Seychelles*. Victoria, Mahe: President's Office, Republic of Seychelles.

Institut National De La Statistique. *Republique Tunisenne Ministere DuPlan, Recensement General De La Population Et De L'habitat*. Tunis, Tunisia: (Undated).

Institut National De La Statistique et Des Etudes Economiques. 1982. *Résultats Du Recensement De La Population Dans Les Départements D'outre-Mer*. St. Louis, Réunion.

Lotka, Alfred J. 1907. "Relation Between Birth Rates and Death Rates." *Science* 26: 275-282.

_____. 1956. *Elements of Mathematical Biology*. New York: Dover.

Mauritius Annual Digest of Statistics. 1984. Rose Hill, Mauritius: Central Statistics Office.

Pearl, Raymond. 1920. "On the rate of growth of the population of the United States since 1790 and its mathematical representation." *Proceedings of the National Academy of Science* 275-288.

_____. 1923. "On the mathematical theory of population." *Metron* 2: 6-19.

Pearl, Raymond, Lowell J. Reed, and Joseph F. Kish. 1940. "The logistic curve and the census count of 1940." *Science* 92: 486-488.

Population Census of Nigeria, 1963, 1968. Combined National Figures, vol. 3. Lagos, Nigeria: Federal Office of Statistics.

Shryock, Henry S. et al. 1971. *The Methods and Materials of Demography*. Washington, DC: U.S. Bureau of the Census.

Tarver, James, D. and Billy M. Thompson. 1976. "Projecting Regional and Subdivisional Populations Through Simultaneous Equation Techniques." *Growth and Change* 7: 13-23.

United Nations. 1982. *Model Life Tables for Developing Countries*. New York.

15

Population Policies

Policy may be defined as a set of goals and objectives, along with appropriate guidelines of the means and procedures of accomplishing them. Thus, specially designed programs and measures are employed by governments to achieve certain goals by deliberately modifying various demographic conditions. Some policies attempt to control population size, some propose to alter certain characteristics, and others try to change the geographical distribution of the people. These policies may or may not be integrated into governmental economic and social development programs.

Population policies, by definition, are designed to influence demographic behavior. Over the years a variety of policies have been used to influence population size and distribution. Even so, there is limited knowledge of the impact of certain policies upon demographic behavior. Despite the many uncertainties, however, African governments are actively proceeding to implement various population policies. Sometimes, however, a country will announce one official population policy but will actually execute another policy.

POLICIES DESIGNED TO INFLUENCE POPULATION SIZE

Rapid population growth occurred in most developed countries following the Industrial Revolution, but the rates of growth then levelled off. In these industrialized countries the low rates of population growth were attained without deliberate governmental population policies and family planning programs.

The recent demographic experience of developing countries has been quite different. For example, crude mortality rates in Africa declined about 40 percent since 1950 while birth rates remained about constant. As a result, the annual

average rate of population growth rose from about two percent after World War
II to three percent. This rapid increase in the rate of population growth added
approximately 330 million people to the African population during the past 35
years.

Growing concern over the rapidly increasing population of the developing
countries prompted the United Nations to adopt a resolution in the 1960s
proclaiming the sovereign right of every nation to establish its own population
policies and guaranteeing parents the basic right to decide the number and spacing
of their own children.

Before 1974, Ghana, Kenya, and Mauritius were the only sub-Saharan countries
with definite population policies (Sadik, 1991). The development of population
policies in Africa covering maternal and child health, family planning, and
population information, education, and communication is presented in a recent
UN Population Fund publication (Sadik, 1991).

POPULATION GROWTH POLICIES OF AFRICAN GOVERNMENTS

Pronatalist policies are designed to increase population size and the rate of
growth. In contrast, *antinatalistic* policies are designed to decrease population
growth and reduce birth rates. In 1988, Equatorial Guinea, Gabon, and the Côte
d'Ivoire expressed a desire to increase their rates of population growth. Although
the Congo also viewed its rate of population increase as too low, it had no plans
to increase population growth. Generally, these governments think that their
numbers of people are relatively small for their unfulfilled development needs and
potentials.

Many pronatalist arguments have been advanced to support rapidly growing
populations. One assumption underlying this position is that successively larger
populations enable countries to utilize more fully development potentials. Also,
a rapidly growing population provides a progressively larger labor force capable
of producing more goods and services. Greater economies of scale and of
infrastructure occur as a result of progressively larger populations. In addition,
there tend to be greater efficiencies, and larger internal and external markets.
The pronatalist position has been employed to advocate growing populations at
least as far back in history as the time of Augustus in the Roman Empire.

In 1988 the following 22 countries had adopted antinatalistic population policies
and planned to intervene to lower their growth rates: Botswana, Burundi, Cape
Verde, Comoros, Gambia, Guinea-Bissau, Ghana, Liberia, Lesotho, Niger,
Nigeria, Algeria, Egypt, Morocco, Tunisia, Rwanda, South Africa, Senegal,
Uganda, Kenya, Seychelles, and Zimbabwe (table 15.1). Ethiopia, Malawi,
Sierra Leone, Tanzania, Swaziland, Cameroon, Central African Republic, and
Zambia considered their rates of population growth to be too high but they
planned no intervention to lower them.

A third of the African countries considered their rates of population growth as satisfactory. Benin, Burkina Faso, Chad, Djibouti, Guinea, Angola, Madagascar, Mauritania, Mozambique, Libya, Somalia, Sudan, and Zaire plan no intervention in changing them. The governments of Mali, São Tomé and Príncipe, Togo, and Mauritius view their rates of population growth as satisfactory and plan to maintain them at present levels. The Côte d'Ivoire is the only country that perceives its rate of population growth to be satisfactory but also plans intervention to raise the rate of growth. The Côte d'Ivoire favors a pronatalist population policy because it faces shortages of skilled workers and relies heavily upon foreign labor.

FERTILITY POLICIES OF AFRICAN GOVERNMENTS

In 1988 three African countries considered their fertility rates too low, 18 considered their rates satisfactory, while 32 countries thought that their rates were too high (table 15.2).

Of the three countries which thought that their fertility levels were too low, Equatorial Guinea and Gabon have explicit pronatalist population policies. Gabon, for example, provides birth bonuses, maternity benefits, and child allowances as inducements to population growth. Many of the Francophone countries have eliminated one of the barriers to family planning activities by repealing the French anticontraceptive law of 1920 (Spengler, 1968). Even though the Congo considers its fertility rates too low it has no plans to raise them.

The government of the Côte d'Ivoire is satisfied with its current level of fertility but would like to raise its birth rates. Even though the Côte d'Ivoire is satisfied with its population growth rate it has nevertheless adopted a pronatalist population policy.

Of the 32 countries that considered their fertility too high, 24 hoped to lower their birth rates. Several countries have established targets for future years. For instance, Kenya has a goal of lowering its total fertility rate to 5.2 by 2000 and Nigeria's policy is to reduce its total fertility rate to 4.0 by the end of the century (UN, 1989). Cape Verde hopes to reduce its total fertility rate to 5.6 by 1990 and to 4.7 by 2000.

Some countries have modified their systems of family allowances in attempting to lower fertility levels. Both Guineau-Bissau and Tunisia have encouraged three-child families by limiting family allowances to three children. In addition, Tunisia prohibited polygyny in the 1960s and raised the legal age at marriage. The legal age at marriage was also raised in Mauritius and the number of maternity leaves was limited to two instead of three.

Table 15.1
Population Growth Policies of African Countries, 1988

I. Population Growth Considered Too Low

  A. No Intervention Planned to Increase Population Growth Congo

  B. Intervention Planned to Increase Population Growth Gabon, Equatorial Guinea

II. Population Growth Considered Satisfactory

  A. No Intervention Planned to Increase Population Growth

     Angola, Benin, Burkina Faso, Chad, Djibouti, Guinea, Libya, Madagascar, Mauritania, Mozambique, Somalia, Sudan, Zaire

  B. Intervention Planned to Maintain Present Population Growth

     Côte d'Ivoire, Mali, Mauritania, São Tomé and Príncipe, Togo

III. Present Population Growth Considered Too High

  A. No Intervention Planned to Lower Population Growth

     Cameroon, Central African Republic, Ethiopia, Malawi, Sierra Leone, Swaziland, Tanzania, Zambia

  B. Intervention Planned to Lower Population Growth

     Algeria, Botswana, Burundi, Cape Verde, Comoros, Egypt, Gambia, Ghana, Guinea-Bissau, Kenya, Lesotho, Liberia, Morocco, Niger, Nigeria, Rwanda, Senegal, Seychelles, South Africa, Tunisia, Uganda, Zimbabwe

Source: Compiled from United Nations, *World Population Monitoring, 1989* (Sales No. E.89.XIII.12).

By 1988 a total of 41 African countries provided direct support for family planning activities carried out through government maternal and child health clinics. However, the relatively low contraceptive rates have been a major concern. For example, the World Fertility Surveys found that only 20 percent of the North African couples used family planning and only 10 percent of those in sub-Saharan Africa did (London, et al. 1985). The use of family planning ranged from about one percent of the married women of childbearing age in Mauritania to 40 percent in Zimbabwe.

Several African countries have set targets for contraceptive use at future dates. Gambia, for example, had a goal of increasing its contraceptive usage to 30 percent in 1992. Tunisia hopes to have 51 percent of all married women using some form of contraception by 1992 and Nigeria plans to extend family planning services to 80 percent of all women in the reproductive ages.

The success of fertility limitation programs has varied considerably in Africa. Birth rates in Mauritius were reduced about a third within 10 years by a family planning program and related measures (Brass, 1976). It was estimated that the family planning program accounted for about 80 percent of the 1972 marital fertility reduction (Hanooanjee, 1982). By 1985 75 percent of the women in Mauritius were using contraception (UN, 1989). Tunisia's fertility control program is more than 20 years old and it reduced marital fertility an estimated 70 percent in 1971 (Jemai and Jemai, 1978, 1979). By 1983 an estimated 41 percent of the women in Tunisia were using contraception (UN, 1989).

Kenya and Egypt, two of Africa's most populous countries, have also employed family planning programs. However, neither has had the success of Mauritius and Tunisia (Simmons, 1986). For example, in 1984 only 17 percent of the women in Kenya and 30 percent of those in Egypt were using contraception (UN, 1989).

MORTALITY POLICIES OF AFRICAN GOVERNMENTS

Despite considerable improvements in health care Africa still has high infant mortality rates, high crude mortality rates, and a comparatively low life expectancy at birth. With the deterioration of economic conditions in Africa, health agencies and organizations in many countries suffered disproportionately large budgetary reductions. Consequently, some primary health care services and immunization programs were curtailed.

In 1988 27 African countries had average life expectancies at birth of less than 50 years, 19 countries had life expectancies of 50-59 years, four countries had 60-69 years, and Seychelles had an average life expectancy of 70 or more years (table 15.3).

Rwanda, Libya, Côte d'Ivoire, Mauritius, and Seychelles were the only countries that considered their mortality levels acceptable, as expressed in terms of the average life expectancies at birth. Overall, the average expected longevity at birth reflects the general health conditions prevailing in each country. Apparently, the attitudes of the three governments with life expectancies of less than 60 years indicate either a misunderstanding or lack of concern about the importance of health care.

Several African countries have established health and mortality goals for future years. For example, Cape Verde hopes to lower its crude death rate to 6.7 by 1995-2000. Liberia plans to reduce its infant mortality rate to 50 by the year 2000, and Nigeria wants to lower infant mortality to 30 by 2000 and lower its crude death rate to eight by 2000. Uganda hopes to increase its life expectancy at birth to 60 years and to lower its infant mortality rate to 50 by the year 2000 (UN, 1989).

Other targets designed to improve health care and thereby lower mortality have been established by African countries. Liberia plans to expand health care coverage from 35 percent to 90 percent of its population by 2000.

POPULATION DISTRIBUTION POLICIES

Only three African governments (Guinea-Bissau, Mauritius, and Tanzania) are completely satisfied with their patterns of population distribution (table 15.4). In contrast, 36 countries desire major changes in population distribution patterns and 12 countries would like minor changes. The widespread dissatisfaction of African countries with their patterns of population distribution reflects primarily the migration and urbanization problems associated with the rapid growth of primate cities. Even though some of Africa's major cities are comparatively small by international standards, Africa nevertheless has the highest rate of urbanization of all major regions in the world.

The prevailing view among African governments is that the problems of urbanization can be solved by rural and regional development strategies. More than half of the African countries have adopted policies to promote the growth of existing small towns and intermediate size cities. Moreover, growth centers have been promoted. In fact, 60 percent of the countries have adopted policies designed to slow the growth of primate cities.

Although Ethiopia has no explicit policy it is attempting to reduce rural-urban migration by establishing schools, hospitals, and small-scale industries in rural areas. Also, it is completing a large resettlement project in a sparsely settled fertile area. Tanzania is establishing villages which provide social services. Uganda's population distribution policy is creating jobs in areas of relatively large out-migration. Also, Zambia is diverting larger investments in rural development projects to retain larger populations in the rural areas.

Table 15.2
Fertility Policies of African Countries, 1988

I. Fertility Levels Considered Too Low

    A.   No Intervention Planned to Raise Fertility Level

        Congo

    B.   Intervention Planned to Raise Fertility Levels

        Gabon, Equatorial Guinea

II. Fertility Levels Considered Satisfactory

    A.   No Intervention Planned to Raise Fertility

        Angola, Benin, Burkina Faso, Chad, Djibouti, Guinea, Libya, Madagascar, Mauritania, Mozambique, Somalia, Sudan, Zaire

    B.   Intervention Planned to Maintain or Raise Present Fertility Levels

        Côte d'Ivoire, Mali, Mauritius, São Tomé and Príncipe, Togo

III. Fertility Levels Considered Too High

    A.   Intervention Planned to Lower Fertility Levels

        Algeria, Botswana, Burundi, Burkina Faso, Cape Verde, Comoros, Egypt, Gambia, Ghana, Guinea-Bissau, Kenya, Lesotho, Liberia, Morocco, Niger, Nigeria, Rwanda, Senegal, Seychelles, South Africa, Swaziland, Tunisia, Uganda, Zimbabwe

    B.   No Intervention Planned to Lower Fertility Levels

        Cameroon, Central African Republic, Ethiopia, Guinea, Malawi, Sierra Leone, Tanzania, Zambia

---

Source: Compiled from United Nations, *World Population Monitoring, 1989* (Sales No. E.89.XIII.12).

Table 15.3
Mortality Policies of African Countries, 1988

I. Average Life Expectancy at Birth Under 50 Years

    A. Current Mortality Acceptable

       Rwanda

    B. Current Mortality Unacceptable

       Angola, Benin, Burundi, Burkina Faso, Central African Republic, Chad, Congo, Djibouti, Equatorial Guinea, Ethiopia, Gabon, Gambia, Guinea, Guinea-Bissau, Mali, Malawi, Mauritania, Mozambique, Niger, Nigeria, Senegal, Sierra Leone, Somalia, Sudan, Swaziland, Uganda

II. Average Life Expectancy at Birth of 50-59 Years

    A. Current Mortality Acceptable

       Côte d'Ivoire, Libya

    B. Current Mortality Unacceptable

       Botswana, Cameroon, Cape Verde, Comoros, Egypt, Ghana, Kenya, Lesotho, Liberia, Madagascar, Morocco, South Africa, Tanzania, Togo, Zaire, Zambia, Zimbabwe

III. Average Life Expectancy at Birth of 60-69 Years

    A. Current Mortality Acceptable

       Mauritius

    B. Current Mortality Unacceptable

       Algeria, São Tomé and Príncipe, Tunisia

IV. Average Life Expectancy at Birth of 70 Years and Over

   A. Current Mortality Acceptable

       Seychelles

   B. Current Mortality Unacceptable

       No country reported gave this response

Source: Compiled from United Nations, *World Population Monitoring, 1989*

         (Sales No. E.89.XIII.12).

231

Table 15.4
Spatial Distribution Policies of African Countries, 1988

I. Major Changes Desired

    A. Explicit Redistribution Policies

        Algeria, Angola, Botswana, Burundi, Cape Verde, Congo, Côte d'Ivoire, Egypt, Equatorial Guinea, Gabon, Gambia, Ghana, Liberia, Libya, Mali, Mauritania, Morocco, Mozambique, Nigeria, São Tomé and Príncipe, Senegal, Seychelles, Sierra Leone, South Africa, Sudan, Swaziland, Togo, Tunisia, Zaire, Zambia

    B. No Explicit Policy

        Benin, Burkina Faso, Ethiopia, Madagascar, Niger, Rwanda

II. Minor Changes Desired

    A. Explicit Redistribution Policies

        Cameroon, Central African Republic, Djibouti, Kenya, Malawi, Somalia, Uganda, Zimbabwe

    B. No Explicit Policy

        Chad, Comoros, Guinea, Lesotho

III. Spatial Distribution Satisfactory

    A. Explicit Redistribution Policies

        Guinea-Bissau, Tanzania

    B. No Explicit Policy

        Mauritius

Source: Compiled from United Nations, *World Population Monitoring, 1989* (Sales No. E.89.XIII.12).

Tunisia is expanding its agricultural sector by improving conditions in rural areas and in the cities and villages of the interior. Also, it is decentralizing public services and investment. Nigeria is constructing a new federal capital at Abuja to alleviate rapidly mounting population pressures on Lagos. Cape Verde is trying to reduce rural-urban migration by creating employment in rural areas and by redistributing land. In Senegal the government is promoting a more balanced regional and urban development. Finally, the government of Sierra Leone is developing industrial growth centers and has subdivided the country into rural development regions.

INTERNATIONAL MIGRATION POLICIES OF AFRICAN COUNTRIES

International migration policies may be considered simply in terms of increasing or decreasing the volume without complex variations of policies. Equatorial Guinea is the only African country which wants to increase its international immigration. Governments like Guinea-Bissau and Mauritius want to halt permanent immigration and Burundi, Gambia, Kenya, Liberia, Sierra Leone, and Zambia want to reduce permanent immigration.

The governments of Ethiopia, Kenya, Somalia, and Uganda are willing to permit a continued flow of temporary workers and their dependents. However, Burundi, Mauritius, Sierra Leone, Uganda, and Zambia want to reduce their numbers and Guinea-Bissau wants to halt the entry of all workers.

Cape Verde and Rwanda continue to encourage emigration, and Tunisia, Morocco, and Egypt desire to increase emigration. In contrast, Ethiopia, Guinea-Bissau, Kenya, Liberia, Madagascar, Senegal, South Africa, and Uganda are encouraging return migration. Seychelles, Mozambique, Uganda, Gabon, Algeria, Botswana, Lesotho, Guinea-Bissau, Burkina Faso, and Guinea consider their emigration rates to be too high and all, except Seychelles, would like to lower them (UN, 1989). For example, Burundi, Comoros, Sierra Leone, Somalia, and Zambia are very much concerned about the brain drain. Many governments are participating in the Return of Talent program which was launched in Africa in 1983 in collaboration with the Economic Commission for Africa, and financed jointly by the European Economic Community and the United States government. Its goal is to attract Africans to return to their countries after acquiring high professional qualifications in the Western World.

SUMMARY AND IMPLICATIONS

Throughout history population policies have been used to control the size of the population. Pronatalist policies designed to increase fertility and population growth have been widely employed. After World War II rapid population increases occurred in the developing countries as a result of major improvements in health care. This sudden population growth encouraged the establishment of antinatalist policies to reduce population growth.

More and more countries in Africa have been attempting to lower the high rates of population growth by adopting family planning programs. A sharp distinction exists between the purpose of family planning programs in Africa and for the rest of the world. For example, family planning outside Africa is considered to be for the purpose of family size limitation. In Africa, on the contrary, family planning programs are specifically designed for the purpose of spacing births to improve maternal and child health. Actually, family planning reduces family size wherever it is practiced. Many Africans choose to emphasize the health benefits of family planning while maintaining silence on the question of population size and level of fertility. Of course, whenever intervals between births are increased, reductions in family size occur, as well as certain health benefits.

Finally, population policies often change over time with changed circumstances. For example, recent surveys in Botswana, Kenya, Zimbabwe, and Senegal reveal definite declines in fertility and mortality. Also, family limitation previously reduced fertility in Mauritius and Tunisia. These changes are likely to effect the policies of the different governments, changing different aspects of the population policies of many countries.

REFERENCES

Brass, William. 1976. "Impact of the Family Planning Programme on Fertility in Mauritius." *International Planned Parenthood Federation Medical Bulletin* 10: 1-2.

Hanooanjee, Esther. 1982. "Application of Methods of Measuring the Impact of Family Planning Programmes on Fertility: The case of Mauritius." In *Evaluation of the Impact of Family Planning Programmes on Fertility: Sources of Variance*, 89-113. New York: United Nations.

Jemai, Yolande and Hedi Jemai. 1978. "Application of Methods of Measuring the Impact of Family Planning Programmes on Fertility: The Case of Tunisia." In *Methods of Measuring the Impact of Family Planning Programmes on Fertility: Problems and Issues*, Population Studies No. 61, 66-106. New York: United Nations.

_____. 1979. "Fertility Projection/Trend Analysis." In *The Methodology of Measuring the Impact of Family Planning Programmes on Fertility*, Manual 9, Population Studies No. 66, 150-152. New York: United Nations.

London, Kathy A. et al. 1985. "Fertility and Family Planning Surveys: An Update. "*Population Reports*, Series M, no. 8. Baltimore, MD: Johns Hopkins University.

Sadik, Nafis, ed. 1991. *Population Policies and Programmes: Lessons Learned From Two Decades of Experience*. New York: United Nations Population Fund.

Simmons, George B. 1986. "Family Planning Programs." In *World Population and U.S. Policy*, edited by Jane Menken, 175-206. New York: W.W. Norton.

Spengler, Joseph J. 1968. *France Faces Depopulation*. Westport, CT: Greenwood Press.

United Nations. 1989. *World Population Trends and Policies: 1989 Monitoring Report*. New York.

16

The Future of Demography in Africa

It is impossible to predict the timing of the future major demographic developments in Africa with any degree of certainty. Some anticipated changes may occur much more rapidly than expected. This chapter examines several important aspects of the overall demographic situation and some changes which seem likely in the foreseeable future.

THE FORMAL STUDY OF DEMOGRAPHY

One of the most pressing needs of demography in Africa is the training of more professionals with skills and expertise. For example, the staffs of central government offices are responsible for performing numerous statistical duties involving the use of demographic data and techniques. About 20 widely scattered statistical training centers provide technical training for government workers from African countries. Of those centers located outside Africa, two are in the United Kingdom, one in the Netherlands, one in Germany, and one in the United States (UNECA, 1985).

The International Statistical Programs Center of the U.S. Bureau of the Census in Washington, DC is widely known for its excellent facilities and successful technical training. Many of its graduates are employed in various African countries. Between 1975 and 1990 over 400 Africans studied in this center, with about one-fourth completing master's degrees.

By 1974 14 sub-Saharan countries had university research and training programs in demography, with master's or Ph.D. degrees offered in five of the 14 countries (Jain, 1986). The locations of these graduate degree programs were essentially the same in 1985. In addition, the United Nations sponsored Cairo

Demographic Center offers a doctorate in demography.

In 1985 15 other universities in sub-Saharan Africa taught demography in undergraduate and master's degree programs in sociology, economics, geography, and history (UN, 1985). The Universities of Botswana and Tanzania offered demography programs, and undergraduate demography courses were being taught at the Universities of Lesotho, Swaziland, Malawi, Mozambique, and Zimbabwe, as well as at a number of institutions in South Africa (Ahmed, et al., 1988).

The United Nations (1986) identified seven demographic centers and 22 different university programs offering demography in Africa. This list, of course, includes many of the university demographic programs identified by Jain (1986) for the Population Council and by Ahmed and his colleagues, but it also fails to include certain programs. However, when the different lists are combined they provide a fairly complete picture of formal university demography programs in Africa.

The Population Council estimates that there are about 100 professional demographers in Africa with graduate training and demonstrated research ability. While the demand for professional demographers will increase in the future, the education and training programs of African universities are likely to continue to be inadequate to meet the anticipated needs, even with the generous support of such donors as the UNFPA, USAID, World Bank, Population Council, and the Rockefeller, Ford, Hewlett, Mellon foundations, as well as other agencies.

National and regional educational institutions in Africa should be able to offer undergraduate and master's level training for demographers, providing they receive continued financial assistance. However, most doctoral students will probably continue to go abroad for study at one of the five major universities in Belgium, Canada, France, the United Kingdom, or the United States which offer specializations in African demography.

Professional journals serve important educational purposes for both students and instructors. However, there are few scholarly African journals devoted strictly to demography or population studies. Among the publications are *Population Studies*, a quarterly published in English and Arabic by the National Population Council of Egypt. This journal began in 1973 and publishes demographic papers mainly about Egypt. *African Population Studies*, a demographic journal, has been published by the Union for African Population Studies, headquartered in Dakar, Senegal since 1988. Since 1970 the UN Economic Commission for Africa has published a quarterly *African Population Newsletter*. The *Pop Sahel*, an international population and development bulletin, is published by the Centre d'etudes et de recherche sur la population pour le developpement, which is part of the Institut du Sahel. This Institute is an international organization sponsored by Burkina Faso, Cape Verde, Chad, Gambia, Guinea-Bissau, Mali, Mauritania, Niger, and Senegal, and is headquartered in Bamako, Mali. Perhaps a future demography journal may emerge from one of the active African population associations--such as the Population Association of Nigeria, the Association

Maghrebine pour L'Etude de la population, the Senegalese Association of Demographic Studies, or the Population Association of Kenya.

CIVIL REGISTRATION SYSTEMS

Both population censuses and vital statistics registration systems have been deficient in the past, but much greater progress has been made in improving population censuses than in improving civil registration systems. For example, 16 African countries scheduled their first population censuses in the 1980 round, leaving Chad, which was the last African country to conduct a population census in 1993. However, about four-fifths of the African countries still have incomplete birth and death figures, even though the UNFPA sponsored pilot projects in about a dozen countries designed to improve civil registration procedures.

Some countries such as Botswana and Ghana collect vital statistics only in designated registration areas. Throughout most of Africa the chief deficiency is due to the overall incompleteness of registration. When accurate birth and death statistics do not exist it is necessary to employ census data, life tables, and specially devised analytical techniques to compensate for incomplete and deficient vital statistics.

When countries have at least 90 percent of their vital events (births, deaths, and other events) registered, they are considered to have complete and reliable registration for each respective event (UN, 1990). Cape Verde, Egypt, Mauritius, Réunion, St. Helena, São Tomé and Príncipe, and Seychelles have reliable birth and death registration systems. In addition, Algeria and Tunisia have reliable birth registration. Infant death statistics are complete in Cape Verde, Mauritius, St. Helena, São Tomé and Príncipe, and Seychelles. Of all 55 countries, nine have reliable birth registrations, seven have reliable death registrations, and five have reliable infant death registrations. Efforts are underway to improve civil registration on this large continent where few countries presently have adequate civil registration systems.

Mauritius, for example, has a well-established system of civil registration that has evolved over many years. It has 50 civil status officers who register vital events on its four islands. Evaluations in 1952, 1962, and 1972 revealed that the registration of live births and deaths were complete. The only incompletely reported vital events were marriages. Only civil marriages are reported in the registration statistics. Marriages performed by religious rites only have no legal sanction and are considered as consensual unions. Each birth must be registered within 45 days after the event, and no burial permit is issued until the death has been registered (Lamy, 1977).

FAMILY PLANNING SURVEYS AND POPULATION GROWTH

Around 85 fertility surveys were conducted in 34 African countries between 1960 and 1973. Afterwards, the World Fertility Surveys and Contraceptive Prevalence Surveys interviewed women in Africa and in 61 developing countries in all throughout the world. Columbia University and the U.S. Centers for Disease Control also carried out family planning and contraception surveys. In all, the surveys cost over 60 million dollars and provided the largest worldwide storehouse of knowledge ever assembled about fertility and family planning. In 1984 the Demographic and Health Surveys of Westinghouse Public Applied Systems of Columbia, Maryland assumed responsibility for these worldwide surveys. During 1984-89 Westinghouse planned about 35 surveys using fertility-and health-related questions, with most studies being undertaken in Africa. The studies put more emphasis upon action and evaluation programs and less upon family planning and contraception surveys. When these surveys are completed there will have been about 130 to 140 fertility surveys conducted in about 40 African countries since the 1950s.

The annual rate of population growth in Africa rose from 2.2 percent in 1950 to 3.0 percent in 1985-90. With the steadily increasing population growth, larger and larger numbers of African governments considered their fertility levels too high. Consequently, over 40 countries now provide direct support for family planning, and the governments of Benin, Chad, Côte d'Ivoire, Madagascar, Mauritania, and Somalia support family planning programs indirectly.

It is too early to measure the impact of family planning programs in reducing fertility in countries that recently launched such programs. However, these programs were effective in reducing population growth in Mauritius and Tunisia. During the past few years they have been responsible for declines in Kenya, Botswana, and Zimbabwe. The effectiveness of the programs vary from country to country and a few pronatalist countries are still advocating higher rates of population growth. However, there is a definite possibility that birth and death rates in Africa may decline after 2000. Unless the rate of population growth is reduced in the future the total number of Africans in the year 2025 may very well exceed the projected 1.6 billion and the projected 3.0 billion by 2125.

THE NATIONAL HOUSEHOLD SURVEY CAPABILITY PROGRAM

The National Household Survey Capability Program, co-sponsored by the United Nations, was initiated in 1977 to assist developing countries in obtaining multi-purpose survey data to implement development programs (UN, 1981, 1982a, 1982b). It was broad in scope and intended to serve as an overall guide for many different types of surveys. For example, under their program nine African countries conducted income and expenditure surveys, seven carried out labor force surveys, seven undertook agricultural surveys, and eight did population and demographic surveys. The responsibility for this very worthwhile program has now been assumed by various other agencies.

SUMMARY AND IMPLICATIONS

Even with the increasing adoption of family planning programs the population of Africa will continue to grow in the foreseeable future, as the 2025 population is projected to be 2.5 times its 1990 population and the projected 2125 population is likely to be over 4.5 times the size of the 1990 population. By 2025 Africa is likely to have more than 1.6 billion inhabitants. A hundred years later in 2125 Africa may have 3.0 billion inhabitants and be the most populous major region in the world.

Both the crude birth and death rates are projected to decline after 1990. Actually, the annual rate of population growth is projected to decline from 3.0 percent in 1985-90 to 1.9 percent in 2020-25. Even so, about 30 million people will be added to the total African population each year during and beyond 2020-25. At the present time it is impossible to make any realistic forecast of the probable date for the total population of Africa to become stable and reach an equilibrium.

REFERENCES

Ahmed, Ghyasuddin, Helge Brunborg, and G.N. Shastri. 1988. "Undergraduate Study of Demography in Southern Africa--Programs, Problems, and Prospects." Paper presented at the annual meeting of the Population Association of America, New Orleans, LA.

Jain, Anrudh K. 1986. *Review of Institutional Capacities, Human Resources and Development Assistance in sub-Saharan Africa.* New York: The Population Council.

Lamy, G. 1977. "The Demographic Situation in Mauritius." Seminar Paper on Population Growth and Development Planning, ECA/UNFPA. Rose Hill, Mauritius.

United Nations. 1981. *The National Household Survey Capability Programme Prospectus.* New York.

_____. 1982a. *National Household Survey Capability Programme, Survey Data Processing: A Review of Issues and Procedures.* New York.

_____. 1982b. *National Household Survey Capability Programme, Non-Sampling Errors in Household Surveys: Sources, Assessment and Control.* New York.

_____. 1985. *Teaching Demography: A Summary Handlist of Universities and Other Institutions Teaching Demography,* vol. 1. New York.

_____ . 1986. *Teaching Demography: Details of Curricula and Related Matters, in Universities and Other Institutions Teaching Demography*, vol. 2, New York.

_____ . 1990. *Demographic Yearbook 1988*, New York.

United Nations, Economic Commission for Africa. 1985. *Directory of Statistical Training Centres and Associate Centres Participating in the Statistical Training Programme for Africa*. Addis Ababa.

Glossary

The glossary terms in boldface below were discussed in the chapters identified.

AIDS (Acquired Immune Deficiency Syndrome) is a complex of diseases that attack the immune system, leaving the victim susceptible to various infections and malignancies that result in death in a degenerative disabling manner. About half of the worldwide cases are in sub-Saharan Africa (Chapter 5).

Agricultural revolution involved a change beginning about 10,000 years ago from hunting, gathering, and fishing cultures to a sedentary way of life involving farming and the domestication of animals (Chapter 2).

Antinatalistic policies are designed to decrease population growth and reduce birth rates (Chapter 15).

Augustus, a grandnephew of Julius Caesar, was the first emperor of Rome (from 27 B.C. to A.D. 14), during which time he ruled North Africa. His adopted name was Gaius Julius Caesar Octavianus (Chapter 2).

Bantu-speaking inhabitants from the modern area of original Nigeria and Cameroon made large-scale migrations thousands of years ago to eastern and southern Africa, spreading their culture of cultivation and herding everywhere they went (Chapters 3, 10).

Berbers were the earliest settlers in northwest Africa who came from either Canaan, Syria, or Yemen several thousand years ago (Chapters 3, 10).

Black Death was a bubonic plague that reached Europe in 1346 and Cairo in 1348. It killed a fourth of the Cairo population. It was the most frightful pandemic ever to occur (Chapter 2).

Cause of Death The 1967 WHO Eighth Revision of the International Classification of Diseases requires that the sequence of events leading to a death be specified and that the underlying cause of death be designated (Chapter 5).

Child-woman ratio is the number of children under five years of age per 1,000 women of childbearing age, usually 15 to 49 (Chapter 4).

Cities first appeared in the latter part of the fourth millennium B.C. in Mesopotamia, then in the Nile Valley (Chapter 7).

Civil registration includes the recording and compilation of births, deaths, marriages, divorces, and other vital events (Chapters 1, 16).

Cohort fertility rates measure the reproductive behavior of women all born or married at a certain time who are then followed throughout their reproductive lives. This rate is especially useful in measuring long-term fertility trends (Chapter 4).

Completed family size is the number of live births to women at the completion of their childbearing, usually 45-49 years of age (Chapter 4).

Completeness of civil registration is attained when 90 percent or more of births, deaths, or both have been recorded in civil registers (Chapter 16).

Constant dollars are used to compare income figures over time to allow for changes in the cost of living (Chapter 12).

Crude birth rate is the number of live births occurring in an area during a year per 1,000 midyear population (Chapter 5).

Cush, an ancient culture in Sudan, stretched from the first to the sixth cataracts on the Nile. It evolved from Egypt about 1700 B.C. and ceased to exist around A.D. 300. Its kings ruled Egypt nearly 100 years around 700 B.C. (Chapter 3).

Dark Ages refers to the first 1,000 years of the Christian era. The stagnation and political and economic crises resulted in a relatively constant population worldwide (Chapter 2).

De facto **populations** include all persons physically present in an area at a designated reference date (Chapter 1).

De jure **populations** include all usual residents of a given area, whether or not they were physically present at a given reference date (Chapter 1).

Demographic transition theory describes the patterns of declining birth and death rates and population growth occurring during industrialization and development (Chapter 2).

Demography is the science of population (Chapter 1).

Developing countries are nonindustrial with low incomes except for the oil-exporting nations. Africa (excluding South Africa), Asia (excluding Japan), Latin America, and Oceania (excluding Australia and New Zealand) comprise the developing regions of the world (Chapter 2).

Disposable income is the amount available for consumption and savings after taxes are deducted from personal income (Chapter 12).

Economic development is reflected by increases in per capita income (Chapter 12).

Economic growth occurs whenever the total wealth of a nation increases (Chapter 12).

Economic welfare is defined as total private consumption expressed in the gross national product at factor cost in constant prices (Chapter 12).

Economically active populations include workers who supply labor for the production of economic goods and services during a specified time-reference period. Individuals above a designated minimum age who were either engaged in or actively seeking productive work are included (Chapter 11).

Exogamy is the custom of marrying outside a group (Chapter 9).

Expectation of Life is the probability of surviving from any given age to any older age (Chapter 5).

Family planning provides birth prevention information, services, and appliances which enable women to have the number of children they desire. Family planning is usually associated with child and maternal health programs which are universally accepted (Chapters 3, 15).

The **general fertility rate** is the number of live births per 1,000 women in the reproductive ages and is computed on an annual basis (Chapter 4).

Gross domestic product is the total final output of goods and services produced in an economy by its residents (Chapter 12).

Gross national product is the total domestic and foreign output claimed by residents. It comprises the gross domestic product plus net factor income from abroad less similar payments made to nonresidents who contributed to the domestic economy (Chapter 12).

The **gross reproduction rate** estimates the number of daughters that women will bear during their lifetime should they give birth to daughters at the same rate of a designated year. The gross reproduction rate assumes that women will live throughout their reproductive years (Chapter 4).

Seven **Hausa states** were created in the northern grassland area of Nigeria around A.D. 1,000. Kano, Katsina, Zaira, and the other four capital cities were walled (Chapter 7).

The **HIV (Human Immunodeficiency Virus)** progresses into AIDS very slowly after the initial infection. Within 10 years after the initial infection about half of the HIV-infected persons will have developed the AIDS symptoms (Chapter 5).

The **Industrial Revolution**, which began in England about 1760 from the replacement of hand tools by machines and power tools, resulted in large-scale industrial production. Urbanization accelerated and the demographic transition accompanied it in many parts of the Western world (Chapters 2, 7, 8).

Industry refers to the activity of the establishment in which economically active persons worked during the time-reference period (Chapter 11).

Infant mortality refers to the death of infants under one year of age (Chapter 5).

Informal sector workers are non-cash workers in family agriculture, market and street vendors, hawkers, and operators of itinerant petty-type enterprises. In Accra, for example, about 85 percent of all food purchases are made from market and street vendors (Chapters 8, 11, 12).

An **internal migrant** is one who changes the political or administrative area of his usual residence within that country (Chapter 9).

Justinian plague probably took 100 million lives in the world between 542 and 600 (Chapter 2).

Labor force is comprised of employed persons and unpaid family workers who worked during a specified time-reference period (Chapter 11).

Louis Leakey discovered the skeletal remains of early modern man (*homo erectus*) in Olduvai Gorge, Tanzania which indicated that man probably developed first in Africa (Chapter 2).

Levant was the ancient region bordering the eastern shore of the Mediterranean Sea, including present-day Greece, Turkey, Syria, Lebanon, Israel, and Egypt (Chapter 2).

The **levels of education** used by the United Nations Educational, Scientific and Cultural Organization are the first level (elementary or primary school), second level (middle school, secondary school, high school, and vocational school), and third level (university, teachers college, and higher professional school) (Chapter 13).

Life table is a statistical instrument designed to measure the mortality of a population (Chapter 5).

A **lifetime migrant** is an individual whose current area of residence differs from the area of his birth, regardless of any intervening moves. This concept measures migration between birth and the date of the census or survey (Chapter 9).

Local movers change their usual place of residence within a political or administrative area. The moves do not cross defined boundaries (Chapter 9).

Lusophone countries of Africa are Portuguese-speaking.

Maghreb is comprised of the northwestern African countries of Morocco, Algeria, and Tunisia (Chapter 10).

The **Mali Empire** in western Sudan flourished in the thirteenth and fourteenth centuries from trans-Saharan trade. Its capital was Niani. Mali was absorbed by the much stronger Songhay empire in 1500 (Chapter 7).

The **Malthusian theory** states that population increases at a geometric rate whereas the means of subsistence increases at an arithmetic rate, resulting in overpopulation (Chapter 1).

Maternal mortality reflects the death of women while pregnant or within 42 days of termination of pregnancy from any cause related to or aggravated by the pregnancy or its management but not from accidental or incidental causes. The Ninth Revision of the ICD recommended that maternal death rates be expressed per 100,000 live births (Chapter 5).

Modernization reflects the recent development of urbanization, industrialization, and rising health education, and living standards, along with related advances. It has accompanied fertility declines and has also been called secularization (Chapter 2).

Multiround surveys match individuals in successive interviews and obtain much more reliable, validated information than is secured in single retrospective studies (Chapter 1).

Neonatal deaths are the deaths of infants under 28 days of age (Chapter 5).

The **net reproduction rate** measures the number of daughters a cohort of newborn girls will bear throughout their lifetime, assuming fixed age-specific birth and death rates. It is a measure of the extent that a cohort of newly born girls will replace themselves, assuming an indefinite continuation of age-specific birth and mortality rates (Chapter 4).

North Africa is comprised of seven countries, mostly north of the Sahara Desert: Algeria, Egypt, Libya, Morocco, Sudan, Tunisia, and Western Sahara (Chapter 1).

Occupation indicates the kind of work a person performs regardless of the industry or the status in employment (Chapter 11).

The term **over-urbanization** reflects rapid urban population growth not accompanied by similar increases in industrial growth. The term has also been used to indicate that the urban population is larger than justified by the level of industrialization (Chapter 7).

Own-account workers operate economic enterprises or engage in professions or trades. They hire no employees (Chapter 11).

The **Paleolithic** period (so-called stone age) was an ancient cultural stage of human development dating from about 2.5 million to 200,000 years ago. Some of the earliest known hand axes were found at Olduvai Gorge, Tanzania (Chapter 5).

Period fertility rates are usually calculated for short periods of time such as a year (Chapters 3, 15).

Polygyny is a marriage in which men have more than one wife. It is still common in West Africa where from 25 to 50 percent of the marriages are polygynous, resulting in many half-brothers and sisters (Chapter 4).

Population pyramids graphically represent the age and sex distributions of populations. Pyramids reflect the demographic histories of populations through changes in their age-sex structure (Chapter 6).

Post-neonatal deaths are to infants 28 days to one year of age (Chapter 5).

The **pre-colonial** period in Africa refers to the period prior to the colonization by the European countries in the modern era and not to the colonization by the Greeks, Romans, and others in the pre-Christian era. The modern pre-colonial period ended in 1462 when the Portuguese made the first African settlement in Cape Verde. Colonization by other European countries followed, and Africa was partitioned by the major European countries at the 1884 Treaty of Berlin when the boundaries of the colonies were drawn (Chapters 7, 10).

Primate cities are the largest ones in each country, usually the national capitals that dominate the commercial, political, and intellectual lives of the entire country. As originally defined by Jefferson, the primate city was at least twice as large as the second most populous center in the country (Chapter 7).

Private consumption is a measure of economic welfare indicating the spending power as it reflects the personal disposable income (Chapter 12).

Pronatalist policies favor increasing population size and rate of growth (Chapter 15).

Provinces in Morocco, *Wilayas* in Algeria, *gouvernates* in Egypt and Tunisia and *Mugataas* in Libya are the major political or administrative units in some of the North African countries (Chapter 9).

According to the **rank-size rule**, city size varies inversely from the largest to the smallest centers. Various formulas were applied to determine the regularity in the distribution of cities of different sizes (Chapter 7).

The **Regional Food Plan for Africa** was proposed initially by the Food and Agriculture Organization in 1978. It called for a growth rate in agricultural production of approximately four percent. Various investments were proposed to reach these goals (Chapter 8).

Return of talent program was created in 1983 to encourage Africans to return to their countries after acquiring professional and technical training in the west (Chapter 15).

Sahel is a semiarid region bordering on the south of the Sahara Desert and stretches from Senegal throughout east Africa. The present Institut du Sahel is sponsored by Burkina Faso, Cape Verde, Chad, Gambia, Guinea-Bissau, Mali, Mauritania, Niger, and Senegal (Chapter 1).

Thousands of **seasonal workers** are absent from their homes for varying periods, such as the international agricultural migrant workers in the Côte d'Ivoire. The usual census practice is to count them as residents of their permanent homes (Chapter 9).

Secondary-size city patterns show considerable differences in the sizes of their three largest cities but not large enough for one to be a primate city. Cameroon and Swaziland, among others, have secondary configurations (Chapter 7).

The Berbers came from the **Semitic** East, either from Canaan, Syria, or Yemen and spoke a Hamitic-Semitic language. Semitic was a major roup of languages of southwestern Asia and North Africa (Chapter 10).

Sex ratio is the number of males per 100 females and is usually about 105 at birth (Chapter 6).

Sub-Saharan Africa is the large area of the continent comprised of the 49 countries south of the Sahara Desert (Chapter 1).

Total fertility rate is the number of children a woman will have if she continues to experience the fertility rates of a particular time period (Chapter 4).

Traffic in African slaves was carried on since the beginning of the Christian era. However, around 20 million were enslaved in the fourteenth to nineteenth centuries and traded to the Americas, North Africa, and Arabia and India. Algiers, Elmina, Benin, Luanda, and Mbanzo Congo served as major slave *entrepôts* (Chapters 3, 10).

Countries with **trinary cities** are those in which the three largest population centers are approximately equal in size. Based upon the last official censuses, Nigeria and South Africa had trinary city patterns (Chapter 7).

The **Tutsi** is a minority group in Burundi that controls the army and the government. It has massacred large numbers of *Hutus* from time to time and driven thousands into exile (Chapters 4, 10).

Urban centers in the African countries range from a minimum size of 100 inhabitants in Uganda to 20,000 inhabitants in Nigeria and Mauritus (Chapter 7).

An **urban agglomeration** includes the population concentrated in a central city and surrounding urbanized localities, and also may include several continuous cities and/or towns and their suburban fringes (Chapter 7).

Urbanization indicates an increase in the proportion of the total population living in urban places. In Africa, of course, urban places range from 20,000 in Nigeria and Mauritius to settlements of 100 inhabitants in Uganda (Chapter 7).

The **World Fertility Survey** was created in 1972 to assist in nationally representative, internationally comparable, and scientifically designed and conducted surveys of fertility. When it terminated in 1984, 61 developing countries had been surveyed with the studies costing more than 60 million dollars. This entire effort resulted in the greatest body of knowledge ever accumulated on fertility and family planning (Chapter 4).

The **Yoruba** kingdom appeared in the forested Guinea of Western Nigeria before 1200, with a possibility of coming from Ethiopia. Yoruba cities were comparatively populous settlements, performing trading and administrative functions for large areas. Ibadan, with a population of about 70,000 in 1850, was the dominant Yoruba city (Chapter 7).

The **Zulus** area a large group of over two million Bantu-speaking Africans living in the northeast part of South Africa. Because of their prolonged warfare most of their lands have been confiscated (Chapter 3).

Appendix 1: Official Language, European Colonial Power, and Date of Independence of African Countries

Country	Colonial Power	Date of Independence	Official Languages
Algeria	France	July 1962	Arabic, French
Angola	Portugal	November 1975	Portuguese
Benin	France	August 1960	French
Botswana	Great Britain	September 1966	English
Burkina Faso	France	August 1960	French
Burundi	Germany, Beligum	July 1962	Kirundi, French
Cameroon	Germany, France, Great Britain	January 1960	French, English

Country	Colonial Power	Date of Independence	Official Languages
Cape Verde	Portugal	July 1975	Portuguese
Central African Republic	France	August 1960	French
Chad	France	August 1960	French, Arabic
Comoros	France	July 1975	French
Congo	France	August 1960	French
Côte d'Ivoire	France	August 1960	French
Djibouti	France	June 1977	Arabic, French
Egypt	Great Britain	February 1922	Arabic
Equatorial Guinea	Spain	October 1968	Spanish
Eritrea	Italy (1890-41), Ethiopia	May 1993	Amharic
Ethiopia	Italy (1935-41)		Amharic
Gabon	France	August 1960	French
Gambia	Great Britain	February 1965	English
Ghana	Great Britain	March 1957	English
Guinea	France	October 1958	French
Guinea-Bissau	Portugal	September 1974	Portuguese, Criolo

Country	Colonial Power	Date of Independence	Official Languages
Kenya	Great Britain	December 1963	English, Swahili
Lesotho	Great Britain	October 1966	English, Sesotho
Liberia		July 1847	English
Libya	Turkey, Italy, Anglo-French military government (1943-51)	December 1951	Arabic
Madagascar	France	June 1960	French, Malagasy
Malawi	Great Britain	July 1964	English, Chichewa
Mali	France	June 1960	French
Mauritania	France	November 1960	Arabic, French
Mauritius	Holland, France, Great Britain	March 1968	English
Morocco	France	March 1956	Arabic, French
Mozambique	Portugal	June 1975	Portuguese
Namibia	Germany, South Africa	March 1990	Afrikaans, English
Niger	France	August 1960	French
Nigeria	Great Britain	October 1960	English

Country	Colonial Power	Date of Independence	Official Languages
Réunion	France	Overseas Department of the French Republic	French
Rwanda	Germany, Beligum	July 1962	French, Kinyarwanda
Saint Helena	Great Britain	British Dependency	English
São Tomé & Príncipe	Portugal	July 1975	Portuguese
Senegal	France	June 1960	French
Seychelles	France, Great Britain	June 1976	English, French
Sierra Leone	Great Britain	April 1961	English
Somalia	Great Britain, Italy	July 1960	Somalia
South Africa	Holland, Great Britain	May 1910 (left British Commonwealth of Nations in 1961)	Afrikaans, English
Sudan	Great Britain	January 1956	Arabic
Swaziland	Great Britain	September 1968	English, Swazi
Tanzania	Germany, Great Britain	December 1963	Swahili, English

Country	Colonial Power	Date of Independence	Official Languages
Togo	Germany, France, Great Britain	April 1960	French
Tunisia	France	March 1956	Arabic, French
Uganda	Great Britain	October 1962	Swahili, English
Western Sahara	Spain	February 1976	Arabic, French
Zaire	Belgium	June 1960	French
Zambia	Great Britain	October 1964	English
Zimbabwe	Great Britain	April 1980	English

Official languages prepared by the United States Department of State, Washington, D.C.

Appendix 2: Recent Population Censuses of African Countries

NORTHERN AFRICA

Recensement Général de la population et de l'habitat, 1977. 19 vols. Algiers, Algeria, 1977-78 (A population census was taken in 1987.)

Population, Housing, and Establishment Census, 1986. Cairo, Egypt, 1987.

Population Census, 1984. Tripoli, Libya, 1987.

Recensement Général de la population et de l'habitat de 1982. 2 vols. Rabat, Morocco, 1984. (A population census was taken in 1994.)

Sudan, Third Population Census, 1983. Khartoum, Sudan, 1985-88. (A population census was taken in 1993.)

Recensement Général de la population et de l'habitat, 1984. 5 vols. Tunis, Tunisia, 1984. (A population census was taken in 1994.)

1982 Western Sahara population census results were included in the 1982 Morocco population census. The 1974 population census figures were published in Censo General de 1974, El-Aaiún (Spanish Census of 1974).

EASTERN AFRICA

Recensement Général de la population, 1979. Bujumbura, Burundi, 1980 (A population census was taken in 1990.)

Recensement Général de la population et de l'habitat, 1980. Moroni, Comoros, 1981. (A population census was taken in 1991.)

Recensement Général de la population, 1983. Djibouti, Djibouti, 1988. (A population census was taken in 1991.)

Ethiopia 1984 Population and Housing Census. Addis Ababa, Ethiopia, 1984. (A population census was taken in 1994.)

Kenya Population Census, 1979. 2 vols., Nairobi, Kenya, 1981-85. (A population census was taken in 1989.)

Recensement Général de la population et des habitats, 1975. 8 vols. Antananario, Madagascar, 1976. (A population census was taken in 1994.)

Malawi Population and Housing Census, 1987. Zomba, Malawi, 1987-88.

1983 Housing and Population Census of Mauritius. 5 vols. Rose Hill, Mauritius, 1984-87. (A population census was taken in 1990.)

1° Recenseamento General da populacão, 1980. 10 vols., Maputo, Mozambique, 1983. (A population census is scheduled in 1995.)

Résultats du recensement de la population dans les départements d'outre-mer, 1982. Saint-Denis, Réunion, 1983. (A population census was taken in 1990.)

Recensement Général de la population et de l'habitat, 1978. Kigali, Rwanda, 1982. (A population census was taken in 1991.)

1977 Census report. Victoria, Seychelles, 1978. (A population census was taken in 1987.)

Census of population, 1975. Mogadishu, Somalia, 1984. (A population census was taken in 1986-87.)

1978 Population Census. 8 vols. Dar es Salaam, Tanzania, 1981-82. (A population census was taken in 1988.)

Report of the 1980 Population Census. Kampala, Uganda, 1982. (A population census was taken in 1990.)

1980 Census of Population and Housing. 2 vols. Lusaka, Zambia, 1981. (A population census was taken in 1990.)

Main Demographic Features of the Population of Zimbabwe, 1982 Population Census, Harare, Zimbabwe, 1985. (A population census was taken in 1992.)

SOUTHERN AFRICA

1981 Population and Housing Census, Administrative/Technical Report and National Statistical Tables. 2 vols. Gaborone, Botswana, 1983. (A population census was taken in 1991.)

1986 Population Census. Maseru, Lesotho, 1987.

Population Census 1981. Windhoek, South West Africa (Namibia), 1982. (A population census was taken in 1991.)

Population Census, 1985. 18 vols. Pretoria, South Africa, 1986-88. Latest Census taken in 1991.

Report on the 1986 Swaziland Population Census. Mbabane, Swaziland, 1988.

MIDDLE AFRICA

3° Recenseamento Général da populacão, 1960. 4 vols. Luanda, Angola, 1964-1969 (last complete census with published results). *Census of Luanda, 1983*, and *Census of Cabinda*, 1984. Luanda, Angola, 1984.

Recensement Général de la population et de l'habitat, 1976. 2 vols. Yaoundé, Cameroon, 1978. (A population census was taken in 1987.)

Recensement Général de la population, 1975. 2 vols. Bangui, Central African Republic, 1980. (A population census was taken in 1988.)

Chad took its first population census in 1993.

Recensement Général de la population et de l'habitat, 1984. 2 vols. Brazzaville, Congo, 1986. (A population census was taken in 1994.)

Censos nacionales I de populación y I de vivienda, 1983. Malabo, Equatorial Guinea, 1986. (A population census was scheduled in 1992.)

Recensement et enêqute démographique, 1960-61. 3 vols. Libreville, Gabon, 1964 (Last complete census with published results). The population census scheduled for August, 1980 was officially repudiated. A 1981 decree declared a population of 1,232,000 including 122,000 Gabonese nationals abroad. (The next census postponed indefinitely).

1º Recenseamento geral da populacão e da habitacão, 1981. São Tomé, São Tomé and Príncipe, 1982. (A population census was taken in 1991.)

Recensement Général de la population, 1984. Kinshasa, Zaire, 1984. (A population census was taken in 1994.)

WESTERN AFRICA

Recensement Général de la population et de l'habitat, 1979. 2 vols. Porto-Novo, Benin, 1983. (A population census was taken in 1989-90.)

Recensement Général de la population, 1985. Ouagadougou, Burkina Faso, 1986.

Recenseamento Général da populacão, 1980. 2 vols. Praia, Cape Verde, 1980. (A population census was taken in 1990.)

Recensement Général de la population, 1975. 9 vols. Abidjan, Côte d'Ivoire, 1976-81. (A population census was taken in 1988.)

Population and Housing Census, 1983. Banjul, The Gambia, 1986. (A population census was taken in 1993.)

1984 Population Census of Ghana. Accra, Ghana, 1985. (A population census was taken in 1994.)

Guinea: The results of the first two national population censuses taken in 1972 and 1977 were never published. The third population census was taken February 1-5, 1983. (A population census was taken in 1993.)

Recenseamento Général da populacão e da habitacão, 1979. Bissau, Guinea-Bissau, 1981. (A population census was taken in 1991.)

1984 Population and Housing census of Liberia. Monrovia, Liberia, 1987. (A population census was taken in 1994.)

Recensement Général de la population du Mali, 1976. 7 vols. Bamako, Mali, 1977-85. (A population census was taken in 1987.)

Recensement Général de la population, 1977. 2 vols. Novakchott, Mauritania, 1977-83. (A population census was taken in 1993.)

Recensement Général de la population 1977. 2 vols. Niamey, Niger, 1978-80. (A population census was taken in 1988.)

Population Census of Nigeria, 1963. 10 vols. Lagos, Nigeria, 1964-68. (A population census was taken in 1991.)

Census of the Population of St. Helena Island and Ascension Islands, 1976. Jamestown, St. Helena, 1977. (A population census was taken in 1987.)

Recensement Général de la population, 1976. 8 vols. Dakar, Senegal, 1976-82. (A population census was taken in 1988.)

1985 National Population Census of Sierra Leone. 5 vols. Freetown, Sierra Leone, 1986-1988.

Recensement Général de la population et de l'habitat, 1981. 2 vols. Lomé, Togo, 1985. (A population census was taken in 1992.)

Index

Mauritius, Republic of, emigration policy of, 146
Middle Africa, per capita income of, 174
Migration: Bantu, 142–43; concepts and definitions of, 117–18; forced, 31; internal, control of, 228–29; internal, patterns of, 118–24; international, 133–47; intracontinental, 142–44; of lifetime migrants, 119–21; and net migration estimates by residual methods, 124–30; and population policies, 233; and refugee problems, 144–46; rural to urban, 110, 124, 228–29; and socioeconomic pressures, 146–47; of temporary or seasonal workers, 142, 143–44. *See also* Emigration, international; Immigration, international
Mortality, 59–78; and historical changes in length of life, 65–66; major causes of, 59–61; policies concerning, 227–28
Mortality rates: infants and children, 66–68; influence of ethnicity, kinship, family patterns on, 77; maternal, 68–77. *See also* Crude death rates

National accounts statistics, 170
National Household Survey Capability Program, 240–41
North Africa: early immigration into, 133–34; per capita income, 172–73; population, prehistoric and ancient, 25, 26; population, 1650 to 1950, 28

Petty, William, 2
Plato, 102
Political unrest, demographic effects of, 30, 31
Polygyny, and fertility, 45–49

Population associations, 238–39
Population censuses and surveys, 7–8, 239; *de facto/de jure* basis in, 7; history of, 7; income data from, 170–71; multiround and single-round, 88; and net migration estimates, 125–30
Population growth (Africa), 25–33; prehistoric, 25; from A.D. 14 to 1650, 26–27; from 1650 to 1950, 27–30; between 1950 and 1990, 30–31; declines and increases in, 17; and distribution variability, 6; and economic growth and welfare, 175–77; future projections of, 22, 31–32, 241; and infectious diseases, 29–30; and political strife, 30, 31; and slave trading effects, 27, 28–29
Population growth (world), 13–22; prehistoric and ancient, 13–16; before 1650, 16; from 1650 to 1950, 16–17; between 1950 and 1990, 18
Population policies, 223–34; and fertility limitation programs, 225–26; and health and mortality goals, 227–28; of population distribution, 228–29; pronatalist versus antinatalistic, 224–25
Population projection: component methods of, 212–18; mathematical methods of, 209–12; through simultaneous equation techniques, 219; of socioeconomic characteristics, 218–19
Population pyramids, 83–84
Population surveys, 7–8;
Portuguese Africa: emigration from, 141–42; internal migration in, 123; refugee problems in, 145
Poverty, and inequality of income distribution, 177–89

Refugees, 144–46

About the Author

JAMES D. TARVER died in June 1996. Dr. Tarver was Demographic Consultant for the United Nations, Professor of Demography at the University of Botswana, Director of Demographic Research and Training at the University of Georgia, and most recently, Professor of Sociology and Anthropology at Howard University. He was the editor of *Urbanization in Africa: A Handbook* (Greenwood, 1994) as well as the author of many journal articles on demography and migration in rural and urban settings.

ISBN 0-275-94885-4

EAN

9 780275 948856

HARDCOVER BAR CODE